From TERRY BRADSHAW
IT'S ONLY A GAME

We grew up mostly in Shreveport, Louisiana. Pawpaw, my granddad, had animals, crops, a salt shed, and a two-hole outhouse on the farm. You knew your family had made it big when you had a two-holer out there. How many holes you got, Terry? We got two! Two! Damn, Terry, you sure gettin' fancy.

Pawpaw taught me how to plow a field, and how to pick cotton, watermelons, and cantaloupe. I learned how to thump a watermelon and tell from the sound how sweet it is. I learned how to drive a team of Clydesdales and stretch out a mink on a board. I learned how to build a sweet potato shed and how to make buttermilk and paste.

This is how I grew up. This was my foundation. This is where I learned my values. I never heard an unkind word spoken about family. Nobody talked about one another. I learned my place, and I learned about love and trust, and more than anything that it is the simple things in life that make all the difference.

IT'S ONLY A GAME

TERRY BRADSHAW

WITH

DAVID FISHER

POCKET BOOKS

New York   London   Toronto   Sydney   Singapore

POCKET BOOKS, a division of Simon & Schuster, Inc.
1230 Avenue of the Americas, New York, NY 10020

Copyright © 2001 by Terry Bradshaw

Originally published in hardcover in 2001 by Pocket Books

All rights reserved, including the right to reproduce this book or portions thereof in any form whatsoever. For information address Pocket Books, 1230 Avenue of the Americas, New York, NY 10020

ISBN: 978-1-4516-6897-1

First Pocket Books paperback printing August 2002

10 9 8 7 6 5

POCKET and colophon are registered trademarks of Simon & Schuster, Inc.

For information regarding special discounts for bulk purchases, please contact Simon & Schuster Special Sales at 1-800-456-6798 or business@simonandschuster.com

Front cover photo by Jeff Katz

Printed in the U.S.A.

DEDICATION

I would like to dedicate this book to my brothers: to my older brother, Gary, who loved me and has been my best friend for much of my life; and to my younger brother, Craig, a fine football player who walked so gracefully in my shadow—which I suspect was a tough place to be. Neither one of them will ever truly know how much I love them and depend upon them. I want them to know that while this book is dedicated to them, they still ain't gettin' any of the proceeds!

ACKNOWLEDGMENTS

I would like to take this opportunity to acknowledge everybody, but in particular those people who have contributed to this book. Many people gave their time and thought to help make this book possible. I sure hope they don't regret it. But I definitely want to thank them for efforts in my behalf.

I especially want my parents to know how much I love them. I write that because I know parts of this book are going to expose you, so I want to say thank you.

I also want to acknowledge the continuing efforts of Bill Bush, the man who helped me understand who I am and why I act the way that I do.

PREFACE

PREFACE

I have never easily fit a description. My life—and the way I've led it—seems to have been a lot more complicated than necessary. I have had fun—amen to that, brothers and sisters—but I also have had my share of the difficult times. Admittedly, a lot of them were self-inflicted.

I've spent a long time trying to overcome an extremely successful football career. That's me. My team set records and I was voted into the Hall of Fame, but I never felt fulfilled. When I look at my personal statistics compared to the truly great players—Joe Montana, John Elway, Dan Marino, Johnny Unitas—I'm almost embarrassed. That's probably the reason I have some difficulty when people define me by my playing career.

So I've tried to become more than a man who used to be Terry Bradshaw. I never wanted to grow old living firmly in my past. And then I found what I believe to be is my true purpose in life: I like to make people feel good. I like the sound of other people's laughter. Not when I was singing or acting, but when I was speaking to them or appearing on television. Laughter makes me happy.

I've been carrying the words that I put down on these pages inside me for a long time. It was my desire to string them together into sentences that make you laugh. And when you laugh, laugh loud, please, so when people look at you funny you can just point to the book and tell them, "That Terry sure makes me laugh. Why don't you go out and buy some copies of this book! You'll be laughing out loud too."

But some of those same words have been long used to cover up some hurt feelings, some pain, and putting them down is a release for me.

I have a lot of regrets about my playing career and the way it ended and even some of the things I've done since. I have no explanations, just the regrets. I played for a coach, Chuck Noll, whom I never understood and who never really understood me; I loved him but we parted badly and haven't really spoken since. I played in a city in which I didn't feel welcome, and to which I have rarely returned, yet in my heart I have such a true fondness for that place and those people.

I regret not having had one of my former teammates or my coach or one of the Steelers' executives present me when I was inducted into the Hall of Fame. I don't regret having invited broadcaster Verne Lundquist, a fine man, to fill that role, but rightfully it belonged to many others.

I deeply regret not having attended Mr. Rooney's funeral. Art Rooney was one of the finest human beings I've ever known. When he died I decided not to go to the funeral because I hadn't been in Pittsburgh in a long time and it didn't seem to be the right time to go. I'm sorry I didn't go.

I regret that until the day this book was written I had never told my two daughters that I have been married and divorced three times. Three times. I sure ought to get some sort of award from the American Association of Divorce Lawyers. I certainly paid for it. But the fact that I have been married and divorced three times is incomprehensible to me as a Christian. I don't just regret that, I'm embarrassed by it, so until recently I never did find the right words to tell my children. To have had such success in my professional life and such failure in my personal life is difficult for me. I would gladly swap them even-up, gladly.

Someone once introduced me by saying, "There is only one Terry Bradshaw and here is all of them." Truthfully I'm as confused about who I am as everybody else. I got the name right, but the person standing behind it tends to change with the wind. But all of the me's try to be kind and entertaining. I've spent a long time trying to be all things to all people, but I think at the age of fifty-two I've finally learned that I need to be honest with myself. That's where contentment lies for me. I hope this book is an honest reflection of the person that I am and maybe the person that I'd like to be.

More than anything, I would hope that after reading this readers will understand there is a truly serious man at work here—although definitely a work in progress—and have many laughs at his expense.

Terry Bradshaw
May 2001

ONE

I had a real job once. It was back about 1990. My ex-wife-to-be and I had moved to Dallas so she could get her law degree and I could learn how to play golf. I was determined to become a good golfer, but the ball seemed about equally determined to go wherever it wanted to go. I was playing golf four days a week and started feeling guilty about it. My buddies couldn't play when I wanted to because they all had jobs. And suddenly it dawned on me that I had never had a real American nine-to-five job. I'd worked hard my whole life and done a lot of different jobs; I'd done all the chores on a farm from baling hay to making buttermilk, I'd been a spot welder and worked on the oil pipelines, I'd been a youth minister. I'd been a pro football quarterback and won four Super Bowls—and called all my own plays—I'd been a television broadcaster, I'd sung professionally and made several CDs, I'd acted on TV and in the movies and coauthored two books. I'd been the world's worst cattleman and owned a horse ranch. I'd been a public speaker, a product spokesman, I'd done commercials, infomercials, and endorsements. I'd worked all my life, just the way I'd been taught by my father.

But I'd never had a real, honest-to-goodness get-up-in-the-morning-when-you're-too-dad-blamed-tired-to-look-in-the-mirror-and-see-this-creature-look-back-at-you-and-think-oh-my-goodness-gracious-and-get-dressed-in-a-tie-and-jacket-and-drive-downtown-in-rush-hour-traffic-having-to-listen-to-Gus-and-Goofy-on-the-radio-and-finally-arrive-at-the-office-to-face-a-pile-of-papers type of job. So I told my wife, "I got to get me an honest-to-goodness nine-to-five real job."

"What?" she said. I have to admit that the things I did often surprised my wife. Well, it wasn't personal—they often surprised me too.

"I got to get a job." My self-esteem was suffering because all I was doing was playing golf. I was feeling very guilty that I was a fully grown man making my living as a sports personality. I felt that I was not part of mainstream America. Somehow it didn't seem right that I could be having so much fun without even knowing how to use a computer, send an e-mail, or even get on the Internet. It wasn't natural.

So I went out and got a job—at Lady Love Cosmetics. So help me Butkus this is absolutely true. My job was to launch a line of shampoos, conditioners, and fragrances for men primarily to be sold at sports clubs.

We were going to change the aroma of the locker room. I went down to the chemical lab and started sampling the different choices of fragrances for our products.

I didn't know how to have a job. So I bought a briefcase, and each morning I would buy the *Wall Street Journal*, wrap it around my *Sports Illustrated*, and put it into my briefcase. I'd put on a starched shirt, a tie, and a jacket and go to my office at Lady Love Cosmetics, feeling proud that people could look at me and say, "That boy has a job." At my job I had a little office and I had a secretary that I shared with another man, and that was definitely fine with me because otherwise she would not have had anything to do. I had a phone, and I would call people to tell them, "I'm calling from my job."

I had no idea what I was doing. I wasn't a very good cosmetics salesman. The truth is I really didn't want to sell cosmetics, I just wanted to have a job. I would go to meetings and sit quietly, occasionally nodding my head, but I didn't understand the terminology any more than those people would have understood my play calling. I didn't even know how to read the stock market results, but I still bought stocks, because that's what people did when they had a job. And from that job I learned a very important lesson.

I didn't *want* to have a job. For almost five months I went to work every morning, just like my buddies. The big problem with my job was that my office window overlooked the eighth fairway of a beautiful golf course, and every day the sun would be shining, the birds would be singing, and I'd be sitting up there watching people playing golf and thinking, Man, I sure wish I didn't have a job. My lunch hour began getting longer and longer till it stretched from about noon to the next morning, and nobody seemed to notice. Soon my lunch break took the whole entire day, starting with a lunch breakfast. Finally I quit, although apparently it took a long time before people noticed I wasn't just on my lunch break, and I did the very thing I should have done months earlier: I found some other people who didn't have real jobs either who could play golf with me.

But it didn't make that feeling that I needed to do something more go away. Nor, truthfully, did it make my golf game better. The fact is I'd had feelings like that my whole life. No matter what I achieved, it didn't seem to satisfy me. In high school I set the national record for throwing the javelin, but I desperately needed to throw it farther. I won four Super Bowls—calling my own plays, thank you very much—and I had to win five. I was the number-two broadcaster at CBS behind the greatest announcer in the entire history of football, John Madden, and I was so unhappy I was ready to quit. Finally I decided to find out why I just couldn't be satisfied living a wonderful life. I went to see a professional therapist.

That didn't work very well at all. I was afraid the therapist wouldn't think that my real problems were very interesting, so I made up a whole character for him. A whole other person. I was actually embarrassed that my problems weren't big enough. I wanted him to be happy that I was so messed up. I wanted him to be able to tell people, Oh man, that Terry Bradshaw has great problems. I just felt that if I told him, I drank too much on Thursday night, or I love beautiful women, or I'm not good with details, he'd be bored. I wanted to have the best problems of any patient he'd ever seen. I wanted Super Bowl–size problems. So I had to make them up.

That was hard for me to do. So I only had two visits. But because I didn't want him to feel like a failure, I told him I was cured. It was a miracle, I told him, he was the greatest counselor I ever saw; two visits and cured.

The truth is that the person I had been telling him about was cured. Me? I felt guilty about lying to my counselor. So I had to start seeing another therapist to resolve my guilt about lying to my first therapist.

There really has been only one thing in my life that has made me feel complete, and that is the game of football. The ability to throw a football was my God-given talent. That was my blessing and my passion; that was my calling in life, and everything that I've accomplished has derived from that. When I was four years old, I would wad up a piece of paper and spend hours lying on the floor throwing it up and down. As I got a little older I'd lie in bed at night throwing my football against the ceiling. Thump! Thump! My dad would yell, "Terry, put the football down right now and go to sleep!" and I would. But five minutes later, thump! Thump! My best friend Tommy Spinks and I would throw the football for hours in our backyard until we couldn't do it anymore. Throwing a football was the most fascinating thing in the world to me. We never got tired or bored, we jut ran out of day.

I got a new football every year. I'd take cordovan polish and just shine it up. As I learned, the more you throw inexpensive footballs, the bigger they get. Those footballs would literally swell up. Eventually the laces would split, I'd take the laces out of my shoes and pull it back together. I loved that, because the bigger the football got, the lighter it got, and the farther I could kick it. In my backyard one day, trust me, this is absolutely true, I popped that baby and it didn't leave my foot good and it—blew up! Bam! Scared me to death. Then there was this real sad-looking flat piece of leather lying there on the ground. Dad, I told him, I kicked that football so hard it just exploded on me. My dad replied real quiet, Don't you go telling no stories, son. Okay, Dad.

I suspect I inherited my love for the game from my father, W. M. "Tennessee Bill" Bradshaw. He encouraged us to play. At times we'd have a dozen kids in my backyard playing football. We had a window with twelve panes of glass; the record we set for one-day breakage was seven. My father used to keep extra panes of glass and putty handy. If we needed an extra player, my mother would jump right in. Maybe she was a step slow going to her right, but we never held it against her. It was in that backyard that she lost most of her teeth.

I played my first game of organized football when I was nine years old. The first person I ever tried to tackle was Tony Poppa. I weighed seventy-five pounds; he was as big then as he was when he went to college. He was Superman. The stud. I was playing safety, and Tony Poppa came roaring through the line right at me. I was the only roadblock between him and the goal line. I saw him coming at me. And I knew a long time before Tony that he was about to make an eighty-yard run for a touchdown. I wasn't real committed to putting my body in front of him. I believe it was at that moment that I decided my future in football was as a quarterback.

I didn't know how to make a tackle. I closed my eyes, lowered my head, and threw all seventy-five pounds of myself at him—and missed completely. Proving once again that there is a God.

I wasn't a very big kid. Often now parents will come up to me and tell me proudly, "That boy of mine there, he wears a size 13 shoe!" Meaning that everybody who's got a big foot is going to be six-foot-six and a football star. "Terry, look at my boy's foot. What do you think about that foot?"

"Oh my," I always say, "that boy's got a nice foot." But what I'm really thinking is, He's a chubby little thing, isn't he? And then I notice that the man who is telling me this also has big feet, but he's five-foot-nine, and he's a welder.

I didn't have big feet, and my father *was* a welder. What I did have was a big heart and a big arm. The first position I played was offensive guard. Maybe I didn't know how to block, but I was always willing to listen to my coaches and learn. That never changed. Never. Even a lifetime later, after a fourteen-year professional career, I still don't know how to block.

After seeing how well I blocked, my coaches moved me to tailback. They handed me the ball and let me run with it. Oh, I liked that a lot, right up until the part in the play where the big guys caught you and everybody jumped on top of Terry. You okay down there, Terry?

Ummmpppff.

Terry's okay.

So I became the quarterback. I was born with a strong throwing arm. Me and both my brothers, Gary and Craig, had very strong arms. Some families inherit intelligence, others get good looks; we got right arms. My younger brother, Craig, in fact, also became a number-one draft pick. Of course, as he likes to tell people, he was the first pick the *second* day of the draft.

We grew up mostly in Shreveport, Louisiana, though we lived briefly in Comanche, Iowa. I spent most of the summers of my childhood on my grandparents' forty-acre farm in Hall Summit, which was about twenty-five miles and fifty years south of Shreveport. Pawpaw, my granddad, had animals, crops, a salt shed, and a two-hole outhouse on the farm. You had to walk through the briar patch to get to that outhouse. You knew your family had made it big when you had a two-holer out there. How many holes you got, Terry? We got two! Two! Damn, Terry, you sure gettin' fancy. I'd go in that outhouse with the Sears catalog and when I was sure nobody was around, I'd turn to the brassiere section and look at those pictures.

That was near as I got to knowing about sex in my childhood.

My brothers and I spent a lot of time back at that outhouse, shoveling and burying, fightin' off the bull flies. Those flies were so big we used to name 'em. Watch it, Craig, here comes Big Al again.

Pawpaw taught me how to plow a field, how to pick cotton and watermelons and cantaloupe. I had my own cotton-picking sack, and written on it in big letters was TP, Terry Pack. That's what all my relatives called me, Terry Pack. I learned how to thump a watermelon and tell from the sound how sweet it is. I learned how to drive a team of Clydesdales and stretch out a mink on a board so its eye sockets would dry out round. I learned how to pull a calf, and if the cow had a prolapsed uterus, I knew how to stuff it back in with brown sugar and sew it up with thread to save that cow and get her pregnant again the next year. I learned how to build a sweet potato shed and how to make buttermilk and paste.

It was four miles to town, and Pawpaw, particularly when I was little, would hook up the Clydesdales, Tony and Shorty, to his wagon and we'd ride to the cotton gin sitting on a bed of cotton. Then we'd go to the general store and buy fifty pounds of flour and ten pounds of Mrs. Tucker's Lard. We bought everything big, and everything got used. Mawmaw made her dresses out of the flour sacks. Pawpaw would make his own anvils and harnesses for the horses. On Saturday nights the men in the family would go into town to Slim's Barbershop for a haircut. I'd sit up on a board, and Slim would give me the high tight one. There were nine of us all getting the same haircut, and I'd listen to Slim and Pawpaw talk coon hunting. In the background the Grand Ole Opry was playing on the radio.

This is how I grew up. This was my foundation. This is my blood. This is where I learned my values. In my whole childhood I never heard an unkind word spoken about family. Nobody talked about one another. I learned my place, and I learned about love and trust, and more than anything, I learned on that farm in Hall Summit that it is the simple things in life that make all the difference.

In addition to football I played baseball and threw the javelin. In baseball, I was always a pitcher. I couldn't play any other position because I just couldn't stand still. I always had to be moving around, doing something. I learned how to throw the javelin by looking at the diagrams in the encyclopedia. Basically, the key to throwing it was . . . throwing it. And trying not to hit anybody. Unlike football, there are no plays in javelin throwing. The strategy is very simple: Throw it. Just throw that sucker as far as you can, and don't cross that little line. Just chunk it, put it out there. The track coach recruited me my sophomore year because he'd seen how far I could throw a football, and the team needed a few points in a meet. I didn't take it seriously. I don't think I ever threw it farther than 150 feet until the district meet. Then I threw it 175 feet and won the trophy. It was just a little aluminum thing, but it said "District First," and I loved it. It was like getting my varsity letter jacket in football; they gave me the heavy jacket in June, and I wore it proudly all summer. Sweated like a plow horse, but I wouldn't take it off because it was my letter jacket.

My junior year I competed against the state champion. This boy was a serious javelin chunker, and he definitely had big feet. People used to say, That boy's got big feet. I had been throwing about 180 feet, but I beat him in the district finals. Everybody just stood there shocked. I didn't even have big feet. Where'd that throw come from? I had no answer. It was like an out-of-body experience. I threw it, and it just went. It just . . . went. It was spectacular. It was pretty. It just hung in the air and . . . went. And it pierced the ground.

The rule was it had to stick in the ground. Like a spear. Several times I threw it 270 feet, 280 feet, but it landed flat on the ground so it didn't count.

During my senior year I'd been throwing it 208, maybe 210 feet. Then at the state meet it did something I had never done before: it got up there and just kept going. Two hundred forty-four feet, eleven and three-quarter inches. A national record. Reporters asked me, "How you'd do that, Terry?" What did they expect me to say? I studied those diagrams in the encyclopedia real hard? I just chunked it. I threw it as far as I could. That was my game plan, and it worked.

I learned something about myself too. When it mattered, I always did what was necessary. For whatever reason, I could produce when it was necessary.

School was not my first priority. My very first day in school I got my hand spanked with a ruler because I couldn't sit still. That never changed. If I enjoyed a subject, like history, I did well in the course; but for the most part learning wasn't fun for me. If I didn't understand a subject, I just ignored it. I went an entire semester without ever opening my geometry textbook, so I flunked every geometry test; F, F, F. The only good thing about that was that I showed consistency. For a long time I believed I just wasn't as smart as the other kids. It was a horrible feeling. Awful. But my real problem was that I could not sit calmly in my seat and focus on the subject for any period of time. I was always moving, always pulling at my hair or biting my fingernails. My mother used to say I was a "squirmer." Or a "fireball." "Terry is a very energetic young man," she used to say. "Terry really likes to hang from the ceiling."

As I discovered much later in life, there is a name for that besides, "Oh, that's just Terry." It's called an attention deficit disorder, ADD, and I could have been the poster boy for it. Of course, my picture on the poster would have been blurred.

ADD is not one of those tragic diseases about which they make movies-of-the-week. If they did, the movie would have to star the Road Runner. But ADD is a disease that prevents children from reaching their intellectual potential and therefore can affect their entire lives. As I've learned, it doesn't mean they're not every bit as smart as the other kids, it means they have difficulty processing certain information. They have difficulty focusing on one task for any length of time. For a child, it makes learning hard. For an adult, it makes life an interesting adventure. I remember telling my ex-wife one time, "We're going to buy just thirteen acres and no more. That's it, just thirteen acres." Next thing I knew I had forty-five acres. Then I had the whole ranch. I had a big ranch, so I had to buy more horses. Suddenly I found myself wondering why I was so deep in debt. To get out of debt I had to sell the ranch and the horses. And then I got so upset when I sold everything that I bought it all back.

I just couldn't sit still and study. When I became a broadcaster, the single hardest thing for me to do was learn all the players' names and numbers. Other broadcasters hated it when they had the same team three or four times during the same season. Not me. I loved it. This is great, I figured, I got these guys down. Hell, let's do their game next week too!

Until the last few years very little was known about ADD, and it was rarely diagnosed. There are still a lot of people who think it isn't an actual problem, it's just boys being active. Real, real active. My mother took me to several doctors, but they had no idea what was wrong. Even when doctors recognized that a problem existed there was little they could do. Medicines like Ritalin or Dexedrine didn't exist. Finally, long after I had finished my playing career, I decided I wanted to know what was wrong with me. So I took a battery of tests and as a result learned I have been ADD my whole life.

I truly wish I had been tested when I was a child so I might have been able to reach my potential academically. Not that I cared about academics, but I wouldn't have had to struggle quite so much. But I wasn't tested, I struggled, and in football I found my answers.

Which is one reason the game of football was so important to me. It was a healthy outlet for all that excess energy, and I loved it. I loved everything about it. I'd throw a football all day and all night if I could find somebody to throw it back to me. When I wore out everybody else, I'd throw it up on the roof and try to catch it when it bounced down. Or I'd throw it at objects. I hung a tire and a five-gallon bucket from a swing set—the tire and bucket lasted, but I broke the metal chains. It was 128 degrees in Shreveport, Louisiana—so hot, flies were sweating—but I'd be outside throwing my football. When we lived in Iowa the snow would be nineteen feet deep, and I'd be outside throwing passes into the snowbank. I threw a football every day of my life, and eventually I got good at it.

When I was seven years old, I told my father that someday I was going to play in the National Football League. Now, did I really believe that? Well, of course I did, with all my heart and soul. And I also believed I would win four Super Bowls and get elected to the Hall of Fame, but I didn't tell him that part. I also didn't tell him the part about me cohosting the Fox network's NFL pregame show every Sunday with James Brown, Howie Long, and Cris Collinsworth and a cast of supporting characters, or having my own television talk show and having to let a tarantula walk on my head, or that I would someday make several movies with Burt Reynolds and Mel Tillis, and I didn't tell him that his very own son would be making speeches to a big bunch of the Fortune 500 companies in the country, and people would actually be listening to what I said. I wanted to surprise him.

For a long time though, it seemed like I was the only one who knew how successful I was going to be. I was not a great athlete; I was tall and awkward and clumsy. All I could do was throw the football. In eighth grade I could throw it sixty yards. But I didn't start on my junior high team until I was in ninth grade. I didn't start at quarterback on my high school team until my senior year. I cared, it was painful for me, but as long as they let me put on a football uniform and play a little, I never complained. I was a team player. I sat on the bench and waited my turn. The same thing happened in college and again in the pros. And when my turn came, I got in the huddle, and I said those two most beautiful words in the English language, "Go deep."

Many kids with ADD compensate for not being able to keep up academically by living on the edge of life. They can be kind of wild. They play harder at athletics or drink more alcohol. If they don't have strong parental supervision, they can have a difficult time. I had strong parental supervision. I had my father.

My dad was a strict disciplinarian. He taught us the value of honesty, discipline, and hard work. We were taught to take responsibility for our actions. We raked our yard and dug up the garden with a shovel—the size of the garden expanded each year as we got older until it covered probably half an acre—and we washed the dishes and cleaned our rooms. My mom hit me a hundred times more than my father, but now I can admit the woman had a weak right arm. "Oh no, Mom, not that," I'd tell her, "not the big Double Whammy!" And when she finished, "Whoa, Mom, you done whup my ass out. My oh my, I just can't take another beating. From this moment on I am going to be a fine young man."

My dad was a lot tougher. He whupped us. I got my strong right arm from him. Like a lot of parents he didn't believe in corporal punishment; he believed in four-star general punishment. When my dad looks back on those days, he says nostalgically, "Today they'd put me in jail for that."

When I did something wrong, he would discuss it with me. The discussion went something like this: whup, whup, whup. End of discussion. Dad had learned that from his father; when he was a child his father had only hit him a few times, but for emphasis he'd used a chain and a whip, and when you do that, it only takes a few times.

Dad insisted that we complete all of our homework every night. That seemed a little harsh to me. But education was really important to him; he was a welder who had gone back to school to work on his engineering degree while supporting his family. We had a desk at which we would all study. Well, one morning my junior year in high school he found out I hadn't done my homework. He marked me pretty good with his one-inch belt. There was no "This is going to hurt me more than it's going to hurt you" stuff. It hurt me and only me. I had welts on my legs. I went to football practice that day, and we were working out in shorts and pads. The coach saw those welts and suggested I wear my long warm-ups to hide them. I wouldn't do that. I believed that I had gotten what I deserved. I was sorry that it happened, but I was wrong.

I would never hit my two girls, but that was a different time, and I was a different child.

And my father was not an unreasonable man. I remember when I was eight or nine years old, a friend of mine got a pool table. A pool table! I had never even seen a pool table. I couldn't hardly wait. But on Saturday my mother sent me to get a haircut and told me to come straight home afterward because I had chores to do. Well, I diverted. I came straight home in a wiggly kind of way that took me right by that pool table. I told my mom I was late because I had to wait in a long line at the barbershop.

The NFL Championship game was being played

the next day, and my brother, my father, and I were going to watch it together after church. That game was the most important event of the year for me. But at breakfast that morning, I made a terrible mistake. I told my brother Gary, "You should see Bubba's pool table. That baby can cook . . ."

My mother said pleasantly, "Terry, didn't I tell you to come straight home? That I didn't want you going by there to shoot pool? You lied to me, didn't you?"

To me, it sounded more like, "YOU LIED TO ME AND NOW YOU ARE DOOMED." "Yes, ma'am," I admitted.

That was followed by the most terrifying sound I ever heard in my house. Silence. That meant she was thinking about my punishment. "I'll deal with this after church," she finally said.

NOT AFTER CHURCH! That was terrible. It meant that I was going to have to wait for about four hours. All the way to Sunday school, I was thinking, You know, Lord, this would be a real good time for a sermon about forgiveness. And while You're at it, a little reminder that "Jesus loved all the little children," would be mighty appreciated.

But through the service, the only thing I could think about was the terrible whupping that was about to be bestowed upon my behind. And rather than forgiveness, the preacher sprinkled his sermon that very day with threats of Satan. Well, even Satan couldn't scare me that particular day, 'cause my momma was *thinkin'*!

But when we got home, nobody said a word. I began to believe in the power of prayer. My mother was cooking dinner, and then the game would be on.

We sat down to eat, and I'm basically pretending to be invisible. Maybe, I thought, just maybe, she forgot. Maybe I was going to get by. Finally, my dad asked, "Son, did you lie to your mother?"

My fault. I didn't pray hard enough. "Yes, sir."

"When you get through eating go to your room. I'll be in there in a minute."

Oh no! I was busy preparing for a momma beating—if you were quick enough you could make her miss a bunch and tire her out—but my dad had persistence, stamina, and the belt. I just sat there on my bed waiting for him. I knew what was about to happen. What did my dad hate more than anything in the world? Lying. Anything else he would listen to reason. Or pleading. But for lying you paid the penalty. When he came in, I apologized. "I don't know why I did it," I said, "I just wanted to shoot pool. It was really neat."

"You going to do it again?"

"Dad, I promise you I will never lie to you or Mom again."

"All right," he decided, "I'll give you a choice. I whip you, you can watch the game. If you don't want a whipping, you stay in your room."

What kind of choice is that? "Dad, I'll take the whipping."

"Son," he said, "I'm real proud of you. Now you keep hollering, okay?" And then he started beating that belt on the bed. As I stood there in astonishment, knowing that my morning in church had been well spent—Thank you, sweet baby Jesus—My dad gave that bed a whipping.

Finally my mother couldn't bear it any longer.

"Honey," she yelled from the living room, "that's enough."

About fifteen minutes later I gathered myself and went into the living room to watch the game with my family. I actually did wipe a tear or two from my eyes. But my mom was there to offer comfort.

Now, admittedly, on occasion I did give my father reason to take a good whack at me. When my father was eleven years old, he got bit by a spider, then rolled over and killed it. His leg swelled up badly. The bite left him with a scar and a phobia. He hates spiders, hates them. Naturally when my brother Gary and I learned about this, we were sympathetic. Naturally. One afternoon we were digging a hole for a tree we intended to plant. My father was holding a piece of wood that we were going to use to hold up that tree until it could take root. I took a shovelful of dirt, flipped it toward my dad, and hollered, "Spider." In retrospect, it's fair to report that he didn't think it was as funny as I did. Here's a good lesson: Never ignite a man's phobia when he's holding a thick stick.

My father balanced discipline with dedication to his family. We spent a lot of time together. My family members are still my best friends. My father taught me how to hunt and fish and enjoy the very basic things of life, and except for those occasional times when I almost killed him, we always had a wonderful time.

Accidents happen, okay? I didn't like hunting. I wasn't good at it. And if there is something you are not going to be good at, it's much better if it doesn't involve guns. But I always went with my father and my brother because I loved being in the woods. I have a passion and a deep respect for the land. I'm always happy just looking at the land as God made it or walking quietly in a meadow or alongside a lake.

I don't enjoy shooting things, but I've done it. The first bird I ever killed was walking on the ground. I only shot it to save my dog. I love all animals, but especially dogs and horses. Horses are limited intellectually, but they are honest and sincere. Treat them with kindness, and they will reward you.

Of course, that was pretty much the way I felt about offensive linemen too.

Dogs have a pretty basic philosophy of life; they live just to live. I had a German shorthaired retriever named Buck. Dad spent hours in the backyard with Buck trying to teach him to point and retrieve. But mostly Buck enjoyed playing with me, maybe because Buck also had a limited attention span. He'd be in the woods ready to sniff out some birds, he'd be so close—and then he would see me and forget all about hunting. That was my fault; when my father was training him, I'd sneak him out of the pen and wrassle with him. My dad had him to hunt, I wanted him for fun. But one day I heard my dad tell someone, "This is Buck's last time out. Hell, he's not panning out for me."

Now Buck did not grasp the gravity of the situation. He just wanted to play with me. He did not seem concerned that his long-term future was in serious doubt here. I knew my father was serious. Several years earlier I'd had a dog named Sandy. Sandy was supposed to be a working dog. I turned her into a pet. At night I'd lean outside my bedroom window, holding on by my toes, and pick her up and bring her in the bed with me. One day I came home from school, and Sandy was gone. Gone. My parents told me they'd given her to a little crippled child. Maybe so, but I never saw her again.

So I took Buck, and we went off by ourselves. He was jumping up and down on me, waiting to play. I was on my hands and knees, crawling through the corn rows, when I saw this bird strutting along. I grabbed Buck, turned his head so he was looking directly at the bird, and held it steady. That got his attention. All of a sudden Buck got rigid; his ancestry was kicking in. I shot that bird's head off. He ran and picked up that bird and proudly put it in his mouth, and together we walked to the end of the road. My father heard the shot and had come running. And I told him in great detail how Buck had hunted down that bird and I'd shot him. It was a miracle, I said. That made Buck's career.

The first time I ever pulled the trigger of a gun, the recoil knocked me down hard. It was a 12-gauge shotgun, and I think my Dad wanted to see me tumble backward. Bam! There goes Terry. During my playing career I got hit hard by some big football players. There were times when I didn't just see stars, I saw entire galaxies. But I never got hit by anything as powerful as the recoil of that rifle. My father wanted me to have a healthy respect for the power of a rifle.

I got even. We were living in Comanche, Iowa, and went to hunt some pheasant. Suddenly this one lone bird came gliding from our right to our left. In the field in front of us a farmer was on his tractor picking corn. My father told everybody to get down real low. I didn't see the purpose in trying to hide from a bird. I was wondering who was going to get to shoot this bird. It was an easy shot. I knew it wasn't going to be me, I never got the easy shots. This bird was just gliding in. It was beautiful. I couldn't help myself. While everyone else was ducking, I raised my double-barrel and fired. Either it was raining pheasant, or I'd hit it. I dropped that sucker right on that farmer. Of course, if anyone had stood up while I was shooting, I might have hit them too. I spent the entire rest of that day sitting alone in our car, "thinking about it," as my father said.

About the only place I could sit reasonably still was in the Calgary Baptist Church of Shreveport, Louisiana, in the presence of Brother Buck Buchanan. Brother Buchanan was a big man with a big booming voice, and I just loved listening to him. He was so good that you could get saved on Sunday, and by the next Sunday you wanted to get saved again. Hallelujah! If there had been TV evangelists back then, Brother Buck would have been a star. He was a fine speaker! He would let it rip! He would raise heaven and hell and let you know in no uncertain terms what evil Satan had prepared for the young man foolish enough to fall for his charms. Brothers and sisters, there is danger lurking out there. Satan has laid his traps, and he will lure you in. Do you hear what I'm saying to you? I said, do you hear me! Satan will win every debate with the flesh of man. He is clever! Some of you, some of you will fall for them, yes you will, because Satan is clever. And when he gets his hands on you, Satan will hold tight and drag you down. But the Lord is watching you, He is looking over your shoulder, He is with you. Lemme have an Amen on that, brothers and sisters! Glory Hallelujah!

Brother Buchanan mesmerized me. He was awesome. I was raised in a Christian household, and there still isn't a day that goes by in my life that some aspect of my faith doesn't make itself known. I've slipped. Oh Lord, I've slipped a lot. Just like a lot of people when things were tough I called on my faith to help me, but when things got good I sort of forgot about it. But I've always come back to my faith. When I was growing up I felt like God had His hand on me. I looked at most things differently than my friends, I acted differently. I was pretty much a loner. I didn't join groups, I didn't hang out, I didn't drink, I wasn't a carouser—although admittedly like most young men on occasion I would dream about one good carouse.

During my career I was never particularly vocal about my religious beliefs. To me, it was sort of like my Super Bowl rings. I won four of them, but I never wear any of them. I know I won them, I just don't feel it's necessary to wear my success on my finger.

I feel the same way about my faith. When I watch a sporting event and I see an athlete thanking the Lord for letting his team win the game, I get real uncomfortable. If they are serious about it, that's fine; but that means they'd better give Him praise after they lose too. When I watch people like that, I wonder, would they still be giving thanks to the Lord if things were bad? To me, that's the real test. I wonder how many people are really going to be like the great football player Reggie White. I've known Reggie White for a long time, and he lives the life he preaches. I know he means it when he gives thanks, and I respect him for it. But there are a lot of players wearing $150,000 crosses around their neck. As I've learned, it ain't the size of the cross you're wearing, but what is in your heart.

When I was in junior high, I would visit different churches around Shreveport to give personal testimony. It was very difficult for me to stand up in front of a church full of people. I didn't know and confess my sins and praise the Lord. I didn't enjoy it. I didn't have any interesting sins to confess—I was just a kid, I had never even had a beer or kissed a girl—and I was too nervous. But I felt it was the right thing to do, and I knew it made people happy. I have always tried to please people, always, and this was simply another example of that. So when several years later I did commit those sins—I did mention that on occasion I slipped—I felt tremendous guilt. I felt like the Lord's hammer was clanging on my head.

When I began speaking in public after I retired, I drew mightily on those early speaking experiences. The difference was that I never did feel guilty talking about appliance sales.

Early in my life I thought I wanted to be a preacher. And one summer, while I was in college, I served as a youth minister for a Methodist church. That job is the reason I now sleep with a .357 magnum near my bed. I don't remember very much of what I told the youth, mostly do good things and don't do bad things, but I do remember getting hit over the head and getting shot at. Of course, that was not a direct result of my work as a minister.

I was staying at an old Methodist parsonage way out on the edge of town. Late one night I woke up, and I just felt that someone was watching me. Maybe I heard something outside, I don't know, but I crawled down to the end of the bed and parted the blinds.

A man was looking right back at me. Oh, my goodness! The window was open, and Bam! He whopped me over the head with a Dr Pepper bottle. I fell back on the bed, and by the time I got up, he was long gone. I was definitely scared, but I wouldn't leave that house. I was doing the Lord's work, and I knew the Lord would protect me.

The prowler returned about a week later. Woke me out of a sound sleep just banging his way through the house. I could hear him clomping around the kitchen breaking plates and glasses and throwing pots around. Under the circumstances I did what any intelligent person would have done. There was an old oak bureau that must have weighed 300 pounds in the room. Like Samson I picked it up and put it in front of the door. Finally, I heard him leave. I immediately waited about an hour, then slowly moved the chest of drawers and walked through the house. It was a mess, but whoever it was, was gone.

I didn't know what to do about it. I told my friend Tommy Spinks about it, and Tommy told me, "Don't worry, whoever it is, he's just trying to scare you."

It certainly was working. I was definitely scared. Then one evening I came home and found a knife stuck clean through my pillow with a note on it reading, "I'll be back." I'll be back! With a knife! I promise you this is absolutely true. I realized then that the Lord definitely did work in mysterious ways. I still wouldn't move out of the house, I still believed the Lord would protect me, but just in case He was busy at the crucial moment, I decided to give Him a little help. I drove home and got my shotgun and bought me a dog, a boxer puppy. I put that shotgun on the floor next to my bed, and I slept just like a baby—I got up every twenty minutes.

Our final confrontation began the middle of one night. The intruder came in and started slamming doors. I could hear him crashing through the house, coming closer and closer to my room. This was the moment I had been dreading—I was either going to have to stand or run. I took a deep breath and made my decision: Run! Run for it! I grabbed my shotgun and the dog and bailed out the bedroom window. I ran to my car. This was a brand-new yellow-and-black Pontiac GTO with an unusual transmission: to put it in reverse, you had to push a button and pull back on the stick. I turned on the car, put it in reverse, slammed down on the accelerator—and drove the car straight ahead into the wall. I smashed up the front pretty good—but I didn't have time to worry about that, I backed up and took off.

I told my buddy Tommy Spinks about my burglar, and we decided to go back to the house. Tommy was carrying a big stick, and I had a club. We decided to circle the house, meeting in the back. I went around the left side, keeping low, being very quiet, making sure that no one . . . All of a sudden this guy steps out in front of me. He was carrying a shotgun. He leveled that shotgun and fired at me. All I saw was flames and pellets, flames and pellets. I turned around and started running as fast as I have ever run in my life. But as I was running I started worrying, Where's Tommy? Where's my buddy Tommy? Oh, Lord, no, I didn't want to desert my best friend in a time of great need. Then I looked up, and there was Tommy—about 500 yards ahead of me. He was way, way ahead of me. I never did catch him. That's the fastest that boy ever ran in his life.

We ran practically all the way to the police station. Several police officers returned to the house with us. They went through the house, and way in the back they found the burglar. The detectives told me he had been living in the attic for who knows how long. The only way to get up into the attic was to climb up on a desk and pull yourself up through the trapdoor. The attic was filthy, littered with beer cans, food cans, girlie magazines, all kinds of dried meat wrappers. He was just trying to scare me out of there, he said. He never intended to hurt me, and had intentionally missed with that shotgun blast. I had only one question: Exactly what constitutes an intentional miss with a shotgun?

While I try to practice in my life what I am taught by my faith, I have never tried to convert anyone. I respect the practice of all faiths. One time, I remember, I attended a Pentecostal service. The Pentecostals are what is called a charismatic religion. They believe that the Holy Spirit speaks through them. While it might sound a little like gibberish, it's known as "speaking in tongues." At this service the preacher was raising the Holy Spirit: "God said we are going to rise to the top of the mountain. We are going to take God's children up. We are going to yadda, yadda, yadda—"

I couldn't understand a word that man was saying. What is that? I wondered. I turned around and asked the person standing behind me, What is he saying? Speaking in tongues, I was told. It didn't matter if I understood it, God understood it. It is the perfect communication with the Lord. That definitely got my attention.

When I was with the Steelers, I would occasionally join several players in a Bible study. At one of these meetings they asked me if I would like to receive the Holy Spirit—meaning would I like to learn how to speak in tongues. Well, of course I would. I'd taken French in high school and could speak a few sentences, but this was something entirely different.

The only way to get the Holy Spirit, I was told, was from people who have received it. God gave it to them, they can pass it along to others. It's done physically through what is called the laying on of hands. We went into my dormitory room at training camp and I sat down on my bed. A group of my teammates surrounded me and started praying loudly and fervently. They laid their hands on my body—and where they were touching me, I could feel heat. Something was definitely happening—the whole room started getting very hot. They started shouting, louder and louder. LORD WE ARE SAVED! SAVED! I don't know if the room got hot because I was receiving the Holy Spirit or simply because I was so nervous, but I definitely could feel the heat rising inside me. People were praying and yelling, they were yabba-dabba-doing all around the room; it was an old-fashioned tent revival meeting right there in my room.

I kept waiting for the message to come through me, I was ready to yadda yadda yadda . . . but nothing happened. Finally, everybody calmed down and they began teaching me how to speak in tongues. Wait a second, I thought, if this is supposed to be a natural outpouring of emotion, why is it being explained to me? If God speaks to me, and the Holy Spirit is in me, then the Holy Spirit should be doing the talking. So why did I have to be taught the words?

That was a question I never could answer. The only conclusion I can reach is that I never received the Holy Spirit because I have never spoken in tongues—although some people who have seen me on television might argue that I have said a lot of things that didn't make any sense.

While my faith was important to me throughout my entire playing career, it was even more important to me during my sitting career. Most football players who eventually make it to the National Football League have been stars from Pee Wee League right through college. Not me. Growing up, I spent a lot more time sitting on the bench than playing. At Oak Terrace Junior High School I didn't even make the seventh-grade team. In eighth grade I was the second-team quarterback, and in ninth grade I was a starting quarterback for the first time. At Woodlawn High School I played for a wonderful man and legendary coach named Lee Hedges. Joe Ferguson, the great Buffalo Bills quarterback, also played for him. Football was big-time at Woodlawn; we would draw crowds of 15,000 people. It was at Woodlawn under Lee Hedges that I learned how to sit on the bench with pride and determination. Years later in Pittsburgh, when we lost our first three games my rookie season and Chuck Noll benched me, I knew how to sit on that bench thanks to Lee Hedges.

At Woodlawn the quarterback playing in front of me was a high school All-American named Trey Prather. But rather than being discouraged because I wasn't the varsity quarterback, and pouting, I practiced as hard as I could, believed in my ability, and waited for my chance. Coach Hedges was always supportive. He treated his players with respect, telling them the truth. I always knew right where I stood with him, I didn't have to guess why I wasn't playing. I wasn't playing because Coach Hedges believed Trey Prather was a better quarterback than I was. My junior year, when we would get a lead, Coach would slip me in for a few plays to get some experience. "Just keep the ball on the ground," he'd tell me, "don't you go throwing any passes."

"Yes, sir," I'd tell him, then go out and immediately start throwing passes. Anybody could run with the ball or hand off; I loved just rearing back and throwing that ball thirty, forty, fifty yards in the air. My brain was making promises my arm could keep. What was Coach Hedges going to do, bench me for throwing touchdown passes?

What I really remember best about playing quarterback in high school is being so scared that when I tried to pass the football I couldn't even do it. In high school I did not call my own plays. In one of my very first games Coach Hedges called a play-action pass, meaning we would fake a run to the right, and I would bootleg it out to the left and look for my receiver. I took the snap, faked the handoff, and ran to my left. I looked up, and my receiver was wide open. He was thirty yards down the left sideline, running with his hand in the air, calling for the football. The closest defender was in Nebraska. There wasn't nothing but air near him. The play was perfect. Perfect! It had developed just as it had been planned. All I had to do was throw it to him.

Ladies and gentlemen, I could not get the ball out of my hand. It was a nightmare. I just held it and held it, I could not throw that football. It felt like it was stuck. Finally, at the very last second, I reared back and threw it—and instead of it going straight to the open receiver, it slipped off the side of my hand. Maybe it slipped, but it was a perfect spiral. I never even looked in that direction. The running back I had originally faked to had continued running down the right sideline. The ball hit him in midstride, seventy yards for a touchdown.

The place went crazy. I danced off that field feeling pretty good; awright, okay, I'm cool, seventy yards, acting as if I knew what I was doing. When I got to the sidelines everybody was patting me on the back, cheering for me.

The next day we looked at the game films. Coach Hedges took me aside and asked me, "Where were you throwing that ball, Terry?"

"Right to that receiver, Coach," I said emphatically. "Where else would I be throwing it?"

"That's what I was wondering." he said. On the game films it was obvious. No wonder that back was so wide open; I fooled everybody. Even fooled myself. I didn't think I was throwing to him either.

I was our starting quarterback my senior year. I didn't have a lot of experience, but I had raw talent and a rocket arm, so I attracted the attention of college scouts.

More than two hundred colleges offered me track scholarships—I even got track scholarship offers from schools in Europe—but as it seemed pretty certain no one was about to start a professional javelin-throwing league, I knew that if I was going to have a career in sports it was going to be in football. Among the few major colleges to offer me a football scholarship was Baylor University. Baylor is a fine Baptist university in Waco, Texas, whose motto is *Pro Ecclesia, Pro Texana,* which roughly translates, "Terry can't even understand the motto, so no way is he going to go there." But I did go there for a visit, and it was an impressive place. Before I visited the campus I believed that Baylor was a fine Baptist university and that all the students there spent their time doing praiseworthy things for God Almighty. During my campus visit I spent time with a player I knew from high school—and I was shocked at what I saw: Shocked! We were in his room, and from beneath his bed he pulled out a six-pack of beer and offered me a drink! I had never had an alcoholic drink in my life, and I wasn't about to attend a Christian college where football players kept alcohol under their beds. It was clear to me that the devil was on the loose there.

I wasn't going to go to a university where football players drank alcohol. In retrospect, perhaps I was a bit naive. But the real truth is, I really didn't want to go to Baylor. It was too far away from home, it was too big, and it was in Texas. In my mind, Texas was always next to Louisiana, even though some people thought I wasn't very good in geography. Like most people who grew up in the great state of Louisiana, I loved it. My dream was to become a football star close to home so my parents and friends could come to all my games.

I was also offered a scholarship to Louisiana State University. LSU had a great football tradition, and there was a lot of pressure on me to accept that offer. I was ambivalent, even before I knew what that meant. While it was an honor to have been offered the scholarship, I wasn't sure I could compete in big-time college football. I had played only one year of high school football. I had no real confidence in myself. And a year earlier LSU had recruited the very same player I sat behind in high school. He was one year ahead of me—and he was sitting on the bench. Now, if the quarterback who had put me on the bench in high school was sitting on the bench his own self in college, what were the chances that I was going to play ahead of him? Maybe I wasn't too good at math, but that was a problem I could figure out. Any big number you multiply by zero is still going to come out zero.

Just about everybody I knew—as well as a lot of people I didn't know—wanted me to go to LSU. I didn't know how to tell them that I didn't feel comfortable in Baton Rouge, so I purposely flunked the entrance exam. I have never much liked people who make excuses for their failures. I am not claiming that I could have passed that exam easily if I had wanted to go to LSU. I'll never know if I could have passed it; I know I didn't study for it, I didn't care about it, and I definitely didn't want to go to LSU. And I also didn't pass the test.

Maybe it was because of my ADD, but I always had difficulty taking standardized tests. I think I got about a 5 on the first test, and they give you 7 points for getting your name right. To qualify for a scholarship you had to get 16—when I took the test a second time I got 15. Instead of being upset about it, I was relieved. All it meant to me was that I couldn't go to LSU. Of course, I absolutely could not imagine how failing that test would affect my life. If I had known how it would damage my reputation, how it would cost me a fortune in endorsements, how embarrassing it would be, I would have put some real effort into studying, and I could have failed that test with style!

Instead I attended Louisiana Tech University in Ruston, Louisiana. My high school preparation immediately began paying big dividends as I sat on the bench for two years. I was sitting on the bench for a small Louisiana college that few people had even heard of, that played teams that few people even knew existed, yet I continued to believe without any doubt that I was on my way to a career in professional football.

That is the definition of faith.

The quarterback playing ahead of me, Phil Robertson, loved hunting more than he loved football. He'd come to practice directly from the woods, squirrel tails hanging out of his pockets, duck feathers on his clothes. Clearly he was a fine shot, so no one complained too much.

I warmed the bench my freshman and sophomore years. After two seasons, that bench was plenty warm enough. At the end of my sophomore year I began to see my dream slipping away from me. I don't quite remember how it happened—my father might have made the phone calls—but we got in touch with a coach at Florida State University who invited me to transfer. My older brother, Gary, and I got in the car and started driving to Tallahassee to meet the coaching staff. But before we could get there, the coaches at Tech found out we were on our way and threatened to inform the NCAA that FSU was tampering. By the time we got to Tallahassee, no one on that coaching staff would even meet with us.

The following season Phil Robertson got knocked out cold during a game against a real tough Delta State team. I took over and played well. Turned out that was the best thing that happened for both of us. During my junior year my body finally caught up with my arm. I set passing and scoring records at Tech, made some All-American teams, and my junior year led the nation in Total Offense. Robertson started making his own duck calls, which he eventually turned into a huge business. He made a fortune. If you need to call a duck, most probably you're going to use one of Phil Robertson's calls.

I worked hard at playing football. I worked out every single day. I lifted weights. I ran sprints and long distances. Maybe Louisiana Tech was a small school, but we had that electricity that we'd heard they had at big schools up north. Ain't that electricity somethin'? Hit one switch, it goes on, hit another one, it goes off! Our stadium had lights, and I learned how to climb a telephone pole and jack on the switches. We'd wait till it got real dark so no one could see us and then turn on the lights. We figured no one would know we were there. Worst camouflage concept since the lightning bug. Then my friends and I would run up and down the field throwing passes. Somehow the campus police managed to discover our secret and made us leave.

Then I would turn on the lights in the gym and throw on the hardwood floor. I absolutely loved throwing a football.

I flew on an airplane for the first time in my life while I was in college. We made three plane trips during my college career, but mostly we traveled to our games by bus. The definition of a long trip is a six-hour drive on an old bus back from Hammond, Louisiana, after you've played a terrible game. While we played by the same rules as the big-time universities, it was still a different game. When someone got hurt during one of our games, for example, we were such a small school we could only afford to give them second aid. Once, I remember, during a game at the University of Southwestern Louisiana I got tackled hard on the asphalt runway also used for the pole vault. Darn neared killed me. They had to wrap me in ice and drive me home stretched out in the back of the trainer's station wagon.

Naturally our trainer was mighty upset about that. The man had to leave his good spare tire behind.

At Louisiana Tech we also did not receive a lot of the rewards for winning that football players at major colleges supposedly received. We were given $10 a month laundry money. Once Tommy Spinks and I were so hungry we decided to have a fund-raising drive. Because we suspected few students were going to donate money for pizza, we decided to collect for the March of Dimes. We wrote up an official piece of paper that said, basically, "These people are definitely not collecting money to spend on pizza. They are raising money for the March of Dimes." We collected about thirty dollars for the March of Dimes and ordered four extra-super-large-family-size pizzas and gallon-gulps, and we still had money left over for dates. The Floor Resident nailed us. He wanted us to return every cent we'd raised. Naturally we couldn't do that, so we had to go room to room and explain that somehow we had made a small mistake, we forgot that we were actually not collecting for the March of Dimes, but that we were collecting for pizza. We got six weeks' strict campus probation and had to pay back every dime.

On another occasion my roommate, Larry Brewer, a fine boy from Minden, Louisiana, and I were alone in the athletic dorm, and we were broke and hungry. For some reason the dorm was pretty much deserted. We were walking all alone complaining that we didn't even have a dime for a soda. And then I noticed maybe a hundred empty bottles stacked up next to the soda machine. At two cents a bottle, I figured that was almost . . . almost two dollars. "Larry, look at these pop bottles. We can cash 'em in and get some money."

"Can we do that?" he wondered.

"Sure," I said confidently, "what can they do to us?"

That was always a bad question for me to ask. They usually could figure something out. This was the day I became Louisiana Tech's most notorious pop bottle rustler. We loaded up pillowcases with bottles and filled the backseat of Larry's car. Then we went to the other dorms and collected enough bottles to fill the trunk. We only stopped because we couldn't squeeze another bottle into the car. I do thank the Good Lord that at that time He did not see fit to give us a truck. But we knew we had enough for burgers and fries and probably a movie. Man, we were stylin'.

As we got ready to leave, a security guard stopped us and asked what we were doing. Now, consider this: You've got two people, one car, and a thousand pop bottles. What did he think we were doing? Going to an art show? Right about then I had to admit to Larry that I wasn't really up on the most recent pop-bottle-rustling laws.

The guard wrote down our license plate number, and we took off. We knew we couldn't unload our haul at the usual local stores. In case the police were tracking us, we stayed off the interstate. We took old Highway 80 and the back roads. We weren't exactly Bonnie and Clyde, more like Moe and Curly. We drove through several small towns until we figured we had made good our getaway and pulled up to the back door of a big store in Larry's hometown, Minden, Louisiana.

We made the deal, leaving with $80! No hamburgers for us. We were in the big time. We had some serious cash. We couldn't even close our wallets. We bought steaks and fries, salads and malts—and we went to the movies.

By the time we got back to school, there was a note on our door instructing us to see the dean of men. Immediately. Faster than immediately. As the dean later explained to my father, "I keep a six-iron behind my desk. I just wanted to take it out an whip 'em with it."

I suspect my dad suggested that instead of an iron he get himself a wood and just drive me home. In the end, we were restricted to campus for six more weeks.

All my childhood dreams came true my senior year. I'd led the nation in total offense—passing and running—my junior year, so the pro scouts found their way to Louisiana Tech to see if I could play the game of football. That was a big deal for Ruston; with all those important football people driving through town, the town council even debated getting the traffic signal fixed

Although we were picked to finish last in our conference, we had a great season and played the Akron Zips for the 1969 NCAA College Division Mideast Championship in the Grantland Rice Bowl in Murfreesboro, Tennessee. The weather was terrible that day, cold and snowy, but I didn't even notice. I was going to be on TV for the first time. It was ABC's regional college game of the week, the region being Louisiana. Just about everybody I knew in the world was watching. At the beginning of the broadcast each player ran right up to the camera and introduced himself: we were told to give our name, position, high school, and hometown. Name, position, high school, hometown. Name, position, high school, hometown. I could do that. This was the coolest thing to me. I started getting really nervous. Finally I ran up to that camera and said my name just as if I'd been saying it my whole life, "Terry Bradshaw. Quarterback. Woodlawn High School. Shreveport, Louisiana." Then I peeled off to the right.

I could just imagine how proud of me my friends watching at home were. Weren't Terry great? He just got up there and said his piece just perfect like.

As it turned out, the scouts were impressed too. I was a big, strong kid who could run and throw deep. Late in the game three Akron players grabbed hold of me, and as I was going down I managed to throw for a touchdown. It was the kind of moment that made me wish someone would hurry up and invent instant replay.

Until that time my dreams of playing professional football had been more in the abstract; suddenly they became real. The scouts were telling my father I was going to get drafted. I was going to get a chance to play pro football. It seemed like just a few years earlier that my father had taken me out to the Fairgrounds to see my first pro game, the New York Titans against the Houston Oilers of the American Football League. Well, actually, it *was* only a few years earlier. The Oilers had players like George Blanda, Charlie Hennigan, and tough running back Charlie Tolar. The old AFL played my kind of football—wind up and throw deep. Defense in that league was mostly a rumor. They played the worst defense since France in World War II. The defense *held* teams to 40 points. The people who formed the league believed spectators wanted wide-open offenses, high-scoring games. That always made sense to me.

But by this time the league was being dissolved, with several teams forming a new division inside the National Football League.

Although I rooted hard for the New Orleans Saints, I really didn't care much who drafted me. While a lot of teams seemed interested in me, they were concerned that I hadn't played against the best collegiate competition. Seems like they would have had more confidence in my ability if I'd sat on the bench at Notre Dame instead of starting at Louisiana Tech. "That ol' boy is a good one, sat on Notre Dame's bench for four straight years! 'Member that great game he didn't play in against Michigan?"

I thought I'd probably be selected in the third or fourth round, which still would have been thrilling for me. But after I played against the best seniors in the country in the Senior Bowl and was selected co–Most Valuable Player, the pros began to take me very seriously. My dad spent time with the great quarterback Y. A. Tittle, who was real high on me. Then we began to hear stories that I might be taken with the first pick. That didn't seem likely; no player from a small college had ever been the number-one pick in the draft. But Don Shula told my father he was ready to trade six people for me. Sure, I thought, Groucho, Harpo, Chico . . . Johnny Unitas told my father he was really high on me. And through all this excitement I remembered my dad's words, "Terry, put the football down right now and go to sleep!"

So, at about that time it dawned on me that my reward for playing so well in college was a chance to play with the very worst professional football team in America. I was first prize for being awful. How bad are we? Bad enough to get Terry Bradshaw! Wow, that's bad.

There were two teams fighting for that dubious honor, the Chicago Bears and the Pittsburgh Steelers. They played each other in a game that became known as the Bradshaw Bowl—because the winner might lose the opportunity to finish dead last and draft me. The Bears were 0-7 and the Steelers were 1-6. By winning, the Steelers lost. The two teams finished the season tied at 1-13.

To determine who would get first pick in the draft, the two teams met the day before the draft and tossed a 1921 silver dollar. The Bears called heads. It landed on the floor tails. That's how my future was determined.

I intended to go fishing draft day. At about two in the morning I got a phone call from the Bears telling me they were in the process of making a trade and they intended to make me the first selection in the draft.

Thank you kindly, I said, and then I went back to bed.

My father told me I had to stay home that day. Our local TV reporter heard that I was going to be the first pick and came out to interview me. Finally, the phone rang and I was informed that I had been the number-one selection in the draft. It really was thrilling, though for a time I thought it was the Bears who had drafted me.

I don't remember too much about that day except that I did a lot of telephone interviews. And instead of being humble, I probably said some things I shouldn't have said about playing in the NFL and winning a championship. I do remember being asked a question about "belittling" an opponent. I responded confidently, even though I had absolutely no idea what "belittle" meant. But I was certain I was going to go to the NFL and belittle everybody!

Eventually I learned I had been drafted by the Pittsburgh Steelers. In thirty-seven years of existence the Steelers had never won a playoff game. In the past the Steelers had released a young quarterback and future Hall-of-Famer named Johnny Unitas. In a draft they had selected future Hall-of-Famer Len Dawson rather than future Hall-of-Famer Jimmy Brown, but let Dawson sit on the bench before sending him to the Cleveland Browns. In another draft they picked Gary Glick over future Hall-of-Famer Lenny Moore. Once they traded draft choices with the Bears to pick two defensive ends and allowed the Bears to take future Hall-of-Famer Dick Butkus.

And now they had picked me.

TWO

According to an old story, Dick Butkus was in the Bears locker room standing at a urinal when the team's legendary owner and former coach, George Halas, came in and stood next to him. Supposedly Halas glanced down and saw a quarter on the bottom of the urinal. He sighed, reached in his pocket, pulled out another quarter, and flipped it to the bottom. "What's that all about, coach?" Butkus asked.

"Well," Halas replied, "I'm not going in there for a quarter"—and then he bent down and reached for the quarters—"but for fifty cents . . ."

People used to say about George Halas, "He throws nickels around like manhole covers." But to Art Rooney, the owner of the Pittsburgh Steelers and a man I grew to truly love and admire, Halas was a profligate spender.

And I learned never to belittle profligate spenders.

The opportunity to play professional football was a great honor available to only a select few people. We

were allowed to play the game we loved in front of de-
voted fans—and we actually got paid to do it! The National Football League had been established and built
by a group of fine businessmen, men who risked their
own money and suffered through many lean years because of their own love for the game. If one year they
happened to eke out a few pennies profit, that was only
a fair return on their investment and hard work.

Least that's what they told me when I was drafted.

This is how smart the owners were: they kept
player salaries secret and somehow managed to con-
vince the players it was for their own good. The owners
did everything possible to keep salaries low. Nobody
knew how much anybody else was making. Nobody
talked about their money. I didn't know what Bert
Jones was making, or Kenny Stabler. When a collective
bargaining agreement finally forced the owners to open
up their books, salaries were made public for the first
time. I had quarterbacked the Steelers to four Super
Bowls—calling my own plays, by the way—I was the
Most Valuable Player in the league, and I was earning
$350,000 a year; Archie Manning, who never even got
to a Super Bowl, was making $600,000. If I had been
an owner, I would have kept that a secret too.

Since then the entire salary structure for professional football has changed, which I believe has gone a
long way toward destroying the game. My complaint
during my career was that players did not get paid a
fair amount for their achievements. That same thing is
absolutely true today; only now players get paid a fortune before they achieve anything at all. The way the
system currently operates, players drafted in the first

round get multimillion-dollar bonuses. In 1998, for example, Ryan Leaf was paid an $11.25 million bonus to sign with the San Diego Chargers. Ryan Leaf may be an upstanding human being, he may be good to his brethren, but what did he do to earn that money? Beat UCLA? Since then Ryan Leaf has mostly been injured, played poorly, or had difficulty getting along with his coaches. I suspect there are a lot of players that could have done that for as little as $5 million.

Being paid millions of dollars is not Ryan Leaf's fault. I don't blame him for it. I don't blame any of those kids for making as much money as they can. That would be like blaming the cow for getting involved with the bull. The cow got no options. But no rookie is worth that kind of money. It's management I blame. I recognize the undisputed right of every pro football team to make a fool of itself. Management is like the bull—it just can't help giving it away. I just don't believe that teams can continue to pay huge salaries to unproven players without it having a negative impact on the sport.

I didn't even have an agent. A lot of players didn't have agents then; we couldn't understand why we should pay an agent a commission for not getting us the same salary we couldn't get on our own. Owners were tougher then, and players had much less negotiating power. The agents today earn more money for negotiating rookie contracts than I made for playing. When I got drafted, my father and his lawyer sat down at a table and met with every agent who wanted to represent me. Eventually they eliminated each of them, and my father represented me. I was real proud of him for doing it for me. Poor, but proud. My dad didn't know what he was doing, and the Steelers helped him do it. The only things that interfered with my father's ability to be an effective agent were his honesty and his ethics. He wouldn't even consider holding me out for several months for a better contract, which definitely cut down on our negotiating position.

Looking back, I really was the perfect draft choice; I wanted to play pro football so desperately I probably would have played for nothing—although if I had have made that offer, the Steelers probably would have offered me 20 percent less. My goal when I went to the NFL in 1970 was to be able to retire someday with enough money invested to earn $50,000 a year. I wanted to own a piece of land. My dad and I agreed we wanted to negotiate a three-year contract. Eventually we signed a five-year deal for a $110,000 bonus spread out over ten years, and a $25,000 salary that escalated $5,000 a year. So at the end of five years I was earning $45,000.

That seems laughable now—although you'll notice I'm not among the laughers. Of course, we weren't playing as many games back then as they play now, so if you divide it by the number of games, it's . . . really laughable. But it was only a couple of years after Joe Namath had stunned the sports world by signing with the New York Jets for $400,000. It was a different era, and truthfully I was thrilled to be paid to play football. And to me it was a lot of money; a year earlier I'd been rustling pop bottles for two cents apiece. With my bonus I bought my mother new furniture for the entire house, and I bought myself a brand new maroon Thunderbird with a white alligator top, spoke wheels with spinner caps, and maroon interior—$4,800, brand-new.

Give me an Amen for that car, brother.

I remember driving home from Pittsburgh to Shreveport in that car. One thousand miles—that includes fifty miles getting lost in Washington, D.C.—listening to Merle Haggard singing "Mama Tried." By the time I got home I could *sing* that song. Who said I was a slow learner?

My brother Howie Long took his signing bonus and bought hisself a fine used Coupe de Ville with spoke wheels, an eight-track cassette player, and a velour interior for $9,000.

In addition to my rookie-year salary and bonus, there was that pile of money I made doing endorsements and signing autographs. I made literally hundreds of dollars. I had never been much interested in going to shopping center openings to sign autographs or telling people, "I wear these pants and they fit just like . . . pants." But there was one word that changed my mind entirely and forever: taxes. After buying my car and new furniture for my family, I had just enough cash left in the bank to pay the taxes I owed. After that I accepted every offer to earn a little extra money. Appearances paid as much as $300, and I was pleased to be invited because that money paid my rent for a month. Make an appearance at the opening of your new Laundromat? Oh man, I was really hoping for this invitation. There's nothing I like more than the clean, crisp smell of a new Laundromat! Make that check out to Bradshaw, with a B.

It's not only the bonuses and salaries paid to rookies that I believe are damaging professional football, it's the impact that money has on the game. The game today is all about money—money and TV ratings. Maybe ratings first, money second; but if you get the ratings, you'll get the money. The league changes the rules every year to make the game more explosive and more exciting, because that is what the TV networks demand. There is no such thing as loyalty anymore: players aren't loyal to their teams, owners aren't loyal to their cities, the league isn't even loyal to the networks that have helped build the game. Everything has a price tag. For example, as soon as owners realized the merchandising value of established old traditions, they immediately went out and began establishing new old traditions.

I know the value of money; I have been divorced—believe me, I definitely know the value of money. In 1996, when quarterback Neil O'Donnell left the Steelers after leading them to a Super Bowl loss and signed a $25 million contract with the Jets, I opined—meaning I said right out loud what I was thinking—I opined that essentially he was trading a potentially very productive career for the cash. In football terms, he was taking the money and passing. As a television network football analyst, this put me in the ironic situation of getting well paid to tell people what I thought about other people getting well paid.

Neil O'Donnell was in an excellent situation in Pittsburgh; he was surrounded by good players and running an offense perfectly suited for his talents. The Jets just weren't as good a match for him, and I said so. Had he stayed in Pittsburgh, I believe he might have had a much more successful career; he would have had a chance to go to Super Bowls just about every season.

And while maybe he wouldn't have earned $5 million a year, at least he would have been paid enough money so that he wouldn't have had to meet me at Laundromat openings.

I was happy for Neil, but not happy for the game of football. And definitely not happy for Steelers fans. One of the few regrets I have about my playing career was that I never was offered the opportunity to make a bad decision concerning money. It would have been real comforting to be able to look back on my career and say, "I truly regret taking that $10 million bonus . . ." The truth is, I don't know what I would have done if I had been put in the same situation. What I do know is that it also feels very satisfying to look back on my career and know that I won it all—calling my own plays, mind you.

Money has never been the prime motivating factor in my life. I always knew that if everything went bad for me, I could sell my ranch, my horses, and all the equipment, then take the cash and buy myself a good trailer with a nice awning and follow the sun from climate to climate. Nothing wrong with that life.

By the end of my career I was being comparatively well paid—compared to my father, who was vice president of a welding company, but not so good compared to other quarterbacks. After twelve seasons and winning four Super Bowls I was earning $350,000. But when I signed my last contract, the Rooneys asked me what I wanted, and I told them that most of all I wanted to pay my ranch off. I think I owed about $80,000. They paid it off for me, so I got what I wanted most out of pro football: a good piece of land.

Even when salaries escalated, some of the players were able to do the same thing. John Elway, for example, earned just enough during his career to buy a nice piece of land. 'Course, his land is called Colorado.

I don't begrudge players being paid million-dollar salaries. This is a hard game in which to have continued success, and any player who does it earns his money. Just about everyone who has played long enough to earn a substantial salary will pay for it in permanent pain or injury for the rest of his life. The players who came before me were paid considerably less than I was; I had people from the 1950s tell me they played for table scraps. But they never complained about my salary, and I'm not going to complain about current salaries. I'm not going to complain that Troy Aikman led the Dallas Cowboys to an 8-8 record and received a $20 million signing bonus. No, I am not going to complain at all. But what I am going to do is point out that lately my passing arm has been feeling a whole lot better than it has in years. And I can still run a lick. . . .

When I was drafted number one, a lot of people believed the Steelers had wasted their number-one pick. And I spent the first several years of my career successfully making those people look pretty smart. There was no way I was ready to play pro football. Emotionally, physically, I just wasn't ready. It was nobody's fault. At Louisiana Tech I had the perfect coach and the perfect system—for me. I played for Maxie Lambright, who came from southern Mississippi and loved the running game. He taught me the running game. What kind of running game did we have? The trapping game. What kind of offense did we have in Pittsburgh? The trapping game. Mickey Slaughter, our offensive coach at Tech, had been with the Denver Broncos. He taught me an improvisational style: call plays in the huddle, change passing routes, take what the defense gives you and be grateful. I learned from these men how to run a team. They allowed me to call my own plays—to make my own mistakes—which is no longer done in college football.

But this was small college football, NCAA Division II. We didn't have a battalion of coaches, we weren't on national TV, we didn't get the blue-chip high school players, we rode old buses to our games rather than flying and played in front of small crowds. It didn't mean we didn't love the game any less or hit as hard as we could hit or throw as long as we could throw.

I was as prepared to play professional football as any player from a Division II college had ever been— which meant I still had a whole lot to learn. There is a story told about Notre Dame's legendary football coach, Knute Rockne. Notre Dame had been upset the previous Saturday, and Rockne was furious. At the Monday meeting he was screaming and hollering, cutting his team up pretty good. "You people know nothing about the game of football," he yelled, "and we're going to have to start at the very beginning." With that, he bent down and picked up a football. Holding it high above his head, he said dramatically, "This . . . is a football . . ."

And from the back of the room Sleepy Jim Crowley, one of Notre Dame's fabled Four Horsemen interrupted, "Please, Coach, not so fast."

I wasn't that bad. At Tech I had been given a strong foundation. I knew how to run a football team, I had been spoon-fed confidence by Mickey Slaughter, and I had learned how to win. But Division II football is just not that sophisticated, so I had a whole lot of details to learn.

It wasn't just that I didn't know football. I didn't even know life. I was raw in reality. I had never even played against a black man until Tech played New Mexico State my junior year. I didn't know anything about handling money or dating women—which in retrospect turned out to be pretty much the same thing; I didn't know about fancy restaurants, buying nice clothes, I didn't even know how much I didn't know.

Pittsburgh was a revelation to me. It was an industrial northern city, and I was a southern boy most comfortable on a farm. What I knew about life just didn't apply: it did not take me long to learn that you can't plow a coal field. I remember my first trip to Pittsburgh. I was driving on a highway and saw a car that had jumped the median and hit another car head on. It was hung up on the retaining wall, and a woman was lying there covered with blood—people weren't even slowing down to look at this carnage. Man, I thought, this is some tough town.

In college I had never been exposed to pressure. Nobody at Tech thought the world was going to end if we didn't beat Delta State. Jump off a bridge because we lost a football game? They wouldn't even jump off the curb. We were so unsophisticated that our fans didn't even paint their faces! Our fans wouldn't even take their shirts off when it was 102 degrees—so just imagine my surprise when I saw Steeler fans stripping down when it was minus 10. I had absolutely no way of anticipating the enormous pressure on me to succeed. Pressure? I figured that the Steelers had finished last without me; they'd won one game; how much worse could I make the situation?

I was about to find out. Even before I arrived in Pittsburgh, I was being hailed as the Steelers' savior. I was the First Coming, "Terrific Terry." I was "Mandrake the Magician," the "Blond Bomber" who was supposed to transform the Steelers into a Super Bowl team. I don't want to imply that the Steelers expected too much from me, but our center Ray Mansfield told *Time* magazine, "This guy is going to be our Moses. He's going to lead us out of the desert!"

Mansfield forgot to mention that it took Moses forty years. Steeler fans expected me to do it in one season. I felt more like Noah. It seemed like things were always gloomy, and if I didn't figure out something pretty quick, I was going to drown. I actually played pretty well in our preseason games, but I was still playing the way I had in college: I dropped back and looked for my primary receiver. If he was open, I threw it to him; if he was covered, I tucked the ball under my arm and ran. I didn't bother looking for another receiver, I just ran. And for a few games it worked pretty well.

Unfortunately, the season started, and the other teams began playing for keeps. It was a different ball game. Nobody had bothered to warn me how much harder the players hit when the games counted. My first game in the National Football League was against the Houston Oilers. When my receivers were covered and I started to run, I got clobbered. In college I was bigger than most defensive backs, I could run over people! In professional football that was like trying to run over a building. An angry building. An angry building with a bad attitude. Until that game I did not fully understand how many players the opposing team was allowed to keep on the field. The answer was—at least fifty. I never saw so many people wearing a different uniform on the same football field at the same time. They were coming at me from all sides. They were coming at me from sides I didn't even know were sides. And there was nothing I could to correct my mistakes. I lacked the knowledge. I had never read a defensive coverage in my life. I didn't know how to find my secondary receivers. The game had always come so easily to me that I had never studied it, I never even watched game films the way a quarterback should. So when they blitzed me, I turned and ran for my life.

I tried to learn how to read defensive formations, but the other team intentionally made it difficult for me. That stuff is harder than bathing cats. Every time I thought I had it figured out, they would change it. I would walk confidently up to the line of scrimmage. I would stand there to see just what defense they were playing; I'd see where the corners were and the safeties and the linebackers. Maybe I smiled at them, they smiled back at me. How y'all doin' today? We're all friends here. Then I'd bend down, way down, under my center, and all I could see in front of me was butt and the eyeballs of the defensive line. And those people were not smiling. I'd call out my signals, take the snap, and stand up and look around and . . . and where did everybody go? While I was busy looking at butt, they had moved around on me. I don't know where they'd gone, and I didn't have time to do real serious investigating because I had the ball in my hand and about thirty-five large people with smoke coming out of their noses trying to break me into pieces. So I'd throw the ball to the first open receiver I saw. Maybe there were five large people surrounding that receiver, debating exactly which three of them were going to drive him into the ground, but I'd throw it anyway. I'd figure I could always apologize later. Or at least I could send nice flowers to the hospital.

It took me one-half of my first real professional football game to get booed. I had never before been booed in my life. I will never forget that sound of an entire stadium booing me as long as I live. Some players claim they don't hear the boos; I heard each and every one of them. I could hear the guy in section 104, row H, seat 6 booing me. That sound went through my body like an angry wife through a bank account. It was painful. Painful. Did they think I was trying to throw interceptions? I felt like I had let down my friends and my family. And not just my friends and family—I felt I had let down my ancestors, who had suffered terrible hardships to get to America just so someday their great-great-great-grandson could stand in front of 75,000 fans and get booed. And not just my friends, my family, and all my ancestors—I felt I'd let down my college, the state of Louisiana, and the entire South.

I was benched for the second half, replaced by Terry Hanratty. This is where my relationship with

Pittsburgh got complicated. Terry Hanratty was a native of Pennsylvania who had starred at Notre Dame; he was the local hero who made fair. The fans loved him and wanted to see him play. I was the reason he was sitting on the bench. The first thing Terry Hanratty did when he replaced me was throw a touchdown pass. I didn't really know how to react to that; it was sort of like having your next-door neighbor win the lottery. But for Steeler fans it was additional proof that the Steelers had wasted their number-one draft pick on me.

As I left the field after the game, the fans continued booing me. During the preseason, when everything was going well and the fans loved me, I was always available to the media for an interview. I answered every question they asked; when I didn't know the right answer, I made it up. All the reporters thought I was good copy, the unsophisticated southern boy seeing the lights of the big old city for the first time. I was Li'l Abner come to Pittsburgh. I played right along with it. I have always wanted to please people, I enjoy making people happy. So I played the role into which I was cast as best I could. And truthfully, I enjoyed the attention.

But when things did not go well that first game, I didn't know how to react. A broadcaster named Myron Cope, a Pittsburgh legend, did a postgame radio show. As I walked back to our locker room, Myron asked me to come on his show. I turned him down. I knew I was a failure, I didn't have a need to broadcast that news. But Preston Pearson, a veteran player, pulled me aside and introduced me to reality. "Look," he said, "you gotta take the bad with the good. You go and do that interview."

In my memory the first question was, "How does it feel to be the biggest failure in the entire history of the National Football League and an embarrassment to everyone you've ever known?" But knowing Myron Cope, more likely it was, "How are you feeling after your first game, Terry?"

How did I feel? What kind of question is that? Most people will never experience the pain of being booed. You ever see customers in a restaurant stand up and boo a waiter? Or walk into a store and boo the salesclerk? Whoa, ma'am, what a bad sale you made! What'd you make that sale for? People don't even boo the income tax collector. But they booed me. Me! After the game I was so upset, I sat in my car in the parking lot outside Three Rivers Stadium and just cried. I just don't take kindly to insults.

I didn't fit in at all with the Steelers. This was a tough bunch of veterans who liked to go out and have a good time. For fun they would rip down buildings by hand and eat the bricks. They had nicknames like Dirt and Mad Dog and Fangs. I was . . . Terry. I didn't go out at night with them, and they didn't come sing gospel with me in church. Well, a few of them did come to see me witness in church. I definitely got into it that day. Oh, my Lord, I got into it. It was a big dose of old-time religion. I could hear Satan coming! I could hear his footsteps! I certainly wasn't like any quarterback most of them had ever played with before.

It was a rough season for me. I had a few good games, but I never felt comfortable. I threw six touchdown passes—and twenty-four interceptions. In the final game of the season our punter, Bobby Walden, got hurt, and Chuck Noll told me to punt. "Just keep your head down," he said. I could kick it as far as I could throw it. I had punted in high school and was the backup punter in college. I was kicking from the back of my own end zone. I stood right on the end line, got the snap, kept my head down . . . and Philadelphia Eagles came at me like hogs being called to dinner. They came in waves, and they buried me. I knew why Chuck had warned me to keep my head down—he didn't want me to see what was coming. An Eagles linebacker blocked the punt, which they recovered for a touchdown. But he also had a cleat missing from his spikes, so as he came down, the screw just ripped open my leg. A simple punt had turned into a touchdown, and I'd been hurt. It was a fitting end to the season.

Naturally, Steeler fans were sympathetic; they would boo me on the street, they would boo me when I stopped for traffic lights. Booing Terry Bradshaw became a favorite sport in Pittsburgh. Hey, what do you guys want to do tonight? Let's go boo Terry Bradshaw. The situation got so bad that my mom came up to stay with me for several weeks. It can't be that bad, Terry, she said. I took her with me to a hockey game, and they booed us. They booed my mother! When my brothers and I booed her at home, that was one thing, but at a hockey game? They were booing her for giving birth to me. How awful is that? Those boos rained down upon us like a shower of nails. It was awful, terrible. Now I understand, she said after the game. And when they couldn't personally boo me, they wrote incredibly nasty letters. I became sort of a recluse. I rarely left my apartment except to go to practice or a game.

I'd like to be able to say Coach Noll helped me. I really would like to be able to make that claim—but it wouldn't be true. Chuck Noll took to me like a duck takes to an oil spill. When I threw an interception or did something wrong as I came off the field, he would be right there in my face. I wasn't used to that type of treatment; the coaches I had played for had always been extremely supportive. No matter what I did, they supported me—"Great pass, Terry. If you'd thrown it to one of our guys, it would have gone for a touchdown sure." But not Chuck Noll. If I had any doubts I was a failure, he certainly did erase them for me. Chuck Noll and I would enjoy as much success together as any coach and quarterback in the history of professional football, but the scars he inflicted those first few seasons never went away. Eventually we learned to respect each other, but there was never any real friendship. Chuck Noll could speak knowledgeably about everything from politics to how to lay a concrete floor, but when it came to the human side, he seemed unapproachable. One reporter wrote that he celebrated the Steelers' victory in Super Bowl IX by shaking hands with his wife. Teammates would tell me that he was trying to motivate me. To do what, I'd wonder—hit him? Quit?

I thought about both options that first season. My confidence was shattered completely. I felt the coach didn't like me, the fans didn't like me, the media didn't like me. Nobody liked me. At one point I was scheduled to be interviewed by Howard Cosell. How-wood Cosell. I'd spent years watching him on television. He had become as big an attraction as any of the players by "telling it like it is." Admittedly, I was excited about meeting him. But as I walked into the broadcast booth I heard him tell a national audience, "Ladies and gentlemen, now walking into the booth, the number-one flop in the National Football League, Terry Bradshaw."

Maybe in this case he should have told it like it wasn't. That was a big thrill, being insulted on national television by Howard Cosell.

I wasn't prepared for any aspect of it. Everything was new and big and different. I was a naive kid, as much a fan in awe of the people I was playing against as I was a player. My first years in the league we played against Johnny Unitas and Bart Starr. Johnny Unitas! Bart Starr! We lost both games, but at the end I made sure I ran across the field to introduce myself to both of them. Well, at least I didn't ask them for an autograph. When I played against the Chicago Bears for the first time, all I heard from Chuck Noll for the entire week before the game was Dick Butkus. The incredible Dick Butkus. I had seen him play on television, and suddenly I looked across the line of scrimmage, and there was Dick Butkus looking right at me. I couldn't take my eyes off him. I was playing in the same football game as Dick Butkus. I was so proud—Dick Butkus was trying to kill *me!* Butkus just stared at me. He reminded me of the way a mongoose stares at his prey and hypnotizes it. That was Butkus and me. I think he hypnotized me. I had the football, and I just said, "Here. You take it, sir." And he did. He intercepted two of my passes. It wasn't tough, I threw them right to him. I felt terrible about it, but there was something thrilling about having two of my passes intercepted by Dick Butkus.

In Pittsburgh, everything in my life was different. For the first time in my life, for example, I had women expressing interest in me. On Fox's NFL Sunday show a very lovely woman named Jillian Barberie does our weather forecasts for the cities in which games are being played, usually wearing extremely form-fitting garments—because if there is one thing that men always associate with weather forecasts, it's sex. Truthfully, though, most men associate anything with sex. Parking spaces. Heavy machinery. Pencil sharpeners. In fact, when I was growing up in Shreveport, about the only thing that I didn't associate with sex was me.

I was a nice-looking boy—maybe not as nice-looking as Howie Long, but I had a headful of nicely groomed blond hair, a friendly smile, and even a little dimple in my chin. I'd been well taught how to be respectful to women. But actually talking with them was something else entirely. I was very insecure with girls, but as I got older I matured to the point where I became very insecure with women. I just didn't have much to talk with them about. What could I say to them: Want to see my javelin?

I never dated a cheerleader. In junior high, high school, or college, never once did I date a cheerleader. We didn't have cheerleaders in Pittsburgh; some players used to joke that they couldn't find ten beautiful women in Pittsburgh. Some players, not me. I did date someone for several years in college, but she broke up with me senior year. Dating was tough in college; Louisiana Tech was such a small school that it seemed like everybody was taken.

But soon as I got drafted, I started getting letters

from women. Women who had never met me were writing to say they wanted to go out with me. 'Course, lacking social confidence, I figured the reason they wanted to go out with me was because they hadn't met me. Even Miss Teen America wrote that she would like to meet me. We dated for a brief time; she was gorgeous. This was my first foray into the world of glamour. She liked me a whole lot. In fact, she liked me so much that after we'd gone out only a few times, she introduced me to her friend and suggested I go out with her.

Her friend, Melissa Babish, had also been Miss Teen America. Melissa Babish and I were married for eighteen months. It made a nice story—the quarterback and the beauty queen—but we did not belong together. This was a learning experience. Missy and I lived for a little while on a farm. We had this little bitty old farmhouse that was raised off the ground on blocks, with a tin roof and tin siding around the bottom. One time her mother came to stay with us for two weeks, although I think she was a bit dubious about this whole thing. The first night she was there, she woke us up just screaming, "Somebody's trying to break into the house! Somebody's trying to break into the house!" Didn't seem likely to me—what did they intend to steal, the tin? But sure enough, I heard something under the house, banging around. It was making a terrible racket. So I got my gun and my English bulldog, Butch, and we went outside to investigate.

We discovered that an armadillo had got under the house and was banging around trying to get out. This was your big-type armadillo. Butch decided to protect the house and those he loved dearly, so he went after him. Those two fought like they were married. When the armadillo started getting the best of Butch, I leveled my gun and took a shot at it. My mother-in-law started screaming, "You're shooting it, you're shooting it." Well, no kidding. That armadillo kept fighting, I kept shooting, she kept screaming. *Rrrwww, bam,* Oh my God! *Rrrwww, bam,* Oh my God! I shot the legs off that thing, but it kept coming. It was like the Butkus of armadillos. Finally, though, I killed it. Butch, being an animal, started ripping it apart. My mother-in-law, being a mother-in-law, kept screaming at me. I was trying to calm her down and get Butch off that carcass. Finally I got it all squared away, and she went back inside and started packing.

She stayed one day. Best way of getting rid of a mother-in-law I ever have discovered.

I had learned so much about marriage from Missy that I only had to get divorced two more times. Of course Melissa wasn't the only woman I dated in Pittsburgh, just the first one I married. So in addition to learning an entirely new offense and learning how to read a defense, I was also trying to understand how to deal with this other species called women.

Dealing with defenses was easier. And they never hire divorce lawyers.

Having black players as teammates was also a new experience for me. The South is in my bones. Shreveport was a town built where the Red River met the Texas Trail, the overland route into Mexico. It was about as deep into the South as it was possible to get and still be in the United States. It was a place with *tra-*

dition. I was raised up right in the middle of the civil rights revolution. When I was young, Shreveport was still mostly segregated. I remember the White Only and Coloreds Here signs. I remember that we went to one side of the store to buy food, and black people came in a separate door. I remember the separate toilet facilities, and I remember that my family could eat at certain restaurants, and black people could not. I remember all the stereotypes; they were not as smart as we were, they were not as ambitious as we were, they were lazy. I was aware of all that. It was sort of hard to believe people, though, who said knowingly, "Them people don't talk no good." Besides, I was raised in a family that believed in the Gospel, and nowhere in all that literature did it even mention the different races. My mother and father taught us to respect each person, and they didn't need to add "regardless of color." Our high school league was all white, and I believe there were two black students in my class at Tech. The first black athlete we recruited was a basketball player from St. Louis, Missouri.

Admittedly, at that time of my life I divided the world into two types of people; those who played football and everybody else. On occasion I would go with a few friends over to all-black Grambling State University, which was only a few miles from the Tech campus, and play tag-team football. In a lot of places they were using guns to integrate society, all we needed was a football.

As naive as it may seem, I was fascinated by black people primarily because I knew so little about their culture or history. In Shreveport, the black people had their part of town and we had ours. As I learned more about America's history, I was amazed by their struggle for basic human rights. It was hard for me to believe that people I knew so well could treat others so badly because of the color of their skin. When I arrived in Pittsburgh I was totally naive. I was surprised when I got to training camp and discovered that at team meals black and white players sat at different tables. Occasionally a black player would wander over to our side, but someone would ask him, "What are you doing?" and that would end real quick. Now, that someone might have been black or white. Like just about all pro football teams, we were integrated on the field but wide apart off the field.

I called them "coloreds." I meant no harm, but I said all the wrong things because I didn't know any better. Finally Jon Staggers took the time to educate me. He saw the truth in me. When I referred to him as colored, he replied, "Am I green? Am I purple?" I learned all about black history, I learned about pomade for straightening hair and black music, I learned all the expressions and all the handshakes. It was called a handshake, but it was a ceremony; it was an under-over-knock-twice-grab-the-wrist-interlocking-finger-how-you-doin'-dude handshake. If we had ever tried to shake hands during a game, we would've been penalized for delay of season. By the time I retired, the Steelers were integrated in every way, and my closest friends on the team were black players like John Stallworth, Calvin Sweeney, Fat Ernie, Mean Joe Greene (my dearest friend), Mad Dog White, and Jim Smith.

Eventually it got very good in Pittsburgh; it certainly could not have gotten much worse. After the first three games of my rookie season I was benched, replaced at quarterback by Terry Hanratty. I'd sat on the bench in high school and college, but that was while awaiting an opportunity to play. And when I was given that opportunity, I was successful. This was very different; I'd been given the opportunity and failed big-time. That had never happened to me before, and I didn't know how to handle it.

Even more painful to me than being benched were the insults from the Pittsburgh media and the fans. I made the transition very quickly from Moses to Ozark Ike. Those people didn't understand me any more than I understood them. As far as they were concerned, I really was Li'l Abner, the slow-witted southerner. I wasn't smart enough to play quarterback for their team. In New York Joe Namath was "Broadway Joe," in Oakland Kenny Stabler was "the Snake," but in Pittsburgh I was "the Bayou Bumpkin." I mean, how smart do you have to be to play for a team that won only one game the year before? Think of it this way: Albert Einstein never completed a pass in the NFL. I may be the only player in National Football League history to have been asked my IQ by reporters. The answer was that I was smart to recognize a loaded question. The assumption was that because I spoke with a drawl and said things like, "It was hotter than a road lizard," I wasn't intelligent enough to lead the worst team in pro football. How insulting is that? If you can't understand how tough that was for me, you must be the dumbest person to ever read this book.

People were cruel. When they learned that I had

failed the entrance exam to LSU, it got worse. I might well have been the very first professional athlete whose image was that I was dumb. Part of it might have been my fault. Trying to please reporters, I once said, "I like being with a loser because I'll play sooner." The media would make jokes about me. I felt bad for my family. I know it hurt my father. I did not take kindly to the insults and the ridicule, but there was absolutely nothing I could do about it. How do you defend yourself against a charge like that? Take a spelling test? Go on *Jeopardy?* What could I say? Hey, I'm smart enough to be the one standing *behind* a line of 250-plus-pound men whose job it is to protect me? That I'm smart enough to start running when a really big defensive lineman is chasing me? That I could find the two-holer in the dark?

These many years later I can joke about it. As I am proud to tell people, I graduated from Louisiana Tech with a 3.6 average, while my friend Roger Staubach graduated from Annapolis with only a 3.1. That surprises a lot of people. Of course, the difference between myself and Roger is that mine was cumulative. You have to add up the averages for each of my four years in college to reach that mark.

The only way I could deal with it then, though, was to ignore it. I didn't read the papers—and contrary to some charges I definitely *could* have read them if I'd so desired—and I never responded directly. I knew I couldn't change my image, but if I could win enough games, at least I could make the fans respect me. I was a professional football player for five years before I learned how to play football. They were difficult years for me. While sometimes I played well, I never played well consistently. The Steelers won, oh my did we win; in 1972 we were 11-3 and won the AFC divisional title, the Steelers' first outright championship of any kind—though it took the most memorable play in pro football history, Franco Harris's Immaculate Reception, for us to defeat the Oakland Raiders.

In 1973 we again went to the playoffs, winning a wild-card spot with a 10-4 record. Much of the criticism diminished; it was amazing, the more we won, the smarter I got. That Bradshaw, he's smart enough to get out of Franco's way. I like that Bradshaw, he sure hands it off nicely to Rocky Bleier. But in 1974 I joined many veteran NFL players in a preseason strike. I was replaced by "Jefferson Street" Joe Gilliam, who proceeded to have one of the greatest preseasons in pro football history. In one quarter alone against the Colts he passed for 151 yards. In one quarter. The man was definitely on fire. When the regular season opened, he was our starting quarterback. After five seasons, after leading the Steelers to the playoffs the two previous years, I was benched.

Joe Gilliam was a black man. At that time black men did not play the quarterback position in the National Football League. Pro football scouts would look at the finest quarterbacks from the black colleges and determine that they would make fine defensive backs or wide receivers. Before Gilliam only one other black man, the Bronco's Marlin Brisco, had started an NFL game at quarterback. It was tough for Gilliam, who received hate mail, death threats, and, he remembered, at least one threat to bomb the stadium.

But it was also tough for me. Now I was more than just run-of-the-mill ordinary dumb, now I was so dumb that I had actually lost my job to a black man! I was making history, too; I was only the second white quarterback in history to lose my job to a black man. I also got hate mail, and some of the things those people wrote were horrifying.

With Gilliam at quarterback we won four, lost one, and tied one, but Gilliam did not play nearly as well as he had in the preseason. Later in his life Joe Gilliam had serious drug problems before dying of a heart attack Christmas night, 2000, but there were some indications of that when he was with the Steelers. Some people claimed they saw him using drugs at that time, but I never did. The last game he started was against the Raiders, and he threw two interceptions, causing some Steeler fans to chant, "We want Bradshaw."

But they didn't say what they wanted me for.

Being benched after five years in the NFL was embarrassing, discouraging, depressing, every other -ing you want to add. I sat down in my living room and had a long personal conversation with myself. I was tough on me. I ridiculed myself. Then I yelled at myself. And finally I got mad, because basically I was giving up.

Giving up was one thing I had been taught was unacceptable. You plow the field till you're finished. You don't quit on a half-milked cow. You don't walk out on your team because you're not playing. I decided I was going to focus on one thing only, winning back my job. I was going to be as tough as necessary, as mean-spirited as required, and work harder than anyone else to do that—and once I had it back, I wasn't going to let go.

To help me accomplish my goal, I used hypnotism. Now, that definitely does not mean I looked across the line of scrimmage and told the defensive linemen, you are getting veeeryyy sleepy, your arms are feeling heavy . . . It was actually a form of self-hypnotism. Things had been going poorly for me, and I was not handling the situation very well. One game against Buffalo, I remember, I rolled out and saw an open receiver twenty yards downfield—and threw the football right into the ground. The one thing I had always been able to do, throw a football, I couldn't do. So one evening our strength coach, a man named Lou Ricke from Louisiana, offered to help me get over my fear. He offered to hypnotize me. Hypnotize me! My goodness. I knew all about hypnotism. I'd seen hypnotists on the TV; they waved a silver watch in front of somebody's face to put him in a trance, and the very next thing that poor person was crowing like a rooster. This wasn't anything like that, Ricke assured me as I looked deeply into his eyes and began feeling tired, this was simply positive reinforcement. No crowing? I believe I asked. I definitely did not want to crow.

No crowing, he promised.

I believe very strongly in the power of positive thinking. Think good things, and good things tend to happen. When I'm speaking publicly my message—whether I'm speaking to a room filled with CEOs or to employees of an appliance company—is always very simple: Keep it simple. That's what I do, and that's my message, keep it simple. In this situation I did exactly that; I focused on three words that would enable me to perform at the peak of my abilities. I concentrated on those three words, and in tense situations I'd wipe my mind clear of the noise and the pressure and think over and over again: relax, confidence, concentrate. Relax, confidence, and concentrate. Even in the most tense situations, when I focused on those three words I calmed down. In fact, I relaxed, I regained any lost confidence, and I was free to really concentrate on my goals.

Of course, when those three words failed, I relied on three other words: Run, Terry, run!

After Gilliam threw two interceptions and we were shut out by the Raiders, Noll put me back in the starting lineup. I started two games, then was replaced by Terry Hanratty for one game. That was the last time in my career I sat on the bench if I was healthy enough to play.

But once you get a reputation, it isn't easy to change it. Throughout his entire career Roger Staubach was the intellect with nerves of steel. Fran Tarkenton was the great scrambler. Joe Montana performed best under intense pressure. Doug Flutie was too short to be a winning quarterback. Bradshaw? No matter what I accomplished, I was stuck with being just another dumb blond. Even after we became the most successful football team in history, the media never forgot it. GQ did an article entitled "The Brilliance of Dumb"; a Pittsburgh magazine that had referred to me as dumb headlined an article "Who Ever Called Him Dumb?" Well, for starters, they did. In San Diego I was "Dumb Like a Fox."

It probably reached a culmination in 1979, when we played the Dallas Cowboys in Super Bowl XIII. A week before the game Cowboys linebacker Thomas

"Hollywood" Henderson told reporters, "Bradshaw couldn't spell cat if you spotted him the 'c' and the 't.'" Only every sportswriter in the Western Hemisphere was covering the game, and Henderson's insult gave them something to write about. That remark almost instantly became one of the most recognizable quotes in football history. *Newsweek* featured me and Henderson on its cover, *Time* did a big story about it. Maybe some people thought it was clever; I thought it was nasty. I tried to kid about it—"It's 'o,' isn't it?"—but it did bother me.

I answered Henderson the best way possible: by halftime of Super Bowl XIII I had broken every significant passing record. For the game I completed seventeen of thirty passes for 318 yards, a 10.6-yards-per-completion average, and threw four touchdown passes in our 35–31 victory. Under third-down pressure I completed eight of nine attempts for 165 yards and two touchdowns, and I was the unanimous choice for Most Valuable Player.

Well, yes, it did feel good. But even that could not erase my image. As the *Pittsburgh Press* reported, "The quarterback whose intelligence is always questioned finally silenced his critics."

Two decades later I interviewed Henderson for the Fox show *NFL Sunday*. It turned out our lives had come together at a crossroads. That week in 1979 had proved to be the highlight of Henderson's professional football career. A year later the Cowboys released him, and eventually he ended up in prison. He abused drugs and alcohol. When we spoke he told me, "I was in prison watching you on a thirteen-inch TV when you were inducted into the Hall of Fame." As I sat opposite him during that interview, I certainly felt no animosity toward him.

About a month later Henderson won $28,000,000 in the Texas lottery. So I hope my good friend Thomas Henderson has no animosity toward me. Actually, Henderson has been using his winnings to help people less fortunate than himself, by working to build affordable housing for poor people.

For a long time my dumb image remained a burr under my saddle. But like anything else, eventually I learned to accept it. As I became more successful in my chosen profession of throwing a football while avoiding the wrath of large angry men, I began to see a bit of humor in it. Gradually I even began to take advantage of it. Just a little, of course.

One year I appeared on a Super Bowl preview show hosted by Burt Reynolds. At that time Burt Reynolds was the number-one box office star in the world. And on that show Mr. Reynolds made several unkind remarks about my intelligence. He called me a "country bumpkin," "Li'l Abner"—nothing I hadn't heard before. But when Burt Reynolds made those remarks, I don't think he realized who he was dealing with: my mother. Furious, she threatened to put in her teeth, get in her pickup, and drive to California. Instead she wrote him a long letter.

Not too long afterward I appeared on Dinah Shore's television show. After the show Dinah, who was dating Burt Reynolds at that time, explained, "Burt was just reading a script. He's really sorry about what happened." Well, at least I knew he'd received my mother's letter. And then Dinah invited me to her home to meet him.

Burt Reynolds had played college football at Florida State. He'd starred in the football movie *The Longest Yard*. The man knew football. And he was truly apologetic.

Subsequently we became good friends, and he found roles for me in several of his movies and television programs. Naturally these were roles that required discipline and focus. I had to learn how to bring all my emotions to the moment. Generally I played a hillbilly.

Each time he gave me a role, I told him, "Burt, honest, this isn't necessary. Just because you insulted me in front of millions of viewers on national television and infuriated my poor aged mother, you don't have to give me this role. And my poor aged mother barely even mentions how embarrassed she was more than once or twice a week." Appearing with Burt Reynolds was the beginning of a television and motion picture career that took me all the way to appearing in many other Burt Reynolds television shows and motion pictures.

As time passed, I finally got smart enough to appreciate the value of being dumb. I've learned to use this image to my advantage. I have learned to play Terry Bradshaw. This character, Terry Bradshaw, is a well-meaning southern boy who may be a little light on the details. He's a nice boy, though. In most of the things we do on the Fox show, I'm the butt of the joke. The writers know I don't mind being the idiot; the idiot has more fun than anyone else. Often I'm the person making the joke at my own expense. In one of the series of television commercials I did for the discount long distance telephone service, 10-10-220, that's 10-10-220, I was in a sushi restaurant. As written, the commercial had no real ending. The agency wanted me to mispronounce the word *su-che*. They thought it would be very funny if I insisted on saying it "su-shi." But I was too smart for 'em, I absolutely refused, insisting on ordering my regular su-che.

The real problem was that the emotional damage done at the beginning of my career caused a rift with the city of Pittsburgh that never really healed. While I was fully aware that many fans were supportive, I never felt embraced by the city. The city of Dallas, the whole state of Texas, loved Roger Staubach. San Francisco loved Joe Montana. After a rough start, New York came to love Phil Simms. But after leading the Steelers to victory in four Super Bowls, being named Most Valuable Player in two of them, I was booed off the field my last game in Pittsburgh.

I am a fortunate man. I've been able to spend my life pursuing my passion. And I never forget that, even when I make out those alimony checks. I had a wonderful playing career for which I will forever be grateful. Many people considered me a great quarterback, although I always believed I was a good quarterback playing on a great team. That's not me being humble—believe me, when it comes to being humble, no one is better than me, I can be the very best humble person you have ever seen—but that is me being honest.

Statistically, during my fourteen-year professional career I threw a lot of passes, some of which got completed—and I threw them for the distance; I didn't throw those tiny five-yard suckers that look good on paper—on occasion I ran with the ball, I gained several thousand yards, and scored a lot of touchdowns. Numbers never tell the entire story: Bill Gates founded only one company. Abraham Lincoln was elected to the presidency only one time. Statistics just aren't important to me. On paper, many quarterbacks have completed more passes for more yards and more touchdowns than I did. Statistically, I wasn't even among the top ten quarterbacks in NFL history. How many passes did I complete? Enough to win. And keep winning. I definitely believe the real measure of success in football is winning. How many games did we win? How many championships? How many Super Bowls?

The Pittsburgh Steelers had one of the great runs in sports history, winning six division titles and four Super Bowls in six seasons. That's the only statistic that matters.

I don't believe even I fully comprehended how seriously people took the Super Bowl until just before we played the Minnesota Vikings in Super Bowl IX. This was my first Super Bowl, and I had been dreaming about it my entire life. I'd been dreaming about playing in the Super Bowl even before it existed, that's how important it was to me. One of the things I always loved were the pregame introductions. I looked forward to hearing the public address announcer's voice reverberating throughout the entire stadium: Forrr the Steellllerrrrs, at quarterback, nummmberrrrr 12, Terrreeeeey Bradshaw . . . Boom! I'd come running through a mob of fans, slapping hands with my teammates, running from the enclosed darkness of the tunnel into the stadium, into the roar of the crowd. The gladiator coming to fight once more for the greater glory of Pittsburgh. Oh, I loved it. I mean, during the introductions my adrenaline was pumping faster than oil in the Middle East.

Now magnify that feeling about a thousand times for the Super Bowl. At Super Bowl IX our path to the field had been roped off, and fans were standing on either side of this path as we ran onto the field. As I stood there waiting to be introduced to a stadium filled with 80,997 fans, I was really nervous. I played in four Super Bowls, and before each one, I was terrified that we were going to lose the game. Rather than exuding confidence, all I thought was, Don't lose this game, don't lose this game, don't you dare lose this game. So as I waited, a fan standing only a few feet from me collapsed and died instantly of a massive heart attack. This was a man probably in his forties, wearing no shirt and a plastic Viking helmet with horns on it. People ran over to help him, but he hit the ground and never moved.

The man dropped dead right in front of me! He died with his horns on. And it didn't stop the program for one second. Nobody hesitated. We didn't even mention it on the sidelines or in the huddle. That was when I realized the Super Bowl wasn't a life-and-death situation—it was much more important than that. Seconds later I ran out onto the field in front of the now 80,996 fans, and we proceeded to defeat the Vikings.

Except for the incredible pressure to win every week from the great city of Pittsburgh, a head coach with whom I had a turbulent relationship, and a slew of angry young men trying to play make-a-wish with my body, I loved every minute of my playing career.

And except for the broken shoulder, broken ribs, broken nose, broken hand, and broken wrist, the four concussions and five herniated disks, torn hamstring, thigh, groin, and shoulder muscles, the smashed knees, jammed thumb, the bone spurs and bone chips, and a badly wounded psyche, I might have even continued playing. Assuming I could have remembered the plays. I certainly wasn't ready for my career to end. I definitely would have enjoyed playing a few million dollars longer. Even after winning four Super Bowls, we wanted to "win one for the thumb."

My playing career began ending on a muddy practice field in Latrobe, Pennsylvania, during the summer of 1982. Ironically, it was the happiest time of my entire career. The great days of the Steeler dynasty were over; we were a football team on the decline. The team needed me more than ever, which is what I wanted; I needed to be needed. On the field the game had finally become fun for me; I'd accomplished about as much as any quarterback in history, I had nothing left to prove to anyone. I was thirty-two years old and at the peak of my skills. My arm was strong, I was healthy. I had learned how to play the game of football and felt capable of responding to any defense challenge. On the field I felt in complete control.

I believed I could play another five or six years. I looked forward to returning to the Super Bowl with a mostly different group of players. That would have been a wonderful achievement. It didn't even occur to me to think, If I stay healthy. No one in the NFL is ever really healthy. Like that battery, I just figured I would keep going and going.

In training camp I dropped back to throw long to John Stallworth. It was the same thing I'd done thousands and thousands of times. But this one time my foot slipped in the mud as I released the ball. Boom! I felt a stinging sensation inside my elbow.

Pro football players learn to live with pain. Even when you come out of a game without being hurt, you hurt. Players become accustomed to chronic pains, begrudgingly accepting them like unpleasant relatives. It's like having your mother-in-law around. You barely even notice her. But if you wake up one morning and your mother-in-law is suddenly gone, you immediately become aware of it. The same thing happens when you feel a new pain. Hmm, what's this? By golly, this is a new pain. I had never felt anything in my elbow quite like this pain. Every time I moved my fingers, it felt like a bee stinging me in the elbow. That's what got my attention.

Pro football players also learn to play with pain. If you can drag your sorry ass out of the grave, you play on Sunday. Even if the hearse has to drop you off on the way to your own funeral, you play on Sunday. For the entire 1982 season I had to get a cortisone shot in my elbow before every game in order to play. I missed only one game, a preseason exhibition game at the World's Fair in Knoxville, Tennessee, because the trainer accidentally stuck the needle into my ulna nerve and put my whole arm to sleep. I had no feeling at all from my elbow down to the ends of my fingers, which I couldn't even move. I was wide awake, but my arm was sleeping like a baby.

I went out to the field and tried to pick up a football. Believe me, a fish would have had more luck picking up a football than I did that day. The longest thirty-yard walk I think I ever took in my life was going up to Chuck Noll that day and telling him that I wasn't going to be able to play because my arm was napping.

I had torn and strained muscles and tendons in my elbow, micro tears of the flexor pronator muscle, but nobody knew exactly what to do about it. The consensus was to just give it a rest, don't even pick up a football for a couple of months, and it'll go away. For me that was a difficult prescription to follow. One thing I've never been very good at was doing nothing. I know experts at it, but I'm not one of them. A couple of months was more than I could wait. After several weeks I picked up a football and started throwing it. That little stinging pain was still there.

Doctors operated on my elbow in March 1983. I was told that it would take three or four months to heal, but eventually it would be as good as new. It was the athlete's version of being pregnant; my new arm was being born. The operation was a success, but the doctor told me he had been surprised to find the tissue was real mushy, the result of too many cortisone shots. As the doctor explained, I would have been much better off if my injury had been more severe. If I hadn't been able to play at all, I would have healed sooner and better; but because I hadn't been hurt bad enough, I played and did more damage to my elbow.

I promised the doctor that next time I would do my best to get hurt really bad, so I could play for a long, long time.

Within weeks after the operation the pain in my elbow was gone. It was gone like my first mother-in-law after I shot that armadillo. I was lifting weights, running, I was in great shape. But I just couldn't live happily without that pain in my elbow. I had to see if my elbow was really fixed. In minicamp before the 1983 season I picked up a football and just lobbed it about five yards. It wasn't even a pass, it was just a little toss.

We were on a practice field at Three Rivers. I just pitched it a few yards, and right where my arm had been sewed up I felt a sharp pain. Although I didn't know it at the time, that moment was the beginning of my broadcasting career. I didn't say a word to anyone. I just dropped my arm and held it tight against my body. When I got home my elbow was purple from internal bleeding. It swelled up to about the size of a tennis ball. But I didn't tell anyone what I had done. I just wore long shirts, kept my elbow hidden, and died inside.

I couldn't do anything for at least two months. I couldn't lift weights, and I certainly couldn't throw a football. As far as the team knew, my elbow hadn't completely healed. Cliff Stoudt became the Steelers' quarterback. When the doctor reexamined my arm, he told me once again to rest it. "Don't even look at a football out of the corner of your eye for the next few months," he said. Don't go near a football field. In fact, he suggested, don't even use words starting with the letter "f." That's how serious he was.

Chuck Noll didn't know what to do about me. The media asked him endless questions about my injury, and all he could tell them, honestly, was "I don't know." When is Bradshaw going to be back? I don't know. What are you going to do? I don't know. Is he getting better? I don't know. How is it going to affect the team? I don't know. Chuck Noll is a man who does not like to not know anything. He likes to know what he doesn't know. Three weeks of questions, four weeks.

I was not really welcomed around the team. I understood it wasn't personal—the game of football is about the players who can help you win this week. Chuck needed to work with the people who were going to play. I wasn't going to play, therefore I was useless to the team, a distraction. It wasn't necessary for me to come to the games. Chuck and I mostly discussed the situation through newspaper columnists. One day he became so frustrated at being asked about me that he told reporters, "I don't know if he can throw or not. Maybe he's ready for his life's work."

Until that moment I hadn't realized that playing quarterback for the Steelers was simply preparation for my real job. Man, that was a head slap. For something that wasn't personal, that sure sounded personal. "He's the head coach," I responded, "and he's going to do what he wants. If he means what he says, he'll either release me or trade me. Then I'll be out of his hair. I'll be seeking employment elsewhere, or maybe I will move on to my 'life's work.' "

Not that I had the slightest idea what that might be, mind you. Lady Love Cosmetics was still a long time in my future. I still expected my elbow would heal eventually and I would return to the field. The Steelers sent me to several physical therapists, but nothing seemed to help. To my surprise I got a call one day from the Steelers suggesting I try a new medical technique: mynah bird therapy. Actually it was someone in the public relations office: "There's a guy who claims his mynah bird has magical healing powers. He wants to put it on your elbow. Are you willing to do it?"

The man wanted to put his bird on my elbow? Heck, yes! Why not. The Steelers had been giving me the bird for years, now we were going to do it for real. The bird's owner claimed that this bird was insured by Lloyd's of London for $12 million, although I never did find out what it was insured against. The owner also claimed the bird had a record of 2,003-78-1 helping people who believed in its powers. He did not explain how you could get a tie in helping people.

I definitely believed in the power of that bird to get publicity for itself; it was amazingly effective at that. But healing my elbow seemed a little more complicated. I let that bird sit on my arm for several minutes. When we were finished, I could say without hesitation that I'd had photographs taken of a bird sitting on my elbow.

It seemed like everybody in Pittsburgh had a remedy to cure my elbow. I got letters from fans sharing ethnic customs, telling me they were praying for me, and accusing me of letting down the team. Noll had pretty much given up on me for the season. Asked by a sportswriter once again when I might be able to play, he said, "Look, he's getting close—but so is Christmas."

I do believe in miracles. While visiting the surgeon in Shreveport who had performed my elbow operation I tested a new gadget, the Electro-Acuscope, a blinking, beeping boxlike machine which supposedly simulated the effects of acupuncture. The doctor explained that most often it was used on animals.

I'll make the jokes here, but thank you very much for trying.

The doctor explained that most often it was used on animals. Well, I might have said, I've often been called a horse's behind. Or, I might have said, Well, don't let them hog it. Or, I might have said, Well, I'm not chicken. But what I probably said was, Let's try it. The doctor ran a thin wand connected to the machine by wire over my elbow. When he was done, the pain was gone. I said, THAT PAIN WAS GONE. Did you read me? IT WAS GONE! I could throw a football. Brothers and sisters, I could throw a football! I was cured! Cured!

Let me have an Amen on that, please.

I felt like I had discovered the Miracle Machine. I was snapping off fifty-yard passes. I called Dan Rooney, and he bought one of the $6,000 machines for the team. Art Rooney ran the wand over his arthritic hand and for the first time in two years was able to make a fist. After watching me work out, Chuck Noll told sportswriters, "I believe in miracles."

I took the field for the first time in a year during a late-season game against the New York Jets in Shea Stadium that we had to win to make the playoffs. As I ran out onto the field, I was almost giddy with happiness; I was going to my job. This was where I belonged. I was back in the saddle again. Man, it felt great.

On our second series as the Jets' Mark Gastineau was about to launch me, I threw across the field for a seventeen-yard touchdown pass to Gregg Garrity. As I released the ball, I felt something inside my arm snap. Pop! goes the career. Everybody on the sidelines was screaming; this was beautiful, Bradshaw comes back after a year away and throws a touchdown pass on the second set of downs. The Steelers were back! Bradshaw was back!

Bradshaw was done. But I was the only one who knew it. I ran off the field without saying a word to anyone, the old pro handling success with quiet confidence. Someone came up to me to offer congratulations. "I just tore my elbow up," I said. What? "I just tore my elbow up. It's absolutely killing me." I was hoping the Jets would keep the ball for a while while the pain in my elbow subsided. They fumbled, and we recovered.

A few minutes earlier I'd run onto the field like the king reclaiming his lands; as I ran onto the field this time, I was silently praying to God, "Please don't make me have to throw a pass." On third down I had to throw a flare out for a first down. I couldn't even pass the football, I sort of flipped. We moved deep into Jets territory. On third and about four I hit Calvin Sweeney over the middle for a ten-yard touchdown and a 14–0 lead.

As far as my teammates and the fans were concerned, the legend of Terry Bradshaw was growing with each pass. I'd completed seven of nine passes for seventy-seven yards. The man comes back after a year and throws two touchdown passes. But I knew my career was over. Chuck came over to me and asked, "You okay?"

"No, sir," I said, "I tore my elbow up." I went into the locker room and iced it, but that was mostly for show. I'd torn a ligament in my elbow. My body knew my career was over, but it took my mind a little longer to wrap itself around that concept.

I stood on the sidelines as we lost the conference playoff to the Raiders 38–10. Almost until kickoff, sportswriters showered Chuck with questions about my availability. "He can't throw the ball," Noll said. "What do you want him to do—direct the running game?"

I insisted that with enough rest I could come back. I tried, but my arm was deader than roadkill. Ironically, it was my passion for the game that had ended my career; if I saw a football, I just had to throw it. If I had stayed away from training camp until my arm had healed completely, if I hadn't picked up that football and tried to throw it, if I just could have waited a few more months . . . If the doctors had told me at the very beginning, Son, you're going to miss this whole season, I would have been fine with it. I would have stayed away from the field and let my arm heal. But instead they gave me hope! That was the worst thing they could have done. It'll take three or four months to heal, they told me. Then as time went by they made the situation even worse; I was told, "You're ahead of schedule." Ahead of schedule? Of course I'm ahead of schedule. I'm a competitor, I want to heal so fast my doctor gets nominated for sainthood because it has to be a miracle. I want to heal faster than anyone has ever healed from this injury. If fast healing was an Olympic event, I would want to make the team. Because I'm an athlete, and athletes want to win at everything they do. That's what athletes do. So instead of accepting the fact that I couldn't play, I was busy healing away. How's it feel, Terry? You got to be a saint, Doc.

When *Sports Illustrated* honored the Pittsburgh Pirates' late, great Willie Stargell and me as their co–Sportsmen of the Year in 1979, I said, "I like to think that when I retire I'll say to myself, 'Gosh, if I could have just one more year, I know I'll get better.' " But when the time came I found that not to be true: I wanted five more years.

Once I accepted the fact that I could no longer play, I never looked back. I also rarely went back to Pittsburgh. When I know something is over, whether it is my playing career or a relationship, I mourn for it for an appropriate period of time, and then I bury it. Deep. That's my form of emotional protection. It's the way I survive. By the end of my career I had reached a level of personal contentment; I no longer needed to play the game to find my identity.

I knew exactly who I was; I was Dr. Terry Bradshaw, compliments of the honorary Doctor of Laws degree conferred upon me by West Virginia's Alderson-Broaddus College.

THREE

After we had won our second Super Bowl in 1976, I was invited to the White House to meet President Gerald Ford and Vice President Nelson Rockefeller. This was a great thrill for me; I had literally gone from the outhouse to the White House. I invited my future second ex-wife-to-be, Olympic figure skater Jo Jo Starbuck, to go with me. Man, I was feeling mighty proud of myself; I was the quarterback of the Super Bowl champions, my sixty-four-yard touchdown pass to Lynn Swann had won the game, I was dating a beautiful and famous skater, my picture was on the cover of newspapers and magazines around the country. I had made it.

During the party following a show starring Carol Burnett, Jo Jo Starbuck and I were introduced to Vice President Rockefeller. This was most definitely the first time the names Bradshaw and Rockefeller had ever been used in the same sentence. The Vice President was very kind to me. "You know, fella," he said, "you're the best quarterback I've ever seen—"

Wow!

"—I've always enjoyed watching how cool you are under pressure—"

Ah, shucks.

"and you're definitely a role model to the young people of this country—"

Hope you're listening to this, Jo Jo.

"Why, from that first game I saw you play at the Naval Academy—"

Uh-oh.

"—and when the Cowboys drafted you I thought—"

Obviously the vice president had heard the name Starbuck and decided I was Roger Staubach, the Dallas Cowboys quarterback, who had not won Super Bowl X.

I didn't know what to do. It was terribly embarrassing, particularly in front of the woman I desperately wanted to impress. I finally realized I had no choice. After a few agonizing moments I stood up tall and straight, put my arm protectively around Jo Jo's shoulders, and said proudly, "Did you see that game we played against Army my senior year?"

If the vice president of the United States of America wanted me to be Roger Staubach, I was going to be the best possible Roger Staubach for the rest of the evening.

Somehow I often found myself in confusing situations like that off the field. But on the field . . . On the field I always felt the comfort of home. It seemed like everything else in my life was simply preparation for playing the game of football. My whole life revolved around the sixty hours a year or so of game time.

I wish I could really describe being on the field in the middle of a professional football game. Right at the end of Super Bowl XIV, we had the game won. We were on about the one-yard line, one-foot line, and I remember the moment as we broke the huddle. There are few great moments in an athlete's life; if you're a jockey on a thoroughbred and you've got maybe five gallops to go and you know you've won the Kentucky Derby, or Michael Jordan at the foul line when you're up by two and shooting two with one second left in the final game of the championships, when you know that the game or the race is over, it's sealed, done. Usually an athlete is so focused on what needs to be done each instant that before it's possible to savor it, it's over. But just this one time, Super Bowl XIV, I decided that this was my moment and I wanted to take it all in, I wanted to pack it away in my mind forever. I felt that for this bunch of Steelers the run was over, we would never be in this situation again. So I did just that. I stood there and I absorbed that stadium.

Usually I was too involved in playing the game to ever appreciate the fact that I was playing the game. I loved every moment on the field, even when I was smashed down facefirst in the mud with a thousand pounds of players lying on top of me. Well, maybe those moments I just liked.

Howie Long once described football as a game in which "grown men put on fiberglass helmets and run into each other from one end of the parking lot to the other." Spoken like a true defensive end. For me, football is a chess match and a war: each team has about sixty-five plays to score points by passing, running, kicking off, punting, exploiting defensive opportunities, and kicking field goals. There are individual matches, substitutions, and penalties to overcome, and it's all governed by a clock. The best part about it is that the whole operation is run by the quarterback.

And I was the quarterback. That meant I made my living putting my hands under another man's butt. Admittedly, the image of me sticking my hands under Mike Webster's butt is not a pretty picture. That's not a natural act. With religion so strong in this country, that's probably the reason you don't see a lot of good Catholic quarterbacks. Fortunately I'm a Baptist, and we never had problems with it. I've always advised women who were watching football games with a man they wanted to impress to wait until the quarterback got in the shotgun position—meaning he was standing way behind the center—and then comment, "That boy must be a Catholic."

As I got better known, I found that people began asking me questions about subjects other than football. They wanted my opinion on the environment. Politicians asked me to endorse them. I replied to all those requests the same way; Hey, I spent much of my life staring at a guy's butt, how does that make my political opinion valuable?

Quarterback was a strange title for my job. I don't know why I was only a quarterback while a man who did nothing but run with the ball that I handed to him was the fullback. I did more than he did, but for some reason he was the FULLback, he was the whole package. As new formations developed they referred to the fullback by other names—running back, blocking back—but I remained only a quarterback.

The only player on the team who handled the ball more than I did was the center. Some players, mostly linemen, could go an entire season without ever touching the football. A football is actually a pretty strange object. A baseball is a hard round white ball with its cover stitched together; a basketball is a big round rubber ball, a golf ball is a small hard dimpled evil ball. But try to describe a football: a football is an inflated ellipsoid with laces.

And every football is different. They may all look the same, they may all be inflated ellipsoids, but just like baseballs, every single football has a unique feel. Some balls are a little fatter on the tip, for example, some are very slippery; some are hard, some are soft, some just feel perfect, others feel horrible. For several years the NFL used a football with white stripes. The only thing different about this particular ball was that it had a painted stripe; but every quarterback in the league swore that the whole ball had been changed. It just felt different. Nobody liked throwing it, so we continued complaining until the league got rid of the stripe.

Most fans don't know it, but before the game we would doctor the footballs that would be used. Until the season of 2000 it was up to the home team to provide twenty-four game balls to the officials for each game. A brand-new NFL football straight from the factory is not easy to throw or catch. It's rock hard and very slippery. So in the privacy of the locker room before the game, players would take the footballs and rub them and scrub them to remove the glaze, or deflate them, then pump them up with air real big to stretch the leather. On some teams the kickers would put them in laundry bags and whomp them against the wall or run them through a cycle in the dryer. Some teams did this, but naturally not the Steelers, because we were righteous folk who would never stretch the rules, and when these other teams—not the Steelers—were finished, they would put them back in the plastic wrapping and right back in the box. Some teams—who were not the Steelers—after the officials had checked and approved the game balls, would let out a couple of pounds of air to make it easier for the quarterback to grip it. A little less air would make the ball spongier. It was what might be called a perceived advantage—both teams played with the same ball.

A lot of people don't know this, but to prevent teams from doctoring the ball, the league changed the rules. The officials keep in their possession right up until gametime footballs with a little tiny *k* on them. In this case *k* is not the symbol used to certify "kosher for Passover." It doesn't even mean kosher for passing. It could mean kosher, meaning nobody's tampered with them, but the *k* actually stands for kicking ball. These balls are put into play by the officials in kicking situations. But that's still better than college, where the teams actually play with different footballs. The home team and the visiting team provide their own footballs, which are put into play when they go on offense. How *k* is that?

To make it easier to catch slick footballs, some receivers would cover their hands with stickum, a really gooey substance that made their hand feel like the sticky side of tape. Often the stickum would come off on the ball. The Oakland Raiders used that stuff by the pound. I didn't know that the first time I played against them. I remember taking the snap from Webster, fading back to throw, finding my receiver and cranking up and . . . and . . . get off, get off of there! The ball stuck to my hand. I couldn't get rid of it. Finally I ended up throwing it straight into the ground. When I complained to the officials, they wiped it down, smearing the stickum all over the ball. My hands felt like I'd stuck them in a jar of peanut butter. I'd go to the sidelines and put my hand on a coach's shoulder, and it would just stick there.

Because of the things people who were not the Steelers did to the football, I had to learn several different ways to throw it. I did have an unorthodox delivery. Unlike most quarterbacks, rather than resting my index finger on the laces, I put it on the end of the ball, and when I released it, I'd give it an extra push with that finger. I'd sort of launch it. Some people are known for their strength of character, others are known for their overall strength; I was known for my strong index finger.

I could always throw a football a long distance, but my arm was never stronger than it was in high school and college. I never threw it as well as a pro as I had growing up. To deal with the different situations we encountered almost weekly—from the heat of Miami that made my hands perspire to the bitter cold in Cincinnati that made it just about impossible to grip the ball, in dry weather and in the snow, on indoor fields covered with artificial turf and grass fields that rain turned into mud swamps—I had to learn a lot of different ways to throw the football. I could heave it, sling it, and shovel it; I could throw bullets or lobs, straight overhand or sidearm. I learned to do whatever was necessary to throw the football.

Throw deep. Rear back and throw long. That was the game we played, that was the game I loved to play. Stand in there when they're climbing the walls of the fort, stand in there until you can determine which lineman hasn't brushed his teeth that morning or, in some cases, that season. Then fire down the field and get ready to take your punishment. That's not the way the game is played today. Today quarterbacks stand back there in their comfort zone and throw dink, dink, dink. Dinky little passes. I was embarrassed when I completed a five-yard pass. Sorry guys, I thought I was playing in the future. I threw the ball too hard to throw short passes; my passes would hit the receiver, bounce in the air, and get intercepted, and then I'd have to make it look like I really wanted to tackle that big lumbering lineman who caught the ball. Let me be honest, I am not a fan of the way the game is played today. Short passes may not win football games, but they certainly do impress the announcers: Oh, Charlie, that boy's more accurate than Trump counting cash, he's completed twenty-two of thirty passes for almost forty-five whole yards.

My mother could complete those passes, and my mother was always the last one picked in our backyard games. A man could be proud of the Steelers offense. The first few years we were mostly a running team. We threw the ball to keep the yardsticks moving, to make first downs, to keep control of the ball, to keep the defense wary so it couldn't focus only on our running backs. But we won or lost our games on the ground. We played each game like it was a heavyweight fight. We attacked with body shots, running running running, until the other team finally let down its guard, then POW! we killed them.

Our running game set up our passing game, and our ability to throw the ball made our running game effective. We didn't peck away at our opponents, we didn't play the West Coast high-percentage passing offense. Our philosophy was strike deep into the heart of the enemy. If I had to throw a little diddly pass, my arm would freeze up. My brain would be yelling at my arm, Now don't you go throwing that junk anymore! I was fortunate, I had extraordinary receivers to throw to; I loved to throw deep, they liked to catch deep. My greatest thrill in football was throwing long; deep ends, deep hooks, take off and run. I loved watching that inflated ellipsoid flying downfield. *WhhhooOOOOoosshhh*. Boom. Complete, Bradshaw to Swann. The crowd goes crazy! I loved play action that allowed me to move out of the pocket and stay loose until one of my receivers got free.

Every time I went back to pass, I knew three things. Number one, if defensive backs were great receivers, they'd be playing on offense; number two, when your receiver sticks up his hand, he wants you to throw the ball to him; and number three, don't worry how bad the pass is, nobody is going to outjump John Stallworth.

Have I mentioned that I called my own plays? Read this: 60 Prevent Slot Hook and Go. Want to read another one? Full Right 19 Straight. I'm extremely

proud of that. There was a time in pro football history
when quarterbacks called all the plays, but this was before the coaches realized that they were geniuses as well
as generals and the game was too complicated for a
simple player to understand. As a result quarterbacks
no longer call their plays; they've got earphones in their
helmets and a voice from on high—well, the press
box—tells them what to do and when to do it. Hey,
Troy, how you doin', sugar? Everything all right out
there, baby? Go open right, 62 Basic. Now stare down
that strong safety, if he moves away from your throwing hand, that's your right hand, you throw away from
where he goes. Now you be careful out there, and I'll
be speaking with you next play.

I played Quarterback Unplugged; I ran my team. I
had on-the-field responsibility for our offense. Kenny
Anderson had his plays sent in from the sideline. Most
often Tom Landry sent in plays to Roger. Vince Lombardi called plays for Bart Starr. I was the one whose
elevator supposedly didn't go to the top floor—but I
called my plays.

Not every play, or even every game. There were
times when I felt the pressure, the pressure of a bad
week, the pressure of a bad game. I felt lost. I couldn't
focus. The fans were on me, the team was struggling,
I needed help. I took a lot of pride in the fact that I
ran our offense, but I was never hesitant to ask for
help when I needed it. There were times I told Chuck
Noll, "Next week you send in the plays. Just let me
relax and settle down. When I'm ready to take over
I'll throw my hand up." In 1977, for example, I broke
my wrist and I had difficulty thinking and hurting at

the same time. I was wearing a cast on my left arm, and I couldn't handle the ball that well, so I thought it would be best if Chuck called the plays from the sidelines and let me concentrate on reading the coverage. That lasted two games. We played poorly both games. I realized that the team was looking to me for leadership that I was not providing. We'd be standing around in the huddle waiting for the next play to come in from the sidelines. When I started calling the plays again, we started winning. It wasn't particularly that my plays were better—we had a fine offensive coaching staff—but when we were making our own decisions, there was more energy and enthusiasm in our huddle. Think of it as the difference between playing lead guitar and playing a record.

There were also times when I got back to the huddle after being hit so hard I was hearing the entire Mormon Tabernacle Choir and Marching Band banging their drums in my head. It wasn't difficult for my teammates to figure out that I was struggling: I was the one watching a formation of birds fly south—and we were playing indoors. You need help? they'd ask. I need a lot of help, I'd admit, what have you all got? I need something here.

Basically, what I needed was another head until this one got all straightened out. But I was grateful for any play suggestion.

When Jimmy Johnson was working on the Fox pregame show between head coaching jobs, he told me that he didn't really believe that I called my own plays. "How'd you do it," he wondered.

I told him that I studied the game plan prepared by

the coaches all week. We went over them time and again in practice. And then on Sunday I threw the game plan away and called whichever plays I could remember. If it worked running it to the right, then we'd run it to the left.

Now that wasn't completely accurate. We did have a plan. The first three plays of every football game are designed long before the kickoff. Those plays are used to get some sense of the defensive setup. What are the bad guys doing to stop you from robbing the bank? Based on studying films of their previous games, we knew what they liked to do in certain situations. Our formations and plays were set up to see if they were actually going to do it. We knew the defensive tendencies against the run, in passing situations, third down, we had them scouted. So we knew what we were going to run on first down and second down; third down depended on whether it was third and just a couple of yards for a first down or third and good luck. Of course, if that first play went for a first down, we had to throw out the planned second- and third-down plays and start again with the first-down package. By the conclusion of our first possession, we had enough information to begin to make adjustments. If our game plan was working, they had to make adjustments; if they were successfully stopping us, we had to make the adjustments.

If I had success running a certain play, I was going to run it at opportune times until it stopped working. Initially I ran my best play at their weakest people. And I continued doing it until they figured out how to stop it. Eventually they would figure it out; even the weakest people on the line are among the very best in the world at playing their position. When they stopped it, I would run other plays, maybe another dozen plays, maybe two possessions—until I suspected that they had forgotten about that play. Then I would run it again; except this time I would change it slightly, maybe throwing a pass from the formation.

Football is a game of cat and mouse—very big and very strong cats and mice. It's a team game of individual combat. The offense tries to set up the defense to make the defense think it has the whole body when all it has is the tail. We may run the same play several times just to lull the defense into a false sense of complacency. Make the defense believe it is the same play, then pull the old switcheroo.

In overtime against the Cleveland Browns one time we ran a Motion Crack Back Fake Flow 38 Reverse Pass. Pretty obvious, right? Basically it begins just like a simple halfback run around the end. We had run that play, just a basic halfback sweep, several times throughout the game. The Browns had seen it enough times to instantly recognize it as it developed. But then we added some wrinkles. We had put our receiver, Lynn Swann, in motion, meaning that instead of going out for a pass, he was behind the line of scrimmage running toward the middle of the field. As he passed the ball carrier, the halfback handed it off to him. Reverse! You could hear defensive players screaming. Reverse! The entire defense had been moving in one direction to stop the sweep, in the backfield the safeties were flowing gracefully across the field following the movement of the ball, and . . . . whoops, after the ball was handed off they turned and started flowing in the other direction—

Now it looked like a straight reverse. Hand off and run. The cornerbacks and the safeties moved to cut off Swann's run. Suddenly, Swannie stopped, turned, and threw the ball back to me.

Whoops. Again . . . The defense turned back toward me. But by now the defensive coverage in the backfield had broken down completely. It looked like a prison break, people in Steelers black and gold running downfield all over the place. I threw a touchdown pass to Benny Cunningham to win the game.

We had worked on that play in practice for a long time. It was a specific play designed for a dire situation. It's called a gadget play—a trick play, street football at its finest. He's got it, no, that guy's got it, you cover him, I'll get that guy, now he's got it . . . what the . . . who's the . . . who's supposed to be covering that receiver?

It was successful because we'd spent the entire afternoon running Flow 38, a basic handoff to the halfback. Fans see a gadget play like that go for long yardage and wonder why we don't run it more often. The answer is that it is a play designed to be used in a very specific situation, a situation that might not come up once in an entire season. If we tried to use a gadget play at the beginning of the game, it would be stopped easily. The defensive linemen wouldn't have been fooled, the safeties would have stayed in their coverage. But much later, after seeing that same basic running play run over and over through four quarters and all 146 television commercials, they responded to it just as we had anticipated.

Call it sleight of football.

We probably had between eighty and one hundred basic plays that we could run. We had a thick notebook full of diagrammed plays. Maybe we should have named that book *War and War*. In preparation for a specific game we might have added a new formation, but we wouldn't make too many changes. In each game we would run approximately sixty-five plays, and of that number maybe twenty plays would work precisely as they had been planned. That does not mean we scored twenty touchdowns a game. Every play is not designed to produce a touchdown. A successful running play gains four yards. It's successful because if you run it three times you gain twelve yards, enough for a first down. If we gained four yards every play, we would never have been stopped. We just would have marched down the field, four yards, four yards, four yards, into the end zone. At the end of the season the coaches chart the plays: 34 Special. We ran it ninety-six times, averaging 3.9 yards per carry. By NFL standards that is not successful. Four yards is the measure of a successful play.

We were a great team because we had a core group of talented players who were well coached and executed their assignments. Our offense wasn't complicated; just hand the football to Franco Harris or Rocky Bleier, or throw the ball to Lynn Swann or John Stallworth, and then start cheering for them.

Calling my own plays made the game fun for me. Generally the situation, the down and yardage, the score and time left in the game, narrowed my decision to a few plays. My favorite down was first down because I had the most options: first down is definitely the best down in any possession. First down was the most fun because we could run, throw, have play action—the defense had absolutely no idea what I wanted to do. Now, second-down play is dictated by the result of the first-down play. Second and ten requires a whole different outlook than second and four. Third down, just like the third child, gets all the hand-me-downs. Third down inherits all the problems created by first and second down. The reason third downs are so tough is that most of the options are gone; if the situation is third and long, we are going to throw the football. I know it, the defense knows it, Forrest Gump knows it: "Yup, they'll be throwing the football now." Third and a few yards we are going to keep the ball on the ground, and the defense is going to put every swinging body it can muster on that line to stop us.

My whole objective in selecting a play was to put my people in the right position to be successful. Often before I decided on the play I asked my teammates for advice. We'd get into the huddle, and I'd ask, "So what you all got?" or "What's it look like? I know we're getting through the safety, but how are the corners playing? Hey, Stall, whattya think?"

"Brad, don't run that anymore," Franco Harris might reply. "The guy is too tight."

Rocky Bleier might suggest, "I could really blow this guy off the ball. Let's go back over here to my side. I can wear this guy out."

I know I was one of very few quarterbacks to ask my offensive linemen for advice. Maybe the only one. Offensive linemen? Most people think they couldn't spell *cat* if you spotted them the "k" and the "a." But when we only need short yardage for a first down, I'd look them right in the face mask and ask, "What would you guys like to run? What do you think would work?"

It was as if someone had finally recognized that offensive linemen are human beings too. Their whole spirit would be lifted. My goodness, Mr. Quarterback is talking to us. But who would know better how to gain a yard or two than the people in the trenches? "Let's shove it up the middle. We can blow them away. Run 35 Special, and I got him."

"Okay," I'd agree, "Let's run 35 Special. Now you're sure you can hook this guy? You're sure now?"

"Yeah," he'd grunt, which is offensive linemen talk for "I will destroy that man and two succeeding generations of his offspring." Now, that was a commitment.

And when I accepted their suggestion, those people were committed to that play. Yes, they were saying, yes, Terry, yes, we can do this! We *will* do this! That play was going to be successful.

Most of the time it was, too.

Two very important things that football players are taught from the first day they put on shoulder pads are that the only person allowed to speak in the huddle is the quarterback and that when the TV camera catches you on the sideline you're supposed to say "Hi, *Mom*." Let's review: Nobody in pro football except the quarterback is supposed to speak in the huddle, and players are never supposed to wave to the camera and say, "Hi, Dad."

We didn't always follow that first rule. I encouraged my teammates to tell me flat out when they had a play that would work. I was fortunate enough to play with two of the finest receivers in pro football history, Lynn Swann and John Stallworth. Both men always wanted the ball. They'd come back to huddle: "Throw it to me, Brad, I got my man set up. We can make this work." "No, Brad, throw it to me, my man's ready to fall." John was much quieter than Lynn, but just as intense. But having played with both of them for several years, I knew they meant what they said when they said it. And they knew if I listened to them and called their number, they had better get free. Because if they didn't get open, if they didn't catch the ball, there was a fair chance I wouldn't throw the football their way again that game.

Chuck Noll was a student of the game. A professor who understood how each piece fit together. He liked things orderly, predictable. And then he had to deal with me.

The essence of professional football is repetition. We would run a play hundreds of times in practice until we could run it the same way every time. I would spend hours each week with the coaches going over the game plan, reviewing the plays we were going to use. We were regimented, robotized, rebuked, rewarded, and constantly reminded: Stick to the game plan. Then we'd get in the game, and when we saw an opportunity we would make up a play. Swannie would tell me, "A double move, and I got this guy." When someone told me that, I called that play immediately. We changed patterns, we ran plays that weren't in our playbook, and many times the result was a big gain.

We learned from every play. My teammates often gave me information that had to be deposited in the memory bank, to be withdrawn later in the game. Maybe John Stallworth would tell me, "If you run that play again, when he comes up on me I'm going by him." I couldn't run that play again right away, the situation had changed. But later in the game if we were back in that same situation, third and seven at our own forty-yard line, I'd go to the ATM in my head and try to remember my supersecret code; that's right, Stallworth. We'd make it up in the huddle, Stallworth would go deep. Touchdown! Darn, that Bradshaw is brilliant!

Everybody on that team knew his own capabilities. Rocky Bleier was a hard-nosed running back. Third and one at a crucial point of the game, we just needed a few feet for a first down, everybody in the ballpark or watching at home eating pizza knew we were going to jam it down the defense. Rocky would look at me and tell me firmly and without any hesitation, "Give it to Franco. I don't want it."

If anyone was the leader in the huddle, it was Franco Harris. When Franco told me he wanted the ball, Franco got the ball. Everybody understood that. With a little over seven minutes to play in Super Bowl XIII, we were winning 20–17 and had the ball inside the Cowboys' twenty-yard line. I got sacked by Hollywood Henderson. Maybe he hit me a little extra hard and just a smidgeon too late. Or maybe that was a solid lead cloud that fell out of the sky on my head. Franco was furious. He jerked Henderson off me, and when we huddled he ordered, "Give me the ball." The play I called was 93 Tackle Trap, a running play designed to make a few yards. But when I got to the line of scrimmage I looked over the Dallas formation. There are times when I'd go to the line and look out and realize the wrath of God was about to befall me, and that the best thing I could hope for was that my heirs would remember me well. But there were other times when I would look at the defensive alignment and know for certain that the sun was shining brightly all over the world, that indeed faith is rewarded in the here and now.

The Cowboys were showing me a blitz, meaning they were coming to get me. The sun was shining brightly, there was hope for all mankind. I had called the perfect play. Cowboys were going to be coming through the line in one direction while Franco was running right past them in the other direction. He was going to score easily, and I was going to look like a play-calling genius.

But the Cowboys' defensive backs had their own secret game plan, so secret Dallas coach Tom Landry didn't even know about it. Cliff Harris and Charlie Waters wanted to mess up my mind, but as I could have told them a long time ago, "You can't do that. There ain't nothing to mess up." The defense was set up to look like a blitz, but it was a fake; it was the RuPaul of football. I was supposed to believe they were blitzing and change the play at the line of scrimmage. But Franco wanted the ball, and I was going to give it to him. They could have been standing back there with shotguns, and Franco was still getting the football.

They were completely out of position. I handed the ball to Franco, and he blasted through the line. Harris and Waters converged on the middle—and ran right into an official. They stopped that official for no gain, but Franco was gone. He rumbled untouched twenty-two yards into the end zone. Touchdown! Ball game! Super Bowl!

If they hadn't tried to disguise the defense, they would have been in good position to stop Franco for a short time. Instead, I looked like the Napoleisenhower of football.

There were times when Chuck Noll would send in a play. The man was the head coach. He won four Super Bowls. He had tremendous responsibility. And he looked really impressive on the sideline watching the rest of us actually playing the game. So many times I ran the play he sent in. But truthfully I wasn't what you would call a real fanatic about it. There's a reason that the word *feel* is almost part of the word *field;* when you're on the field you have a feel for the game that you can't possibly get from the sidelines.

At times Chuck would send in a play, and after dutifully considering its merits I would decide it did not quite fulfill the various and sundry needs of the moment and refrain from executing that specific command. I would share my thoughts in the huddle with my teammates, telling them, "That's a stupid play. He can't see what's going on here. Let's run . . ." In some ways I was setting up the classic confrontation, Chuck v. Everybody Else. The result was that we all worked together to prove that we were right.

Chuck used to have a signal to me when he wanted to send in a play. I remember one sequence when we moved from our goal line ninety yards down the field in about twelve plays. It was a classic beautifully executed Steelers drive, power on the ground, acrobatics in the air. But when we got to about the five-yard line, I looked at the sidelines and saw the coaches frantically screaming at me to wait for them to send in the play.

Oh yeah, I thought, we drive the entire length of the field, and *now* you want to call the play? I don't think so. I turned my back and called the touchdown play: Hand the ball to Franco.

The conversation in the huddle was almost exclusively about the next play, although during a time-out we might talk about anything from the condition of the playing field to a personal situation. One thing I never did in a huddle was remind a player not to do something wrong. I learned that from Chuck, who told me near the end of the first half of a game against the Giants, "You'd better not go back in there and throw an interception. You do, and I'll jerk your ass out of this game." I went back into that game with one thought on my mind: Don't throw an interception, don't throw an interception. I was so worried I was going to be intercepted and get chewed out by Noll that I couldn't concentrate on what I was supposed to be doing. I had been programmed to fail. My first throw was intercepted.

But invariably when I went over to the sideline toward the end of a game, some coach would urgently remind me, "Tell them to hold on to the ball." Tell them to hold on to the ball? What kind of advice was that? Now, there was about as much chance of me telling Franco or Rocky not to drop the ball as there was of Little Orphan Annie finally getting adopted. It just was not going to happen. These people had been playing football most of their life. To reach the NFL, obviously they had succeeded on every level. They knew they were not supposed to drop the football on the ground, and I was not going to remind them.

But if they did fumble, I was willing to take the

blame. Sorry, Franco, it was my fault you fumbled the ball, I forgot to remind you not to do it. To me, being a leader means taking responsibility for your actions. I never made excuses. When I screwed up, I was vocal about it; I don't know why I threw that ball into coverage, I don't know why I threw that ball over your head, I don't know why I messed up that handoff—but I did it. During my career I heard all kinds of excuses for making a physical error; I lost it in the sun, the wind took it, that sumbitch held me, the balls were bad, the field was torn up, it was too cold to get a good grip, the meteor shower made me nervous, I had a bad hair day—but I never heard them from the group of players who stayed together through our four championships. This was a stand-up group of people. If we screwed up, we admitted that we screwed up.

When people took responsibility, when they apologized, we always forgave them. I was a great forgiver; Oh, man, anybody can drop a pass thrown right into their arms, I'll get you again later. Hey, everybody fumbles on the two-yard line once in a while, don't worry about it. Ummggh, anybody can miss a block on a 300-pound tackle once in a while, I'll just . . . I'll just . . . let me just pull my head out of the ground here, and I'll be okay. . . .

One thing I can say with great certainty about every single play I called: every one started out correctly. I can say with pride that in my entire career never once did I go to the line of scrimmage and, as some quarterbacks have done, line up for the snap behind a guard. I suspect it's pretty embarrassing to try to explain to 82,000 people in the stadium that you were only kidding, that you really knew that wasn't the center.

The plays might have gotten off to a good start, but then again so did the Hindenburg. Running plays developed very quickly; there wasn't time for a lot of improvisation. But because we liked to throw downfield, I had to stay in the pocket a little longer waiting for my receivers to get free than those people who threw that wimpy short junk. It's pretty much impossible to accurately convey the feeling of standing in the pocket looking for a receiver as several large people are clawing their way to you. It's sort of like being the doorman in *Night of the Living Dead*. Arms and bodies are coming at you from all sides, accompanied by a sound track consisting of grunts and the crash of equipment. You kind of have to pretend that you are so cool that these people are nothing more than a minor irritation: I'm cool, I don't even notice you, I'm co— My, you are a big fella, aren't you? Sir.

Even the best offensive lineman can only protect the quarterback for a few seconds. Then the pocket begins collapsing. That's the time that the quarterback "feels the pressure," meaning he realizes his time is just about up. Quarterbacks have a built-in alarm clock in their heads that tells them, right about now you'd better evacuate the premises. It is generally accepted in pro football that a quarterback has 3.2 seconds to get rid of the ball or get out of the pocket. After 3.2 seconds that alarm begins screeeeaming, "Attention, brain, you have now gone way past the limit of safety. The rest of us wants to move, and we want to move RIGHT NOW!" I learned how to tell time in my head; the technical term for that is "survival." After you've retreated into the pocket several thousand times, you know from experience when you've run out of time. When I give a speech, if I'm asked to speak for sixty minutes, I will speak almost exactly sixty minutes, without even glancing at a clock.

I've never really felt "pressure"; rather, I've felt a time restraint. Thousands of years ago nautical maps identified by name those places on Earth that had been discovered and explored. But areas known to exist that had not yet been explored were marked, in Latin, "Beyond this point there be dragons." As any experienced quarterback will tell you, beyond 3.2 seconds there be dragons.

It takes courage to stay in the pocket. In any sport when the force is coming at you and you are not delivering that force, it takes courage to stand there. It takes real guts for a baseball player to crowd the plate when the ball is moving toward him at nearly 100 mph; I have great admiration for batters. It takes real courage for an ice hockey goalie to put his body in front of a hard rubber puck fired at him from a few feet away. I admire those people greatly. But when time runs out on a quarterback, he has three options: try to complete a pass, intentionally throw the ball away so that no one can catch it, or run for your life. For a lot of quarterbacks the key to that decision is based on how much confidence they have in the team doctor.

"Running for your life" sounds more professional when you call it "scrambling." I was a scramblin' man, made a lot of yards. . . . Early in my career I had reasonable speed, but as I got older I got slower. For a quarterback, being fast isn't as essential as being quick.

You only have to be one step quicker than the player pursuing you. The key to being successful when you have to scramble is to sit in that pocket, show your patience, and when it gets to that time you have to burst out of the pocket. No pussy-footin' around, son, you got to get to that promised land. Once you're outside the pocket, you can start gliding, because the pressure is on the defense to commit: Do they come up and try to tackle me, which means one of my receivers is going to get open, or do they drop back and let me have a short gain?

I could do that; I was more of a drag racer than a Formula One racer. For the few feet needed to save a play, I could move fast. Fear and defensive linemen will do that to you. I had ignition, I could just burst out of the pocket when it was necessary. And I never lost that quickness.

When I was scrambling, I probably could best be described as a cross between a fullback and a sissy. I was a big kid; I had strong legs and arms, and I wasn't afraid to get hit. I didn't want to get hit, I tried hard to avoid getting hit, but I was strong enough to push off people and—just occasionally, mind you, I'm not trying to rile anybody up—I could run over a tackler.

There is only one objective you need to remember when you're scrambling: Don't get hit. Scrambling can be fun, particularly if you don't end up being carried off the field in the rear of a cart, of course. When you're scrambling, you've got to keep moving, keep ducking, keep low to the ground, make yourself as small a target as possible. There is no intuition involved; the object is to keep your eyes constantly scanning the field, looking for holes in the defense, always moving toward open space, ready to stop and turn instantly when that hole closes, throwing fakes, never standing still, being ready to shake off a tackler, being aware of the line of scrimmage, and until the walls of Jericho come tumbling down on top of you—keep looking for a receiver.

Basically, what goes on in your mind when the pocket begins to collapse around you is, Uh-oh, gotta move, watch out, oops, turn tha—Go, move it, whoa, don't—Get away, watch it, watch it, whoops, oh boy, not that way, duck, go, go, go. . . .

Literally, I've run back and forth across the width of the entire field in one play. The best thing about scrambling is sitting in the team meeting watching yourself do it on the game films. That's really when you get a feeling for it, and truthfully, sometimes it's pretty impressive. Watching those films definitely made me appreciate the power of the human survival instinct. There were times when I truly amazed myself. I'd see myself making moves I couldn't believe. I'd really want the coaches to run the film over, but I'd be too embarrassed to ask. My teammates loved watching me squirm on the films, especially after a win. People would be screaming, hollering and laughing—until I got caught. Then there would be a collective "Oooouch . . ."

Defensive linemen absolutely hated it when I got out of the pocket and they had to start chasing me. A little traveling music here, maestro, da-da-dum da-da-dum, da-da-dum-dum-DUM. . . . On some scrambles the same defensive player would get two or three shots at me; they'd miss me once, then when I was coming back in their direction, they would miss me again. And as I went by them I'd hear them shouting "%#(*$^! you!" I always thought it would be like trying to tackle Jell-O. I remember a Monday-night game against Kansas City; none of my receivers were open, so I started scrambling, looking for somebody to throw the ball to. The great defensive lineman Buck Buchanan was chasing me like Tommy Lee Jones chased Harrison Ford, like the posse chased Butch and Sundance, like Detective Javert chased Jean Valjean. The man was persistent. Relentless. Determined. And pissed off big-time. We went back and forth across the field. No matter which way I turned, he was behind me. And old Buck was fast. I kept looking downfield, waving to my receivers, and nobody could get free. Finally I got tired, and Buck nailed me. I was lying on the ground trying to catch my breath, and his huge leg was flopped over me, and the man was not moving. I felt like I was trapped under a fallen tree trunk. So I got angry; I took my fist and started pounding on his leg.

Then Buck Buchanan stood up. And up. And up. All six-foot-seven 280 pounds of him. Even for a big man, Buck Buchanan was BIG! And he was angry; not only had I worn him out, I'd punched him. So he started coming after me, warning me, "I'm gonna kill your ass."

Fortunately, several people stepped between us. Uh-oh, I thought, this is definitely not a good thing. I tried hard to patch up our differences: "Buck, you all right, man? I'm really sorry." "Nice stop, Buck, we thought we had you that time. I'm really sorry, you know."

After listening to my attempts to apologize, number 99 pointed at me and said again, "I'm gonna kill you."

I remember one of my teammates trying to reassure me. "Now don't worry about him, Brad," he said. "If he does kill you, we'll take care of him for you."

Hey, thanks, guys. Now I feel better.

Actually Buck was a peaceful man. Within a decade he had forgotten all about that incident.

One of the biggest and fastest people ever to chase me was the late and very great John Matuszak. The Tooz was about eight-foot-fifteen; he was so big that some people blamed his shadow for global warming. In Oakland once he started chasing me across the field. There were probably 65,000 people in the stands, but I could literally hear him behind me. He was flat-out moving. As I was running, I was begging, Come on feet, don't let me die. Get my ass out of here.

I made it safely to the sidelines, and he pulled up near me. "Oh, I'm sorry, John," I told him. "Don't worry about me. I've gotten accustomed to looking this scared."

I remember playing against the Los Angles Rams the last game of the season and being chased by Deacon Jones. Deacon was closer to me than my shadow; I just couldn't shake him. He chased me around the field, on the sidelines, up in the stands, out to the team bus, back to my ranch in Louisiana. I mean, that man just would not give up. Finally, he got me. The two of us were exhausted, lying there, and the strangest thing happened to me: I started laughing. And Deacon started laughing. The two of us were just lying there hysterical. It's difficult to explain why we laughed; maybe it was the fact that two grown men had exhausted themselves playing tag on national television, or maybe it was the joy of playing this game at that level finding a way to release itself. I didn't know how the broadcasters explained it— "It looks like Bradshaw pulled a muscle in his brain"— but I couldn't stop laughing.

Among those people who did not get the joke was Chuck Noll.

The problem with leaving the pocket is that you are really vulnerable. Blockers and rules protect the quarterback when he's in the pocket, but when he takes off, he is fair game—or, as defensive players might say, meat on the run. Most of the time the worst injury a quarterback can suffer is a shoulder separation, but when you leave the pocket, the defense looks for a full head separation. One time I was scrambling against Miami, I believe, and I saw one of my receivers break free, so I stopped and got set to throw. Suddenly the referee, Tommy Bell, screamed at me, "Terry! Duck!"

I ducked. Two players went flying over me and collided. I never saw them coming. That's as close to being the makings of a Terry sandwich as I ever came. I don't know what surprised me more, the two defensive players or the fact that a neutral official had saved me. I didn't know many officials by name, but Tommy Bell and I were together in the league for at least a decade. We got to know and respect each other. He was a great man, just a great person. Maybe you're not supposed to admit that, but Tommy cared about the players. He didn't want to see anybody get hurt. Tommy actually used to coach me on the field. After a play he'd stand next to me and without looking at me say, "Terry, you can't be standing there like that. You got to get rid of the ball or you got to move around."

On another occasion two defensive players had me in their grasp and were trying to drag me down, but I was still fighting, still desperately trying to find a receiver. Tommy blew the play dead, and as he took the ball from me, he said, "Terry, when the whistle blows, you got to go down."

That was hard for me. Getting tackled was part of the game, but I hated to go down holding on to the football. I hated having to take a loss. When I got sacked, I was furious with myself. I'd start screaming, I'd curse myself out. One time I remember we were playing Houston at the Astrodome, and I was playing terribly. Some people might say I was playing like a dog, but that would be an insult to dogs. I was totally frustrated. We were getting beat and it was my fault. But as badly as I'd played, with a few minutes left in the fourth quarter we still had a chance to win the football game. We got the ball on our own twenty-yard line. I knew if I could march us eighty yards down the field, everything that I had done before would be forgotten. Why after playing so badly for three quarters and thirteen minutes I would expect things to change, I cannot tell you. That is the hope that lives inside us all, but does not understand statistics.

But to my amazement we started moving down the field. All of a sudden passes I'd been missing all day were connecting. It was a great feeling—until I held on to the ball too long and got sacked for a big loss of yardage and time. Basically, that was the end of the game. Oh, man, I was mad. I erupted. I was using every nasty word I knew; when I ran out of them, I was making them up. If my momma had heard me, to this day

I'd be picking Ivory Flakes out of my mouth, and that was thirty years ago.

I don't remember the player who tackled me, but obviously he knew I was a Christian. Maybe he even knew I'd written two books about my beliefs for the religious reader. He was still lying right on top of me when I paused to take a breath, and he said incredulously, "Terry! I thought you were a Christian!"

That was hitting me below the Bible belt. I had never been so embarrassed in my life, but there wasn't much I could do about it. I wasn't exactly in a position to quote Scripture to him, with him lying on top of me like that. So I apologized to him. And Him.

Running with the ball was not listed in my job description. Or if it was, it must have been in the real tiny print underneath the heading "Not Covered by Health Plan." My job was leading the offense on the field, handing off the ball to runners, or throwing it to receivers. But on occasion I did have to run with the football. I liked it; if my receivers were covered after I got forced outside and I saw some open field in front of me, I wasn't afraid to tuck the ball under my arm and run for it. It is amazing though, how rapidly open field can become crowded field. Fact is, when a defensive player sees a quarterback in the open field, he starts to drool. Well, drool more than normal, I mean.

I had a few good long runs in my career. The longest run from scrimmage of my entire career, with the possible exception of my backyard, was a ninety-yard run against the Raiders in a preseason game. There are a lot of people who believe that what happens in preseason games doesn't count. Believe me, the hits hurt just as much in a preseason game as they do during the regular season. A muscle is just as pulled preseason as regular season, so I'm gonna count this run. Ninety yards from scrimmage against the great Oakland Raiders.

We were on our own ten. It was play action—fake a handoff to a running back and throw to a receiver. The play was 119. I took the snap and retreated to our own end zone. I felt the pressure closing down on me, tucked the ball under my arm, and ran to the outside. Two guys had shots at me, but I made them miss and turned upfield. Our secondary did a great job of cutting off their defensive backs. Nobody could get a good angle on me.

Look at that boy go! Run, Terry, run! Ninety yards is a long way to sprint, but I never slowed down. There was somebody on my tail the whole run. But I clamped my eyes on that end zone and just kept pumping. I was running on adrenaline. The whole trip downfield I expected to get tackled or pushed out of bounds. I suspect I was as surprised as the Raiders—and all of my teammates—when I reached the end zone.

When I crossed the goal line, I casually tossed the ball on the ground as if I'd been making ninety-yard touchdown runs my entire career. Within seconds a couple of my teammates came running up to congratulate me. I looked at them and said, "Uhhhhhhh-gggggg. Uuuuhhhhhhhgggg." Man, I was dying! I could barely catch my breath. That run had absolutely exhausted every bit of energy I had. I earned every one of those 270 feet; so far as I'm concerned, it counts as the longest run of my career.

Unfortunately, one of my people was called for holding, so the entire play was nullified. I still don't care—I ran that whole distance, it counts as a run!

The toughest runs I made in my career were only three or four inches, maybe a few feet. They weren't as much runs as dives. They were called "quarterback sneaks," and I only called that play when we needed a foot or maybe two for a first down. It's totally inaccurate to call this a sneak. That's like being in a restaurant with your wife and pretending not to notice Michelle Pfeiffer. Oh, Michelle Pfeiffer, was she there too? Where was she sitting? Come on, every person in the stadium knew I was going to be carrying the ball. Maybe once quarterbacks used to try to get down real low and dive forward under the defensive line for a few yards. But doing that is like running into a brick two-holer house. So quarterbacks started leaping over the top of the linemen trying to gain the necessary few feet. Instead of "sneak," this might better be called "a death-defying leap into the air at the same time big people are hurtling forward through the air from directly opposite to try to meet you head-on and stop your forward progress."

Now, when we needed only a few feet, it would have made sense to hand off the ball to Franco or Rocky and let them grind out that yard. It would have made sense, but we didn't do it. If we were really concerned about making sense, we wouldn't be playing the game in the first place. The basic theory in support of the quarterback sneak is that when you hand off the ball, you greatly increase the chance of a fumble and the play takes too long to develop; that extra half-second allows the defense to stack up the line, to build a human barrier in front of you. The quarterback sneak is almost instantaneous—hike-go. The quarterback sneak is also one of the scariest parts of the quarterback's job. There is where the basic physics I learned at Louisiana Tech became important: I knew that two objects in motion cannot occupy the same space at the same time without the quarterback being smashed.

I remember going over the top one time and being met there head-on by the Empire State Building. On steroids. That is definitely not an enriching experience. When you stay on the ground, you've got some leverage, you've got the opportunity to make decisions, you can cut, you can retreat, you can put down a shoulder and try to power your way forward. But when you leave your feet, you're at the mercy of your decision—you can't make a cut, you have no recourse, you're just a toy to be played with. That's me: Bradshaw putty. Bradshaw Slinky. Hey, Mom, I broke my Bradshaw toy.

But when you finally score, all the mistakes, all the bruises, are forgotten. 'Least temporarily. Scoring in the NFL is so special. No matter how often we won—which was usually just one game less than necessary to satisfy Pittsburgh's fans—I never got over the thrill of scoring. As a quarterback I got just as much of a thrill out of directing a scoring drive, no matter who finally scored the touchdown, as taking it in myself. I understand completely why players celebrate in the end zone by dancing. A lot of people don't think it's seemly, but I like it a lot. I know what it took to get there. What I don't like is showboating. I don't like it when people take off their helmets, those people who are saying by their actions, Look what *I* did. Whenever I see that, I think, Just who do you think you are? Do you not think you had help getting there?

I loved watching Barry Sanders score. He got into the end zone, handed the ball to the referee, and went to the sideline. You watched him, you knew, you absolutely knew, he had been there before.

Scoring on a quarterback sneak was not a big deal. That was like cheating. I just threw my body forward and held on to the ball. What I did love was running the ball in from twenty-five yards—but only if the run had some theatrics to it; for example, breaking a tackle and diving into the end zone. I loved that. Diving was great. My absolutely favorite way to score was diving for a corner of the end zone, sticking the ball out in front of me, grazing one of the flags in the corner. Oh my, that was sweet. I did it, lemme see, counting all the games I played, including playoff games and preseason exhibitions, it was . . . one time, I believe. But man, that was football as it oughta be.

As a rookie I was an illiterate when it came to reading defenses. But as I gained experience, it became a great deal of fun. I'd see players moving, I'd know exactly how they wanted me to react, and I'd counter by changing the play. Responding to different defensive sets became natural. Only one time did I regret it. We were beating Don Shula's Miami Dolphins badly in the fourth quarter of a game played in Pittsburgh one Sunday. Shula was a terrific coach and person—I loved him. We were winning by twenty-something points, and the last thing I wanted to do was embarrass Shula by scoring again. That's turning the knife one last time, and is a memory tucked away for another game. Essentially, the game was over; there were less than four minutes left, and I was killing the clock with running plays. I was really enjoying myself. Those are great times for a quarterback, when the game is won and all you have to do is run down the clock, and you're just moving slowly on the ground, two yards, five yards at a time. Finally it got to be third down and maybe two yards. I got to the line of scrimmage, and the Dolphins line up to blitz. Blitz! My brain went into hyperdrive: I knew that formation, I'd been practicing against it all week, Chuck had prepared us for this exact situation—and I had been taught to respond to that blitz by throwing a short pass.

The ball was hiked, the Dolphins came at me, I threw a pass to Theo Bell—and as the ball is in midair I see that I have called the perfect play; there isn't a defender between Theo and the end zone. This is going to be a touchdown. But I don't want it to be a touchdown. Bell catches it in midstride and is gone. Gone! I started running down the field after him: "No, Theo! Don't score! Stop."

And as I'm running downfield, Shula is running along the sidelines right next to me, mother-blanking me every step of the way. "You no good mother-blank—"

In addition to stopping Theo, I had to respond to Shula, "Stop, Theo! Hey, Don, what are you talking about? Why'd you blitz me? Theo, wait!"

Bell got tackled on the one- or two-yard line. Thank you, Lord. That might be the only time in my entire career I was happy not to score. For the rest of the game, I killed the clock. I think I even got booed for my conservative play selection. But I didn't care. After the game, I found Shula to explain to him. The Dolphins' great quarterback Bob Griese, who hadn't played because of an injury, was standing next to him. Griese understood what happened. "Coach," I said, "you don't understand—"

He didn't. "$%#$!!! you," he said and walked away. That was the first time an opposing coach had cussed me out after we hadn't scored a touchdown.

It would be impossible even to estimate how many times I got down there under the center, took a snap, and ran a play. Tens of thousands, certainly. I studied every play in our playbook, I looked at films, I went through the same motions. I threw innumerable passes. Fourteen years after my first game, I was still doing the same things. For me, for Chuck Noll, for the Steelers, we spent a glorious decade pursuing perfection. We were a legendary team. We performed the fundamentals, and when we needed a great play, we could make it happen. But the ironic thing was that with all that repetition, with everything we practiced, the single most remembered play in football history was an accident. I threw the pass, and two days later I finally saw the play.

FOUR

During the season we always had off the Monday following a game to give the aches and bruises and cuts a chance to settle in quietly. I usually played golf on Mondays, but one Monday morning I went out to offensive lineman John Kolb's place to look at a roping horse he owned. I'd had a roping horse and it hadn't killed me, which made me an expert on the subject. I was sitting on a rail with Moon Mullins, my right guard, watching John riding this horse. It was a nice horse, big and sturdy. As John came riding up to us, we jumped off the rail. Then John roped me and hopped off his horse. Hey, rope the quarterback. That was one way of capturing Bradshaw.

Everybody laughed. We knew it was all in fun. Unfortunately, the horse didn't know that. Horses don't have a real well-developed sense of humor. That was a roping horse, and there was a warm body on the business end of the rope. That horse knew its job. John popped the rope to make the horse back up, to keep the rope tight. The horse backed up—full speed—and kept backing up. Uh, John, maybe you'd better no—

I went flying into the air—and then I hit the ground. That horse started dragging me through the rocks and weeds. One of my arms was pinned against my body, so I couldn't protect myself. The gate was wide open, and that horse went galloping through it, out into the pasture. For a second, I think, Kolb and Mullins were too stunned to move. This wasn't funny; I was in a pretty serious situation. Suddenly they realized what was happening; if they didn't do something really quick to stop that horse, Chuck Noll was going to be furious!

Meanwhile, I'm screaming for help loud as I can.

Kolb and Mullins start chasing the horse. Naturally, being a horse, he saw people running after him and started running faster. For several years I had been dependent on these men to protect me, but they never had to outrun a horse to do it. If blocking that horse would have helped, these were the people who could have done it.

That horse dragged me through the pasture, the weeds just cutting me to bits. Finally the horse turned. That's good, I thought. I thought that, but I was wrong. My foot grazed a telephone pole as the horse pulled me through a rocky creek bed, then over a little mound into another creek, then back and around again.

I must have been dragged at least 500 yards. Finally the horse was exhausted and slowed down enough for either Kolb or Mullins to tackle it. They knocked that horse right off its legs. They were really worried, but then they determined that the horse was fine. Meanwhile, I'm lying on the ground semiconscious, moaning.

Of course, they'd seen me like that on the field many times before. But I really was a mess. I was bruised and battered. One of my teeth was broken. My clothes were just ripped to pieces. My boots had been torn off. "You okay, Brad?" Moon asked.

"Ummmgghhhhuckenhorse," I said.

"Don't worry about him," John said. "He's fine."

Kolb and Mullins picked me up and drove me up to the trailer. They filled a bathtub with cold water and dumped me in it. Then they plotted strategy. One thing they knew for certain they were not going to do was call Chuck Noll for help: "Hey, Chuck, how you doin'? This is John. You know, I got this great roping horse here, and I don't have any calves to rope, so I roped our starting quarterback. Terry Bradshaw. Remember him? It was pretty funny for just a little while, but that horse didn't do what it was supposed to do. You know, it's a horse. So I slapped the rope to make him back up to tighten the rein up on the rope. And Chuck, you're not gonna believe what happened next. You would have had to see this to believe it. That horse just took off. But Chuck, Terry was still in the rope when he took off. It took us about 500 yards to catch that horse, but we tackled him. You want the good news or the bad news first?

"Okay, the horse is all right, but we aren't sure Terry's gonna make it."

We had a saying in my family that came from my uncle Bobby. One time Uncle Bobby's boss came over to his place to ride his horse. It had been raining, and the whole lot was filled with big mud holes. Uncle Bobby, being polite and considerate of his boss, pointed out that conditions were poor and that maybe it wasn't a good day for a ride. But Uncle Bobby's boss wanted to ride. The boss wants to ride, the boss rides.

Uncle Bobby schooled this man on the horse. "Now, you don't want to hold too tight—" The boss did not want to listen, he wanted to ride. Finally he got up on this horse and started riding. But he wasn't satisfied with the horse's gait; he wanted speed, so he sort of goosed the horse. The horse reared straight up into the air and dumped this sucker on his back in a mud hole.

When he hit, the only sound Uncle Bobby heard was a painful "Oooohhhhhhsss!" He had splattered into that mud hole and lay there flat as a slow squirrel on I-95.

The man was covered with mud. Uncle Bobby picked up his head by the hair and asked, "Mac, you all right?"

The man replied, "Oooooohhhhhhh."

"I said, are you all right?"

"Oooohhhhhhh . . . yeah, guess so."

It was becoming clear pretty quick that all the air had been knocked out of him, but the mud had cushioned his fall. But Uncle Bobby asked him one more time, "You're sure you're all right?"

The boss started climbing to his feet. "Yeah," he said, "I'm all right now."

With that Uncle Bobby looked his boss right in the eye and asked politely, "So would it be all right if I laughed now?"

When I finally began to understand that I had been lassoed by a lineman and half killed by a roping horse, this was the first thought that came into my mind. Once I became completely conscious, naturally. I almost expected John and Moon to ask me solemnly, "So Brad, would it be all right if we laughed now?"

Well, sure it would have been. What good is getting roped and dragged if you can't see the humor in it? Eventually they took me in to see the team doctor. Basically, I was put on ice until all the swelling went down. Bradshaw on the rocks. But I didn't miss a minute of playing time. And I wasn't hurt. I could always take a good hit.

Football is a violent game. If you play football, you are going to get hit. You are going to get tackled or blocked, beaten, smashed, pounded, poked, pounced on, clobbered, clouted, jabbed, smacked, swatted, or slugged. You are going to get whomped, whacked, punched, hammered, creamed, slammed, battered, pummeled, whupped, kicked, banged, and butted. You are going to get bruised, cut, scraped, scratched, and wounded. And then you've got to go back in the huddle and run the next play.

One question I have been asked many times by people who have watched me get hit during a game is, "Did it hurt?" The answer is, Well of course it hurt! What kind of question is that? You don't get hit by 270 pounds of muscle without it hurting. Even in a ball game in which every player walks off the field at the end, people are going to be very sore, people are going to be hurt. You get rug burns from the artificial surface, bone bruises, welts, bumps, sore ribs. The offensive linemen's hands are cut and battered, the defensive linemen's hands are cut, and their knees are ripped up. It's brutal. Absolutely brutal.

And a great deal of fun. Assuming you are able to walk off the field. There are people who claim that the hitting in pro football isn't as rough as it appears to fans. The people who make this claim are definitely not pro football players. Players are able to successfully survive this level of contact because they have grown up with it. When I began playing football, I didn't like the contact—which is like saying I like everything about parachuting except the height—until I got involved in a few plays. Then I found out it didn't hurt too much when I got hit—and I got praised for hitting other people. This was my kind of game.

Growing up, you're always playing against people mostly the same size as you are, and generally within the same skill level. When you weigh seventy-five pounds, it doesn't hurt to get tackled by other seventy-five-pounders. As you progress in football, you grow at the same rate as the people you're playing against. The difference is similar to learning to ski as a child or as an adult: children have no fear, they come barreling down the mountain with a sense of joy. Adults kind of poke their way down the hill, going slow, watch it, careful now, don't turn too fast, whoops, close, watch out for that tree! Too fast, going too fast . . .

After my first tackle I was never intimidated again. By the time I was drafted by the Steelers I had played junior-league football, middle school, high school, and college football, always against people on my own size scale. When I got to the NFL and people were just incredulous about the ferocity of the hitting, I wasn't overwhelmed by it. If I lined up and saw Butkus or the Tooz or Buck Buchanan staring at me, I knew from experience that the worst thing they could do to me was rip my head off my shoulders, put it on a stake, and parade around the field with it.

I didn't enjoy being hit, I didn't like it at all, but it was part of the game, and I wanted to play the game. I also had tremendous confidence in my protective equipment. In college I wore foam rubber padding in my shoulder pads. When I got to the pros, trainer Tony Parisi threw them out and gave me big-time fiberglass shoulder pads. Those pads made me look great in team pictures, even if I could barely throw the ball with them on. It took some adjusting to get used to them. I also changed the face bar to see a little better. The only pieces of equipment I didn't wear were a chin strap and a flak vest to protect my ribs, and I never had a problem with my chin or my ribs—though eventually the league made a chin strap mandatory. The team tried to make me wear the flak jacket, but it felt too restrictive for me. I never liked feeling restricted. I didn't like my uniform too tight, and I don't like my clothes too tight. I even wore my wrist bands, which supposedly absorbed sweat, way up on my forearms. That made them basically useless. But I wore them that way anyway, and never had a problem with my shoulders sweating.

One part of my uniform that was important to me was my socks. My socks had to stay up. I had to wear them up high. Socks that flopped down bothered me more than linebackers. There is a legging you can wear instead of socks, but I didn't like the feeling. Socks. I wanted socks. I was playing professional football. We were the best team in the best football league in existence. I was the quarterback. I was the two-time Most Valuable Player in the Super Bowl. I was the league's Player of the Year. *Sports Illustrated* picked me as the co–Man of the Year with Willie Stargell. And all I wanted was my socks to stay up. Any society that could invent self-adhesive scrap paper ought to be able to invent socks that would stay up by their very own selves. Some people might have wrapped their socks with tape to hold them up, but I was a purist. The tape felt too restrictive, and the last thing I wanted was restricted calves. I finally solved the problem by wearing *two* pair of socks.

Other players also made adjustments to their uniforms. I remember once before a Monday-night game in the early 1970s I walked back in the locker room where we kept the offensive linemen. They were putting on their shoulder pads. I noticed they put two-sided tape on top of their pads so when they pulled on their jerseys, they would stick to them. That made it much tougher for a defensive lineman to grab hold of a jersey and use it to gain control.

Before another game I was going over defensive coverages with Chuck Noll when we heard a lineman shaking what sounded like a can of paint. When he shook it, a ball inside rattled. "What are you doing?" Chuck asked him.

"Spraying liquid silicone on my jersey, Coach," the player responded. This was a new old trick that everybody was using. The silicone made the jersey very slippery. It also came off on your hands, so if I touched a jersey coated with it, I could barely grip the football. I was certain Chuck knew we were using it, but he acted as if he were shocked, absolutely shocked, to discover that one of his players would do something illegal. He gave him a major-league chewing out. This player would have been better off spray-painting graffiti on his uniform. I think what Chuck meant to say was, "How stupid can you be to let me catch you?" Chuck was so angry that I couldn't help myself, I started laughing—after he left the room, of course.

But the most important protection I had was my offensive line. These were men who willingly laid down their bodies for me, the Pittsburgh Steelers, and the Internal Revenue Service. After one Super Bowl victory, as a means of expressing my appreciation, I gave each of them a portrait of himself.

Now admittedly, there were times during my career when I might have wanted to recall those portraits. I took my share of hits during my fourteen-year career. Some of them I will never forget, some of them I still can't remember. Concussions will do that. I do remember getting my neck just about broken by the Cleveland Browns' defensive end Joe "Turkey" Jones in October 1976. For some reason Moon Mullins was playing tackle rather than guard. As he remembers it, "I wasn't having a great day that afternoon."

Turned out to be a whole lot better than my day was about to get. Turkey Jones slipped by Moon and grabbed me around the waist. In those days officials didn't blow the whistle quickly. That was fine with me, I always thought I could get out of a defensive player's grasp. Jones had me around the waist, and I continued fighting to get free. So he simply picked me up, drove me backward about six yards, turned me upside down, and drilled for oil with my head.

My whole body was interested. I had pain running through places I didn't know I had places. I could barely move. My arms and legs were quivering involuntarily. Once again, Moon Mullins thought I was dead.

When I managed to open my eyes, I thought I was seeing stars. Instead it turned out to be our team doctor and trainer, who were well-respected professionals, but hardly stars. At first I thought my neck was probably broken. The pain was tremendous. For a time I couldn't feel a thing in my arms or legs. I was terrified. It shakes your personal resolve big-time when you see them put your hands on your chest and they just fall right off and there is nothing you can do about it. They carried me off the field on a stretcher, and on that journey I have to admit I did have a private conversation or two with the Lord.

I hurt so bad even my two pair of socks didn't help.

The officials were so outraged they immediately called unnecessary roughness against Jones. Cost the Browns fifteen yards. I guess that sure taught them a good lesson. You can't turn Terry Bradshaw upside down and try to send him the short route for Chinese food without paying a bigggggggg price. Fifteen yards, yes, sir!

After the game Chuck Noll said, "It was an enthusiastic tackle." Enthusiastic tackle? Believe me, if NASA showed that kind of enthusiasm they'd be serving McDonald's on the moon right now.

Many people thought it was a cheap shot. I didn't. As I told a reporter, "If I'd gotten up, nobody would have said it was a cheap shot." However, that would have required me to actually get up, which was impossible at the time.

Jones really was upset. While I was lying on the stretcher he told me, "I'm sorry, man. I just got caught up in the game. I didn't hear the whistle. I didn't try to hurt you."

To which I gasped in reply, "Then get your foot off my neck, please." Okay, that's not what I really said. What I told him was, "It's okay. I understand."

A few hours later I learned with great relief that my neck wasn't broken. But two years later, two years, when my neck continued to bother me I had my neck reexamined—and discovered I'd broken some transverse processors. One of the side benefits of playing professional football is that you discover all these body parts that you never knew you had until they got broken. I missed four games.

To me, the most astonishing thing about pro football is, considering how big, fast, and strong the players are, how few truly serious injuries there are. People who have played the game their entire lives have learned how to take a hit. You know from experience that when you are about to be hit, you lower your shoulder and keep your head up. You know how to dip and tuck and fall. If you see the hit coming, even if it's a vicious hit, most of the time you are going to be fine. Pained, but fine.

We even took pride in taking big hits. We played the Cincinnati Bengals during Cris Collinsworth's rookie year. Cris made the mistake of trying to come across the middle of the field and catch a pass. It was a sad moment; he just didn't know any better. Our future Hall-of-Fame middle linebacker Jack Lambert educated him. I mean, Jack Lambert drilled him. It was a three-surgeons-operating-all-night kind of hit. Then Lambert warned him, "You come back over the middle, Collinsworth, I'll kill you."

Collinsworth went back to his huddle with a big smile on his face. One of his teammates asked him, "What are you smiling about? Lambert almost killed you."

"Yeah," Cris told him, "but he knew my name."

The hits that hurt the most were the ones I didn't expect, when I got blindsided. Those hits even hurt me when I was watching them on the films two days later. But truthfully, when one of my people missed a block and I just got buried because of it, I did tend to take advantage. In the huddle the player who missed the block was devastated: Oh, man, TB, I'm so sorry. That just is never gonna happen again, I swear on my mommy. You awright? Yo'kay?

I definitely should have been nominated for an Academy Award for my performance inside the huddle. It's okay, just give me a minute. Wait, now, there it is, the feeling's coming back now in my legs. No, no, I'm fine, really, I didn't need all those fingers anyway. Is my nose still attached to my face?

As a quarterback there was nothing better than having a teammate apologize to me. Now he owes me. I have paid the price for the error of his ways. It's similar to the great Japanese tradition created by Hollywood movies; if a person saves your life, your life belongs to him. If I took a beating because someone missed a block, his body was mine.

I almost never yelled at a teammate. I just didn't feel it would have accomplished anything. There are great quarterbacks known for screaming at their people. Johnny Unitas, Dan Marino, they were vocally active in the huddle and it worked for them; they knew their teammates, they knew how to motivate them. I knew my people. They were champions, they knew when they screwed up without being reprimanded by me. Although sometimes I threw in an extra couple of moans for effect. Really, what could I have said—See that 280-pound tackle standing directly in front of you? I don't want to dance with him again. I also had enough experience making my own mistakes to know that pretty soon I was going to screw up enough for everybody; they would have every right to remind me of that.

So there were precious few times in my entire career that I screamed at a teammate in the huddle about anything. One time against the Cowboys on Monday night I was letting the thirty-second play clock run down nice and easy. With about four seconds left, Mike Webster didn't believe I knew how much time was left and called a time-out. I was all over his behind for that—but I knew I could do that to Mike, and he would respect me for it. If I had to, I knew I could climb all over Rocky and he would understand, probably Franco too. But the fact is that because I was calling my own plays—I did mention that I called my own plays, I believe—I didn't have time to waste over past history.

Being hit too often led to being hurt. I have been hurt so often that when I fill out a form for an insurance company asking me to list "all surgical procedures," I simply write, "Too many to name." If they insist, I explain, "Okay, but I'm gonna need some extra forms."

I'm breakable. Also bendable and foldable. Some people played hurt, I stayed hurt. I just get hurt a lot. I have my whole life. When you ask my father to mention some of my childhood injuries, he'll tell you, "Let me sit down over here. We're gonna be a while." My mother says calmly, "We spent considerable time visiting the doctor." When I was three years old, I fell on a gas heater. It took my father and two nuns to hold me down while they closed the cut above my eye with four stitches—and those nuns were tough. One time I was in the back of a pickup truck, and I cut open my hand on a knife trying to stick a hole in a pop bottle cap so I could suck it down and make it last longer; we were going up to Clear Lake for a family picnic, so I kept it hidden best I could. When I got home that night I went fishing for guppies in a dirty sewage ditch—and four days later my hand swelled up bigger than a boxing glove and gangrene set in. Seriously, gangrene. The infection went about halfway up my arm; a day or two later, and I would have been dead. Then the Steelers would have had to get somebody else to call my own plays. These are only the highlights now. In junior high school I broke my collarbone playing football. The doctor put me in a sling for six weeks. The day it was supposed to come off, I went up to the school very early to shoot some baskets. My mother had warned me every which way: Do not play basketball until your shoulder heals! I was shooting all by myself; I figured, what could possibly happen.

What did happen was actually pretty amazing. As I was shooting baskets by myself, one of my friends happened by. I missed a shot, and the ball bounced between us. When he went to pick it up, he slipped on the wet grass and fell on top of me, snapping my collarbone in exactly the same place. I walked up to the gym, listing badly to one side, and called my mother.

They operated on me the next day and put my collarbone together with a pin.

I would get the strangest injuries. My father met my mother through her father, because the two men welded side by side in a Panama City, Florida, shipyard. So I had welding in my genes. My dad taught my brother Gary and I how to weld and got us summer jobs machine welding. One summer I was tack welding a railroad tanker car under construction. Industrial welding lines are very heavy and you need to be very careful with them. Eventually I had to climb on top of the car to complete the job. So I was standing on top of the car when I sort of snapped the line to get a kink out of it, just like I would have with a hose. But this time the line just fell right down the center of the car and pulled me through the manhole cover—which is what we called the round hole in the top of the cars. I went flying right through that hole; I fell down about ten feet and got smashed into the concrete floor. My brother Gary was naturally concerned. I believe his exact words were, Wow, Terry, the way you went shooting through that hole was pretty impressive. I didn't break anything, although my pride was damaged! I just hurt all over.

All my injuries just drove my mother crazy. I take full responsibility for the way she is today. That's why I'm always the first one there with the bail money.

In pro football I took great pride in my ability to play damaged. The Steelers replaced Terry Hanratty with a fine young quarterback named Cliff Stoudt, who became my backup. Stoudt almost became the first NFL player to get the four seasons necessary to qualify for a pension without playing a single down during the regular season. "Coach Noll doesn't want me to get hurt," he told a reporter, "because I'm so good at carrying the clipboard."

During my career I broke my shoulder, my nose, several ribs, my left wrist, and several fingers. I tore my hamstring, thigh, groin, and shoulder muscles. I had surgery to remove bone spurs from my left wrist and bone chips from my right elbow. Two times I twisted my knees so badly that I had to be carried off the field. That doesn't even include concussions: I can't even remember how many times I got hit in the head so hard I lost my memory.

Some of these injuries I remember more than others. The most painful injury I suffered in my career occurred at the end of a scramble during an exhibition game in Baltimore in 1978. Colts linebacker Stan White swung his arm around and accidentally shattered the cartilage in my nose. On the Bradshaw Pain Scale this rang the big bell. This was to pain what Johnny Unitas was to quarterbacks. Oh, my, did it hurt. I never had anything hurt so badly in my life. My teammates didn't take it very seriously. They assumed it was just a bad nosebleed: "Hey, TB, talk to me when a couple of the bones are popping out of it." On the sidelines they put cold compresses on it to try to stop the bleeding. The bleeding won. At halftime they put me in the shower room, and when they went out to play the second half they left a security guard there to watch me. He watched me bleeding. "Boy," he said, very impressed, "that sure is a lot of blood you got there."

"Thank you," I mumbled. I lost so much blood I just about bled to death. Now that would have made a great headline: "Bradshaw Dies from Nosebleed." My friends would have been too embarrassed to attend my funeral.

A doctor finally got the bleeding stopped, and I flew home with the team. But when we reached a high altitude the pressure caused the bleeding to start again. Blood was just pouring out of my nose. When the plane landed, I was taken directly to the hospital and they operated the next morning. After the operation, newspapers reported, "Bradshaw Is Listed in Fair Condition." Fortunately, however, they did not finish that report, "with a bad nosebleed."

A pretty common injury that I just hated wa—oooppppphhhh! "Getting the wind knocked out of you" just sounds like a weak excuse for an injury. Oh, my, the poor young lad has had a bit of oxygen expelled from his lungs. But maybe it would be more accurate to think of it as blowing air into a paper bag, then smacking it so it explodes. In this case though, my lungs were the paper bag. Pro football might have been the only job in which this was considered an occupational hazard. I never heard a mathematician complain that a problem was so tough it knocked the wind out of him. I never heard a salesclerk say that a sale was so tough it knocked the wind right out of her. But I have heard pro football players say, Uggghhh . . . Uhhhhhhh . . .

Even broadcasters tended to treat it lightly. Ah, Rex, he's all right, he just got the wind knocked out of him when that ton o' tackles leaped on top of him. He's just taking a breather on the sidelines.

Now, what they really meant was that I was on the sidelines desperately trying to force oxygen into my lungs because I couldn't breathe and I thought I was going to die. Getting the wind knocked out of you is painful; it hurts practically as bad as breaking a bone. If I could make it to the sideline, I'd sit all alone on the bench trying to remember *why* I was Terry Bradshaw. People would amble on up to me and ask, How y'all doin' TB? "Uggghhhhh," I'd say. They'd reply, that's real good, keep it up, and maybe pat me on the shoulder in a gesture of sympathy. "Uggghhhh," I'd add. Eventually I wouldn't exactly come back to my senses—if I had any sense I wouldn't have been out there in the first place—but I would come back to reality.

Maybe the most difficult moments I had ever had on a football field took place during preseason 1980. My second wife, Jo Jo Starbuck, and I had been having difficulty, but we were trying to make our marriage work. At times like that football became just about the only thing in my life I had to hold on to for stability. The field was my office, and I didn't allow my personal problems to intrude. While we were in training camp in Latrobe, Pennsylvania, I was in a quarterback meeting with Chuck and several other players when there was a knock on the door, and the sheriff was standing there. "May I speak with Terry Bradshaw?" I really didn't know what it was all about. I knew the statute of limitations had long passed on the great Pop Bottle Robbery, so I went to meet him.

"Sorry, Terry," he said, "but I need to personally hand you these papers."

It's never a good thing when a law enforcement officer hands you papers and apologizes. But I didn't even open them, I didn't even give it any thought. During the meeting, Chuck kept staring at the envelope. His curiosity was ripping through him. Finally he asked, "Don't you need to read that?"

I opened it up. Terry Bradshaw, yadda, yadda, yadda, hmmm, hmmmm, hmmm, DIVORCE, hmmmm, hmmmm, GET A LAWYER, hmmmm, hmmmm . . . Sincerely yours . . . Man, I started bawling. I hadn't known I was getting divorced until I opened that envelope.

I was devastated. Devastated. I have a lot of difficulty with much of my relationship with Chuck Noll, so sometimes I tend to overlook the many wonderful things that he did for me during my career. During this time of my life he could not possibly have been more supportive. He was definitely there for me when I most needed him to be.

It was tough, but on the field I was able to set it out of my mind. Chuck gave me the option of playing in an exhibition game the next weekend, and I said yes.

I needed an outlet for my frustrations. I played very well in the first quarter, and he gave me the option of playing the second quarter. Again, I wanted to play. Right before the end of the half we were running a two-minute drill, trying to move the length of the field in less than two minutes, when I got blindsided. Whomped. I got the wind knocked out of me.

I was lying flat out on the turf surrounded by the doctor and trainer and a couple of teammates. I was lying there for a long time. As my breath came back, they helped me sit up—and all of a sudden I started crying. Crying! On a football field! In front of a filled stadium! But I couldn't help myself. It was uncontrollable. I had been keeping all my emotional pain deep, deep inside, and I'd gotten hit so hard it knocked it out of me. I was surrounded by people I had known and cared about for a long time, and they were supporting me. The doctor was holding my back up, trainer Ralph Berlin was holding my hand, Tony Parisi was right there; and I was bawling. They understood what was happening. "Don't worry about it," Tony said, "just let it go. Don't worry about the time, they'll wait. We're right here, just go ahead."

Nobody else knew I had suffered a badly broken heart. Up in the booth the broadcasters were probably speculating on the extent of my injury. How many weeks would I miss? As far as I know, nobody has ever gone on the disabled list for a broken heart.

That time I walked off the field by myself, but there were other times when I was carried off on a stretcher. Here is another admission: at times maybe I did play a little to the fans. In an article about the Steelers, the great *New York Times* wrote about me, "[Bradshaw] has a low tolerance for pain and sometimes falls to the ground on contact, writhing startlingly. Once the initial pain subsides, however, and there is no serious injury, Bradshaw can play with residual pain that would sideline many other athletes."

Now that hurt. Truthfully, there were several times in my career when I suffered nerve damage. I got hit the wrong way, and the nerves throughout my body lit up like somebody hit the million-dollar slot machine. I laid there on the ground "writhing startlingly," probably just like the Frankenstein monster "writhed startlingly" when the electricity juiced him alive. I was kicking and screaming and hollering, flapping around like a chicken with its head cut off. The pain was intense— but it went away quickly. The fact is that there were times when I was actually embarrassed I could return to the game.

Against the Cardinals once I got a painful stinger! My arms and legs were flailing about, I wasn't thinking, I just flopped. But as I relaxed and remembered to continue breathing, the adrenaline slowed down, and the pain mostly disappeared. But I had put on quite a display of being hurt. "It's okay," I told Ralph Berlin. "I'm okay. Let me get up."

Ralph may have been concerned I had suffered serious injury, and he wanted to be extremely careful. They tied me to a board, lifted me up onto a stretcher, and carried me off the field. The whole time I was telling him, "Honest, Ralph, I'm fine. It just stung real bad."

Meanwhile, the fans watched practically silent.

This was potentially a solemn moment: Yeah, son, I was there the day Terry Bradshaw flopped around like a chicken without a head and then up and died. They buried him right there on the forty-three-yard line.

As they carried me off on the stretcher, the fans stood up and began applauding. The cheers started slowly, then spread throughout the entire ballpark. It was amazing. I was getting a standing ovation for being hurt! God bless Terry, they were saying, I sure hope he lives. I sure hope he don't die. Hey, you see how hard he got hit? Wadn't that cool?

I definitely heard the fans every time I was carried off the field or assisted to the sideline. When I was hurt, those people appreciated me. Naturally, I didn't want to disappoint them, so I laid on the stretcher motionless. Well, maybe I did let my head sort of flop to one side—but I definitely never let my tongue hang out.

They carried me into the trainer's room and laid me down. I could see my teammates peeking around the corner to see how I was doing. How y' doing, TB? Hang in there? If you don't make it, can I have those lizard boots? The medical people were working on me, maybe they even gave me a little boost to help speed the healing process. Then they taped me up. Chuck came in and asked, "Can you go?"

"Yeah," I said, "I think I can."

The team was already on the field when I got back outside. After watching me flop around, people were astonished I was alive, much less ready to play. It was like, It's alive! He has risen! My own teammates were throwing me skeptical glances: Hey, TB, nice act. Way to go, Brad, you sure did fool 'em that time. That's when I was awarded my first Oscar for fine acting, although there were some people who wanted to name the award the Terry.

In Baltimore I got kicked in the leg and had to be carted off the field. After receiving medical treatment I was able to return to the game. I was able to, but I was embarrassed. Bradshaw? Didn't we give him a big ovation for getting hurt just last quarter? Make him give back the flowers.

Running out onto the field was my big mistake. What I really should have done was limp out onto the field. Look at that Bradshaw fella, my God, that man has courage coming out of his teeth. Momma, send the flowers.

I did get a bit of a reputation for grandstanding. My brother Craig, my very own flesh and blood, has described me as "a great actor." That was a fine thing to say—until he added, "on the football field." He claims to remember a play in which I got hit hard on the side of the head after throwing across the middle to Swann. I was just lying there on the ground. Now as Craig tells the story, while I was supposedly out cold, I lifted up my head to see if the pass was caught, then laid it back down. After several minutes I regained consciousness and was helped off the field, leaning gallantly on the shoulders of my teammates.

Maybe that's true, but as I was busy being temporarily unconscious I don't remember it at all—although I'm told Lynn Swann made a great catch for a touchdown.

Lying on the ground was not an unusual place for me. There was a risk-result factor in our passing game;

with the great receivers we had, if we gave them enough time, one of them was going to get free—but the longer I waited, the higher the chance I was going to be sacked. That was nobody's fault but my very own. I often put too much pressure on my offensive linemen—who were generally underappreciated by everyone but me and my health insurance carrier. I risked waiting until I felt the hot breath of doom on my neck before chucking that inflated ellipsoid. As a result I often got slammed to the ground an instant after I released it. So there were a lot of plays that I never saw completed. But it was usually pretty easy to tell what happened by listening to the crowd. If we were at home and I heard the crowd cheering, that was good. If we were on the road and I heard the crowd cheering, that was bad.

There were many times when I had to ask someone in the huddle what had happened.

But there were at least two times the roar of the crowd didn't help me at all. In Super Bowl X, played in 1976, we were beating Dallas 15–10 with three minutes to go in the game. We had a third down and four at our own thirty-six-yard line. Everybody knew if we made another first down, we could take much of the time remaining off the clock, so they expected us to go for the four yards we needed. That was the percentage play. That was the smart move. But that's why defensive coordinators had such a hard time figuring out what we were going to run. I just hated to throw those dinky little passes. The play I called in the huddle was 68 Basic. I was just going to throw it as far as I could, and Lynn Swann was going to catch up to it. Man, this was going to be fun, we were going to fool everybody. Nobody could have expected it.

Except the Cowboys. Dallas blitzed! They were going to get me before I could get rid of the ball. Webster hiked the ball, and I dropped back. Swannie got on his horse and took off. Linebacker D. D. Lewis was coming from my blind side; the safety, Larry Cole, was right behind him. I waited, maybe humming a little ditty, when I *felt* Lewis coming and stepped to my right. That truck just missed me as it went whizzing by. Okay, time to throw. I wound up and let it fly.

Larry Cole hit me an instant after I released the ball. He caught me flush on the jaw. I was out cold before I hit the ground. The ball traveled almost seventy yards in a parabolic arc—in a movie they would show a close-up of the ball spinning through the air in slow motion—and Swann caught it without breaking stride and scored what turned out to be the winning touchdown. It was the play every boy spends his childhood dreaming about.

I didn't know any of that. I was on the ground. If you like big loud marching bands, you would have enjoyed being inside my head. Particularly the gong players. A couple of days later I learned that as they led me to the sideline, they told me about this great play. Then they told me again when I sat down on the bench. Man, that music was loud. I wanted someone to turn down the volume in my head. They told me again when they led me into the locker room. But I don't remember any of it.

The first clear memory I have is my father standing right next to me when I opened my eyes. My dad had always been one of those men who'd say out of the side of his mouth, so no one would see him getting soft, "I'm real proud of you." But this time he was openly emotional. He kept hugging on me and telling me how proud he was.

Never saw the pass, never saw the catch, never saw the touchdown. I definitely never saw the victory celebration at the end of the game. I celebrated each of our Super Bowl victories with my family in our hotel room. An athletic shoe company paid me $2,500. to wear their shoes in the Super Bowl. I did it because I needed the money to pay for my family to come to the game. I'm not forgetting any zeroes, it was twenty-five hundred dollars. Notice I'm not mentioning the name of the company, because they already got their $2,500's worth. But I had to do it because I wanted my family with me on the most important occasions of my life. We played some wild card games. That hotel room was about the warmest place in the world to be. But I was in no condition to party after Super Bowl X. I ended up staying alone in my room that night.

The most famous play I never saw was the Immaculate Reception. Decades have gone by since I threw that pass, but I can still close my eyes and not see it as if it were yesterday. Where this play is concerned, though, even people who did see it don't believe they saw what they saw. In 1972 we were playing the great Oakland Raiders in the first round of the playoffs. These were the fearsome Raiders coached by John Madden, owned by Al Davis. With a few ticks over a minute left in the game, we were losing 7–6. I threw three incomplete passes, so we had a fourth and ten with twenty-two seconds left in the playoffs unless some sort of miracle occurred.

As an athlete, I don't believe in miracles, and I don't believe in luck. I do believe that if you work hard, if you practice hard, if you play hard, you put yourself in a position to take advantage of opportunity. When a close game is decided on a tipped ball or a fumble, an unforced error or an official's call, people tend to call it luck. But being prepared to take advantage of that opportunity, and turning it into something positive, is the result of time, training, and dedication. I believe that completely.

And then sometimes you do get lucky. Either I had been having a terrible day, or the Raiders' defensive backs had been having a great day; I'd completed only ten of twenty-four attempts for 115 yards. I wouldn't have wagered my momma's last tooth on our chances. Chuck Noll sent in the play, 66 Circle Option, a pass over the middle to our rookie receiver Barry Pearson. In the huddle when I called the play, another rookie, Franco Harris, sort of moaned, "Oh no, not that play." Franco's assignment was to block.

The ball was snapped, and I waited for the play to develop. I just kept looking for a spot of Steelers gold in what appeared to be a sea of Raiders black and silver. I felt the pressure coming, and I scrambled out of the pocket to my right. Defensive tackle Art Thoms took a shot at me and missed. Now, all this was taking place in much less time than it takes to read this description. The clock in my head was chiming; I knew the very worst thing I could do was get sacked. If I went down, the ball game was over. Even if I just threw the ball up for grabs, that was better than a sack. There were Raiders to the left of me, Raiders to the right of me; somebody grabbed hold of my leg and I pushed him off. I shoved another Raider away with my left hand. Another Raider came flying at me; I ducked as he just missed me.

Finally I got caught. Somebody had one of my legs. I was going down. At the last instant, at the last instant of the last instant, I saw a black jersey get free for an instant in Raider territory. I had no idea who it was, but I knew it was one of my guys. He was way downfield, well beyond what we needed for the first down. I found out later it was John "Frenchy" Fuqua. Frenchy was tough—although he was the only player on the team to wear platform shoes with live goldfish in the heels. I fired the ball at him about as hard as I could throw—and then I went down.

Frenchy, the Raiders' Jack Tatum, and the football arrived at the same place at the same time. The ball hit one of them—and precisely which one of them it hit will forever remain one of football's unsolved mysteries—and bounded into the air about twenty feet away. Frenchy had no shot at catching it. Pass incomplete, Raiders win! John Madden was already on the bus. But Franco happened to be maybe thirty feet away, looking for someone to block in case Frenchy had caught the pass. And while the Raiders were celebrating, Franco miraculously caught the ball inches above the turf and took off.

Franco scored the game-winning touchdown with five seconds left on the clock.

It was an incredible play not to see. I was lying

there on the ground listening to the crowd to try to figure out what was going on. First the crowd cheered, then it moaned, then it cheered again, and then the crowd really let loose. The stadium shook.

Lying on the artificial turf listening to this, I could really only reach one conclusion. I had done the impossible, I had threaded the needle with an elephant, I had completed the pass to my receiver, and he'd scored a touchdown. Damn, I thought proudly to myself, you truly are amazing!

It seemed like I was the only person who knew what had happened, even if I was completely wrong.

As I got up, I began to see all kinds of strange things taking place. John Madden was irate. He was chasing the officials, screaming about something. That was John Madden, I thought, always trying to teach people about football.

As I soon learned, the rules of football prohibit two offensive players from touching a pass consecutively. In other words, you can't throw a pass to one player who would bat it to a teammate. Just like soap operas, somebody had to come between them. Madden was insisting that the ball had bounced off Fuqua right to Franco Harris. If he was correct, the play was dead and the pass was incomplete.

What was he talking about? This was definitely a case where not seeing was believing. I knew exactly what had happened. The ball had bounced off Tatum directly to Harris, who rumbled in for the touchdown. The fact is that people who saw the play apparently did not have a much better view of it than I did. Referee Fred Swearington had not immediately signaled touchdown. He wasn't sure what had happened. He conferred with other members of his crew, and nobody knew for certain what had happened.

Well, shucks, why didn't they just ask me? At that time the NFL had not yet introduced instant replay, in which the officials review tapes of the play and based on what they see can change their decision, but the networks were using it. Swearington didn't care about the rules; he wanted to make the correct call. The officials initially ruled that Tatum and Fuqua had touched the ball simultaneously, then Swearington went into a dugout and called upstairs to the NFL's supervisor of officials, Art McNally. Swearington wanted to look at the videotapes to try to determine the order in which the ball had been touched.

I had gone to the sideline and kept asking people to tell me what had happened. Franco scored! they said. We did it, we won! Franco scored, I thought—that isn't right. How did Franco get the ball? The only thing I could figure out was that Fuqua had been trapped and lateraled to him. Man, what a play! What a play! I couldn't believe it, and the fact that it didn't happen did little to dampen my enthusiasm.

Meanwhile, on the field, Tatum was practically begging Frenchy, "Tell them you touched it, go ahead, tell them." Now there was about as much chance of that as me sincerely telling people I used a horse shampoo and it made my hair grow. Well, I did do that, but Frenchy was not saying a word.

Officials actually set up a TV set on the sideline so Swearington could watch the replays on television. This was totally against the rules. Millions of people watching television at home were watching an official watch television. This was the first time instant replay had been used by an official to make sure he got the call correct. The instant replays were inconclusive; it was impossible to tell by looking at video or even still pictures whether it was Fuqua or Tatum who touched the pass before Harris caught it. It was just as difficult to tell if the ball had touched the ground before Franco caught it, which also would have nullified the play. The officials finally ruled that it was an incredible, unbelievable, astonishing, amazing touchdown.

It's still hard to believe? Only $2,500 to wear their name-brand shoes.

On TV later that evening Pittsburgh broadcaster Myron Cope referred to it as "the Immaculate Reception." Few plays in football history had ever been named. Mostly it was just "Namath's touchdown pass to Maynard" or "Bradshaw's intercepted pass." But "the Immaculate Reception" was so exactly accurate that its place as one of the most renowned plays in sports history was assured.

But if you should ever happen to meet John Madden, it'd probably be best not to mention it to him right off. In fact, you probably shouldn't even mention Franco or Fuqua. Try to talk with him about that big bus he travels on. Food is always a good subject, talk about food.

Frenchy Fuqua and Jack Tatum are probably the only people who will ever know for certain exactly what happened. I believe Tatum is still shouting at Frenchy to tell someone, anyone, that he touched it. I do know that the only person Frenchy ever offered to tell the whole story to was Art Rooney. And to Mr. Rooney's credit he didn't really want to know, telling Fuqua, "Let it remain Immaculate."

Now, not every pass I threw turned out that well. In fact, in the entire history of pro football that's pretty much the only one like it. But in my career if you sort of mumble and speak real fast "reception" and "interception" sound a lot alike. Oh, yeah, Howard, I certainly did throw a lot of *mmm*ceptions in my career, and thank you very much for asking. Truthfully though, most of the interceptions I threw, I earned. Very few of my passes were intercepted as the result of a great defensive play by a defensive back or linebacker. Most of them were pretty much bad reads on my part.

I had a strong arm. I could throw the football as hard as anyone who ever played the game. That's not bragging, that's reporting. I was confident I could whip the dadblamed thing through a keyhole. I didn't think I could do it, I knew I could do it. I absolutely knew it. I had my people get open five yards past the line of scrimmage, but I wouldn't throw the ball to them. I wouldn't embarrass myself or my teammates by throwing a pass like that. I was going to throw a fifteen-yard deep end, and I was going to throw it even if nobody got open. The technical term for this commonly used in the National Football League is "How could you throw that $$##@!# pass!"

I was a gambler. I insisted on forcing my passes even when I did not have an open man. There were times when I would see the defensive player between myself and my receiver, I saw him standing there big as

Butkus, but I believed I could throw it around him or over him or, if necessary, through him. Most of the interceptions I threw were caused by my own ego. I can throw that ball past the defender. Yes, I can! Man, I had confidence. I said, I HAD CONFIDENCE! And I also had a lot of interceptions.

The second reason I had a lot of passes intercepted was that I locked in on one receiver and was determined to throw it to him. My other receivers might have been so open they could have sat down in a chair and popped open a cold one—but they were not going to get the ball from me. I was determined! I was committed! I was throwing that ball to Lynn Swann, and there will be no further discussion about it. So I dropped back, I turned, and I fired. And I was intercepted!

In fact, it is a lot easier to throw an interception than it is to complete a pass. But I was good at it. One afternoon against the Bengals I believe I had five passes intercepted—in the first half! I was so rattled that later in the game I had a receiver wide open, I can still see him begging for the ball, and I threw it right into the ground. But on most of my interceptions I saw the defensive back, and I believed if I made a perfect pass or threw it with enough velocity it would get there.

I had been retired and working as an announcer for about five years when I finally accepted the fact that in the National Football League I just couldn't do that.

Nobody feels worse than the quarterback after he throws an interception. You think you've done everything correctly. You think you called the right play. You set it up, you go to the line of scrimmage, and it still looks good. The coverage seems to be exactly what you anticipated. Then you turn around and gun that football, and somebody is standing where nobody is supposed to be standing. The feeling is just awful. You feel like you've let down all the good people in your life. Momma, I'm sorry I threw that interception.

There is an old football adage known to all quarterbacks: The moment the ball changes hands through an interception or a fumble, you become a defensive player.

But I didn't want to be a defensive player. I hadn't spent four years in college to learn how to play defense. I was the tackle-ee, not the tackle-er.

The very first thought that came into my mind after a pass was intercepted was, Shoot, now I've got to go tackle this guy. Well, maybe the Shoot part isn't precisely accurate. I didn't want to try to make the tackle, I wasn't used to tackling, I didn't want to get hurt doing something I knew I shouldn't be doing. But I was responsible for this situation, and I had to do my best to set it right. Without getting wiped out, of course. Maybe I did cause the herd to stampede, but that didn't mean I should stand in front and get run over.

During a Monday-night game in Minnesota I had a pass intercepted, actually three passes intercepted if you insist on the details, and I didn't really try to make the tackle. Chuck Noll just ripped into me on the sideline. By God, he screamed at me, these guys are busting their ass out there, and you're throwing into coverage . . . if you get another one intercepted, you'd better get your ass over there and make that tackle—

Interception, ass. Interception, ass. I got it. Later in the quarter I had another pass intercepted. Sho—I started to think. Then, instantly, I remembered: Interception, ass! I took off after the defensive back who'd intercepted my pass. I was doing just like Chuck warned me, moving my ass to make the tackle. I had a good angle on him, I was going to bring him down, make him pay. Go, Terry!

I never did see the player who wiped my clock. Who cleaned my plow. Who cooked my goose. But he ate me for lunch. He flattened me like a junkyard press. Left me lying there like turf-kill. I definitely did make the effort, though. And when I went to the sidelines, I'll bet Chuck Noll was right there telling me that.

I couldn't hear a word he said. All I heard was *rinnnnnnnnnnnnnnnngggggggggggggggggggggg*. Man, that was some echo inside my helmet.

The very worst moments on a football field are those few seconds it takes to jog off the field to the bench after having a pass intercepted. That is the loneliest feeling I ever experienced. Not only did I feel as if I had let down my teammates, I also knew that Chuck Noll would be right there to remind me. I never did escape the wrath of Noll. He'd grab me and get right up there in my face and tell me in an unkind way what I already knew. And then I'd have to go sit on the bench while the defense was on the field trying to save me. It's easy to be the quarterback when the team is playing well; but when I got intercepted, our defensive players were angry because they had to go back on the field, and our offensive players were mad at me because I'd turned over the ball. The only people anxious to talk to me were the fans sitting behind our bench. And they always had a lot of interesting opinions to express.

I always heard the fans. The harder you try not to listen, the louder it gets. I always preferred to have my bad games on the road. If I played badly in Pittsburgh, I had to face the loyal Steelers fans, but if I played badly on the road I got cheered. Way to throw those interceptions, Bradshaw! Do it again, we love you!

On the sidelines after you've thrown an interception, nobody wants to stand too close to you. It was as if they were reminding the fans, Hey, don't blame me, Bradshaw's the one who threw the pass. Or perhaps they were afraid whatever I had would rub off on them, Oh boy, I got a bad case of the Bradshaws. What do I take to get rid of it? Occasionally somebody would give me a friendly pat on the shoulder pads and tell me, "That's okay, Brad, get 'em next time." 'Least, it seemed to me that it was a friendly pat.

On occasion I also fumbled the football. In football, as in life, fumbles happen. The big difference is that if I happen to fumble my car keys, for example, and they fall on the ground, twenty-two large men don't dive on them and try to kill each other for possession. Late in my career the only time I ever really got nervous on the football field was when we played a team that had a big talented nose tackle. A team with an odd-man front. The nose tackle lined up opposite my center, Mike Webster. In those situations Mike had a tendency to lower his butt so he could gain some leverage against the tackle. That made things a little more complicated for me. When he snapped the ball, his butt would go down and then he'd shoot forward;

at times that would push my hand down and I'd end up missing the snap.

I'm not blaming Mike Webster's butt for my fumbles, I am simply explaining a technical aspect of the game that most fans don't understand. Fans just naturally assumed I fumbled the ball because I was clumsy, not because Mike Webster's butt wasn't big enough. So if anybody is to blame for my fumbles, it would be Mike Webster's parents, who raised a strong boy but he definitely needed a bigger butt.

I just hated to see a ball bouncing loose, especially when it was in front of me—which meant it was between my bones and defensive linemen. In that instant the football became the most valuable possession in the world. Everybody went after it. Fans came out of the stands to get it. Players parachuted in from other games to get it. So I had to do my part.

When that football was rolling loose on the ground, my instinct took over. I knew I had to dive for that sucker. And I knew I would have to do it with my arms and fingers extended. So admittedly at times maybe I didn't dive as hard as I might have. I definitely made the effort, no one could accuse me of not making the effort, but it was not like a 270-pound lineman making the effort. I didn't bring quite as much enthusiasm to the pile as he did.

I've been on the bottom of a number of piles. The bottom is not a good place to be. There is a great community spirit in that pile, but only if the community you live in is Hell. That pile is Desperation City. Everybody in that pile is pulling and grabbing and shoving, doing anything to get hold of the football. Nobody says please or excuse me; mainly they just grunt. The wrestling keeps going until the officials tear bodies off the pile to get to the bottom of it. It doesn't really matter who recovers the football; what matters is who has it in his possession when the officials dig it out. When I had the ball I just tried to wrap myself around it as tightly as possible and hold on for Chuck Noll until the sheriff arrived with help.

That didn't always work. There is only one rule at the bottom of the pile: There is no rule. Force wins. That's the rule. Do it if you can do it. Several times I had the football yanked out of my hands at the bottom of the pile. I was holding it tighter than a bank book, but it's almost impossible to move with that mountain on top of you, and if you don't have it gripped tightly in both arms, someone is going to yank it away. Believe me, it is unbelievably frustrating to be lying there squashed under hundreds of pounds of humanity—and still lose hold of the football. But once it was ripped from my possession, there wasn't too much I could do about it. After a fumble, possession is ten-tenths of the law.

I never blamed a teammate for dropping a pass or fumbling the ball, and I never made excuses when I called the wrong play, threw a ridiculous pass, or fumbled the football. I never made excuses. Never.

Maybe once. After I retired, I told a reporter that during my career my depth perception had been poor. That was absolutely true. In fact, until 1977 I wore reading glasses to study the playbook. Then I started getting bad headaches, so there was only one solution: I quit studying the playbook.

I never did see clearly inside domed stadiums. It always looked hazy and blurry to me, and I had a very difficult time judging distances. I was nearsighted, and at night it would be pretty bad. During the game it would look to me like my receiver was fifteen or twenty yards away, but when I'd see the game films, he might have been twenty-five or thirty yards away. I compensated by throwing the ball as hard as I could.

When I started broadcasting, I found I needed glasses to see uniform numbers from the press box. I remember sitting up there and looking out at the field with my new glasses. Everything looked so crisp, I could see the uniform numbers clearly, I could see the leaves on trees. Gee, I thought, how long has this been going on?

Now that is not an excuse, that's an explanation. An excuse would be an attempt to avoid responsibility for the mistakes that I made all by myself. That's not me. When I screwed up, I was the first to admit I screwed up. I wasn't proud of it, but I admitted it. Sometimes even I was impressed by the magnitude of my screwup: Oh, man, did you see that? That was by far the greatest bad pass anyone ever threw! No one in the entire history of the great game of football ever did anything quite that ridiculous. Believe me, when I stunk up the joint, I didn't hide from the reporters. When you play a game in front of a hundred million viewers, it's pretty tough to blame someone else for your own mistakes. What was I going to say, a hundred million viewers missed it? It's more honorable to stand up straight and face the firing squad.

The one thing I never forgot, even when I was getting carried off the field after getting hurt or hearing people criticize me or watching a pass go directly into the arms of a defensive back, the one thing I never forgot when I sighed and dived into the pile after a fumble or had Chuck Noll in my face discussing my intelligence, was how incredibly fortunate I was to have the God-given ability and the opportunity to play football.

I've loved football my whole life. While the game has hurt my feelings, it has never spurned my affection. And after all the distractions of a fourteen-year career, what I remember most are those times on the field when everything went perfectly; when I got set and watched as the play unfolded in front of me just as it had been designed, when I anticipated my receiver arriving at a spot and I just laid that baby right in there and everything came together perfectly—naturally I didn't get hit—and he caught that pass. There is nothing I have ever experienced to compare to the thrill of a good read, a perfect pass, a nice catch. It's the quarterback's dream. The Steelers ran the ball, we didn't throw it thirty-five times a game, so I probably savored those completions more than most other quarterbacks.

There were times in my career when the game was easy. I say, EASY. I could do no wrong. Maybe it was my biorhythms. Maybe the moon was right; we wean horses on the full moon, why shouldn't it affect quarterbacks? We castrate horses on a full moon; now don't you even begin to think I'm going to mention quarterbacks in this sentence. But for whatever reason, there were times when the game was simple. I felt in complete control. In 1975, for instance, it seemed like I had the game licked. I just went out there and threw touchdown passes. It was as easy as getting wet in a car wash. But the following year I couldn't throw a touchdown pass if my receiver was wide open. It was like falling out of love, I couldn't tell you the reason why it happened.

Of course now that I've been retired longer than I played, and have spent much of that time carefully analyzing the game, trying to understand each of the small details that must come together to create the larger canvas, working with some of the most brilliant minds ever to apply their intellect to football, I have finally reached the conclusion that the real beauty of the game is that there is no way to really understand it.

FIVE

Most of the skills pro football players master during
their playing careers have almost no value after they retire. There is very little tackling needed in management,
for example. No one blocks for lawyers. Stockbrokers,
restaurateurs, law enforcement officers, or farmers
rarely need to run backward at full speed. Truckers
don't throw passes. And teachers don't need to catch
them.

My playing career ended exactly the same time as
every other professional athlete's: too soon. I didn't expect to play forever, just one more year after my last
year. And maybe one more year after that. And then
maybe one year after that. To my mind I still might
have played several more years if I hadn't been hurt, although the *Chicago Tribune* announced the end of my
career with the headline, "Bradshaw Finally Retires."
Finally? I finally retired? I was sorry they felt so bad
about it.

During the press conference held to announce my

retirement, I said, "I'm extremely excited about my future because I don't know what it holds."

I was widely quoted as saying that I didn't know what was going to happen in the future. Think maybe it was a real slow news day?

It's tough to be closing up shop at the same age most people are just getting established. When my playing career ended, I really had no idea how I wanted to spend the rest of my life. The only thing I knew for certain was that I didn't want to spend it having been Terry Bradshaw. I didn't want to spend the rest of my life talking about my past. And I knew I had one big advantage; whatever I did, no matter how terrible it was, it would still be better than the pipe-laying job my brother and I had one summer.

That was my summer of heartache. After five years of dating, my high school girlfriend had broken up with me. She found herself another man and left me devastated. This was the first time a woman had broken my heart. I like to refer to it as practice. If I really could have seen the future, I wouldn't have. It was painful enough to make me a country-western singer.

My dad finally got tired of seeing me moping around the house feeling sorry for myself, so he decided the best way to get this boy straightened out was to get him out of the house. Way out of the house. He shipped me and brother Gary to Hutchinson, Kansas, to work on a pipeline project.

We were skid haulers. A skid is a used railroad tie, a big, long piece of lumber. These particular skids weighed about fifty pounds each. Our job was to load about 150 of them onto a flatbed truck, piling them as high as possible. Normally this requires four people: a driver, someone on the truck to keep the pile orderly, and Terry and Gary to do the heavy lifting. As it happened, we didn't like the two men assigned to the truck; fortunately they quit. The straw boss asked us if we could handle the truck by ourselves.

Skid hauling is definitely the suck-ass job of pipelining. It requires absolutely no intelligence. It is lifting, loading, driving, and unloading. If you can lift those skids, crank a truck, and drive, you're qualified. This was a job for the Bradshaw brothers.

The only requirement was that we stay ahead of the pipeline welders. When they were ready, the skids had to be on site, or the whole schedule got messed up. We agreed to handle the truck without help for a $1-an-hour raise. That straw boss couldn't put one over on us.

It was rough work. We were out in the middle of the Kansas wheat fields in the middle of August. Those wheat fields hold the heat real well. But we were doing fine. We were doing a ten-hour job in about eight and a half hours and turning in twelve hours on the worksheet. We stayed about a quarter mile ahead of the welders. Gary and I, we stacked and drove those babies all day. The only time we saw the rest of the crew was when we went flying by them with another big load.

We saved every penny we earned. We lived in the attic of a Mennonite family's house, for which we paid $5 a week. There were no windows in that room, and at night it cooled off in there to about 100 degrees. We ate at McDonald's. We wore shorts and gloves to handle the skids.

We were given the company's worst truck. That truck was pitiful. It didn't even have a windshield. So even though we couldn't drive very fast, bugs were still smacking us in the face. One morning we were cruising along just being in our normal state of miserable—hot and sweaty and tired and poor and on our way to work—when we hit a skunk. I mean, we slammed into that skunk. And in return he sprayed the entire truck. It was like we were engulfed with warm death. The minute that spray hit us, we started screaming. Then we started throwing up. We were desperate to get out of that truck. Finally we pulled into this field and started running, stripping off our clothes as we ran, doing anything we could to get away from that stink.

We found this creek and just dived in. We were washing ourselves, covering ourselves with mud, doing anything we could to get rid of that awful smell. But it was stuck to us tighter than Dion on defense. As long as we stayed in the water, it was tolerable, but whenever we tried to get out, that stink hit us. The straw boss found us there and couldn't stop laughing—although naturally he was laughing from a considerable distance.

We stayed in that creek all day. I believe someone brought us mustard, a lot of little mustard jars, which we spread all over our bodies, trying to remove the smell. To get the stink out of the truck, they lit bonfires to burn it out. We went home that evening wearing towels.

So whatever I ended up doing after I retired, I had this job as a basis of comparison; and as long as it didn't involve skunks, I knew it would be better than hauling skids.

When I had to retire, I did what anybody else looking for a job would do: I analyzed my marketable skills. Exactly what could I do that potentially had value to an employer?

Well, that certainly didn't take very long.

My first choice for a second career was anything to do with working the land. Sometimes in the evening I'll just grab a cup of coffee, get into my Jeep, and drive on out to a hillside overlooking a meadow. I'll just sit there and watch the setting sun. I don't need much more than a piece of land to make me content.

Some people look at a beautiful piece of land and think, This is a perfect spot for a house. I look at that same place and wonder, Why would anybody want to ruin this beautiful piece of land by putting a house on it? I am fortunate enough to live in a lovely community in Texas. The businessman Ross Perot owned a considerable amount of property in my town and decided to develop it. "Develop it," in this particular situation, meant taking something magnificent and transforming it into something profitable. I looked at his land just the way it was, and it seemed to me that it had already been developed. Several million years ago somebody had put the most beautiful rolling hills on it, and a lake, and much later some trees had been planted. What these people meant was that they wanted to destroy it and turn it into something else.

We had a town meeting during which Ross Perot's people presented their plans to the community. I don't remember ever speaking at a town meeting before, but

I did this time. I stood up and told those people that if I had all the money that Ross Perot had, I would park my family up on that hill and spend my time looking across that 2,500 acres and marveling at its beauty. I said, just think how wonderful it would be if your children could play in that fifty-acre lake and ride their horses across the meadow, looking at those longhorn cattle and buffalo, instead of bringing in houses and factories and buildings.

I defended the land. I said my piece and never said another word. They began construction less than a year later.

So my first choice for a career would have been working the land. Two things held me back from that—money and knowledge. Three marriages ago I bought 400 acres of beautiful farmland in south Louisiana. A lot of kind people offered opinions about what I should do with that land. One guy said, Oh, dude, you gotta have some cattle.

Cattle sounded fine. I'd like to, I explained, but this land cost me just about the all the money I've got.

But you can borrow money. That's no problem.

So I got into the cattle business. What I lacked in experience, I also lacked in common sense. I used to listen to the host of the farm report on the local radio station, KWKH. He seemed very knowledgeable; he knew all the right words; pork bellies are up, hogs are down, corn is up, cotton is down. Damn, that man knew his farm words. He had all the right talk. And he volunteered to help me get established in the cattle business. I guess you might say he was going to help me develop my bank account.

I envisioned myself with a herd of real longhorn cattle. No, sir, he told me, what I really needed was shorthorns. I had never heard of shorthorns; the only breeds I knew anything about were Hereford, Angus, and Brahman. As I learned, shorthorn cattle are pure-bred; they've even got papers to prove it. So I went to the cattle auction with my first wife, Melissa. We were standing around talking cattle with several other men, among them the auctioneer, whose name was the Colonel. He had never been in the military, but his name was the Colonel. Now, Melissa, being from Pittsburgh, didn't know anything about cattle. And me, being from Louisiana, also knew nothing about cattle, but I certainly wasn't going to let these cattlemen know that the quarterback of the Pittsburgh Steelers didn't know his cattle.

While these men were talking cattle prices, I was looking at these fat cows and thinking, I don't have any money. But several times during their conversation I heard them mention limousines. Man, I was impressed. The cattle business must really be lucrative, I thought; here's a guy making so much money selling cattle he's also selling limousines.

Apparently the limousine business was very good. But before I could say anything, Melissa said to the Colonel, "You mean to tell me you make more money selling limousines than these registered cattle? I didn't know those cars—"

The men started laughing. The cattlemen were laughing, I started laughing. Whatever we were laughing at, it sure was funny. "Oh no, little lady," one of the men explained, "a Limousin is a breed of cattle."

"Oh yeah," I agreed immediately, "didn't you know that? I thought everybody knew that. I knew that, definitely, no problem." And I thought, thank you very much, Lord. Nice save there.

We didn't buy any shorthorns at the auction, but fortunately my adviser had some shorthorns on his own spread that he was willing to sell me, just to help me get started in the business. It was a real friendly gesture. I bought about fifteen head from him. What he failed to tell me was that these cattle also had short teeth, meaning they were old. I bought old cattle. They were ready to retire. They seemed to believe my farm was an assisted living facility.

They didn't breed. Not one calf. This was the sorriest herd of cattle I had ever seen. I lost all the money I paid him.

Then people told me, Terry, what you need out here is some crossbreed cattle. Crossbreed means they were a mixture of all the breeds, Hereford, Angus, and Brahman. These cattle are called little ear. I was told to make sure I got little ear, because that meant they had just a touch of Brahman. It's that little bit of Brahman that gives cattle the vigor to withstand the heat and humidity of the Deep South. One thing I had learned was that it was very important to buy cattle acclimated to your area. Don't buy cattle in Arizona or Montana and try to breed them in Louisiana. So I looked all over Louisiana for some crossbreed cattle, and finally a good friend of mine told me he had found "a good set down in South Louisiana."

A "set" is a complete herd that someone is selling. So my friend and I drove way down south—we even had to take a rowboat to get to this place. It seemed like he had hundreds of little bitty crossbreed cattle. They were little tiny things. "How many acres you got?" the man asked.

" 'Bout fo' hunnred," my friend said.

"Oh jeez," the man said, "that'll run two, three hundred head easy."

Wow, I thought, I didn't know that. He finally agreed to sell me 220 head of these sickly-looking cows. And I began to explain that we would have to work out payments because I didn't have that kind of money.

"That ain't no problem," he said, "you're a famous professional athlete. You just go on down to the Professional Credit Association, and they'll loan you the money."

I borrowed $100,000 and bought 220 wiglings, which means baby cattle. No one explained to me that it was going to take at least three years, possibly longer, for these cattle to mature enough to breed. So I wasn't going to earn any money from them for four years. Worse, just being from Louisiana was not quite good enough. They were going to be leaving the swamps and moving to the hill country, and they liked the swamps. I had bought a set of swamp cattle. A lot of them were not going to be able to adjust to the different grasses and were going to die. And those that lived probably would jump the fence or break it down and head for the woods.

But I was a cattleman. I believe I was the only member of the Pittsburgh Steelers to have my own set. Two weeks later, about midnight, Melissa and I were awakened by an air horn just blasting through the night. I got dressed and went outside to find a huge semitrailer in my front yard. "Here's your cattle," the man said. He had somehow managed to wedge 220 head of cattle into this truck.

This definitely was a substantial problem. It was the middle of the night, and I didn't have the ramp we needed to safely unload the cattle. Now, this rancher could have dropped off the cattle up in Mansfield, which would have enabled me to drive there with my trailer and bring them back in several loads, but he wanted to get rid of those suckers.

Maybe I have my suckers wrong here.

"We'll just have to have 'em jump out," he said. It was approximately nine feet from the truck bed to the ground. Nine feet to these small cattle was about a mile and a half in people distance. But he backed the rear wheels into a ditch, which dropped down the truck bed several feet. I opened the gate to the yard and lit up with the headlights from my Jeep. I figured they would hop out of the truck and go into that yard. Like any proud owner, I was ready to thoroughly enjoy watching my cattle exit in a calm fashion. Then he opened the back door of that truck.

The first hundred came shooting out the bottom of that truck like it was the Kentucky Derby. Pow! They were smoking. They had been stuffed in there on top of each other for who knows how long. They stampeded. Then I heard a sound I will never forget: sort of like ping, ping, ping. As I learned, that was the sound of them taking out my barbed wire fence. They just went right through it and were gone. I mean, they just disappeared into the dark.

I had never seen anything like that in my life.

'Course, we still had to unload the top bunch. While the bed was only a couple of feet above ground, the top layer was much higher. "Won't they get hurt jumping out?" I asked.

He assured me these particular cattle were good jumpers.

It would be near impossible to accurately describe what happened next. Remember the fable about the cow jumping over the moon? Notice they never tell you how that cow landed. There's a good reason for that. Cows don't jump! They're cows, they're not supposed to jump! Of course they were going to get hurt jumping out of that truck. The first eight or ten that hit the ground never got up. The rest of my set used them as springboards. They were leaping onto this pile of cows, then hitting the ground. There were cows flipping, flopping, and rolling.

The cattle that survived took off across my field. Ping! Ping! Ping! My fence was already gone, so they couldn't go through it; instead they went through my neighbor's fence. And then they were gone into the night.

The cattle business was definitely turning out to be a lot more difficult than I had anticipated.

The next morning the sun rose on the biggest mess I have ever seen. I had dead cattle, I had cattle with broken legs. My nice fence was just a jumble of mangled barbed wire, I found pieces of hide, ear, and tongue in it. Several of the surviving cattle had wads of stuff pouring out of their noses, which I found out meant they had pneumonia. The cattle that weren't broken or sick were spooked. If I went anywhere near them, they just took off running again. Oh man, it was just awful.

I lost about 40 head just getting them unloaded. That's like fumbling the kickoff. I had 180 head surviving and not the slightest idea what to do with them. My adviser told me, "You got to breed them."

Breeding. Now we were talking cattleman talk. But I didn't know anything about breeding.

"Heifers like this," I was told, "young cows, you need to put an Angus bull on them because Angus bulls produce small, tiny babies."

For my 180 head I needed thirty or forty Angus bulls. Young Angus bulls, I was told. So I went back to the credit association and borrowed more money to buy more bulls than my little cows needed.

Now I needed to cut hay for my cattle, which meant I had to buy a tractor and a cutter and a baler. By this time I had a lot less money than I didn't have when I got into the cattle business. But I had made some real good friends at the credit association. They smiled big-time when I walked in again.

Turns out I bought very particular bulls. I looked out in the field one day, and there were my forty bulls chasing one cow. It was like a dance at a high school; all the boys were chasing one girl, and 179 other girls were standing in a corner by themselves. It looked like an ordinary cow to me, but as I've learned, there is no understanding women. The next year my 180 cows had a total of 30 calves.

This was how I got poor. I wasn't so much learning the business as I was being given the business. Eventually I sold my set and took a $50,000 loss. That still remains the best deal I ever made, even better than my deal with the toupee company that distributed my head to beauty shops around the country.

I learned an important lesson. I could have learned the same lesson for less money, but it probably wouldn't have had the same impact: after I retired from football, I was not going to raise cattle.

I also was not going to raise homing pigeons. I tried that too. I've raised pigeons at various times of my life. I even raced them for a while—I once won $9,400 in a pigeon futurity, a 200-mile race. I raised them because I love animals of all kinds, and I need to be busy. So in Pittsburgh, for example, I was always holding them or feeding them, cleaning the cages, pairing them up, paying for their dates, raising their babies. Trained them myself.

Pigeons are a lot less expensive than cattle. Homing pigeons do one thing well. They come home. Once they lock in on their home they can never be trained to go elsewhere. The only possible way to change that is to take them to another loft and let them have their babies there, and then they will come back to their babies. I like that loyalty about pigeons.

I also was not going to go into politics. While I have known some fine people in politics, among them former senator and secretary of defense William Cohen, my basic feeling was that anyone who would spend millions of dollars to get a job paying thousands of dollars did not have my interests in mind. And with all the problems I have in my own life, I would feel less than honest telling people I knew how to solve the problems in their lives.

There were a lot of jobs for which I wasn't qualified. I didn't have the patience to be a good teacher. I didn't understand finance well enough to become a banker or stockbroker. Last time I drove a truck, I ended up spending the day in a creek. Summing up, basically I had no marketable skills.

That made me perfect for television. I could go on television, and people would listen to me, and I would make them feel good about themselves. Because they would know that if Terry Bradshaw, who had no apparent skills, could be successful on television, there was hope for them in whatever they chose to do with their lives.

I have never watched much TV. That is probably, not a wise confession from someone who appears on TV as much as I do, but if I did have the opportunity, I would definitely watch myself whenever I appeared. It's all those other shows on which I don't appear I probably wouldn't watch. Basically, I watch the movie channels. I love classic movies. There are certain movies—and I am not exaggerating—that I have probably watched at least one hundred times. I take them with me when I travel and put them on at night and go to sleep to the familiar dialogue.

The first few times I was interviewed on television, I tended to emphasize my faith. But as time passed, it became obvious to me that I definitely was not practicing what I was preaching, I definitely wasn't the role model I wanted to be. I wasn't reading my Bible. And when I was out with a beautiful woman, there was only one thing I was praying for! I felt I was being hypocritical. So eventually I stopped talking about my religious beliefs on television.

Reporters always liked me because I was consid-

Here I am in my
"one-gallon" hat.
COURTESY OF
THE BRADSHAW FAMILY

The Bradshaw Boys
(my brother Gary
is on the right)
looking for action—
or at least
a change of diapers.
COURTESY OF
THE BRADSHAW FAMILY

The graduate—
of first grade.
COURTESY OF
THE BRADSHAW FAMILY

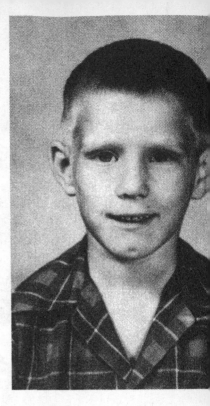

The graduate—
to first-string quarterback
at Woodlawn
High School.
COURTESY OF THE
SHREVEPORT JOURNAL

Many people have said I must have played without a helmet,
as in this publicity shot taken at Louisiana Tech.

The graduate—
to the National
Football League.
COURTESY OF THE
PITTSBURGH STEELERS

The postgraduate to TV sitcoms—like this appearance on *Blossom*.
COURTESY OF BUENA VISTA TELEVISION

In high school I set the national javelin-throwing record—and got to meet my first television star, Michael Landon.
COURTESY OF WOODLAWN HIGH SCHOOL, SHREVEPORT, LOUISIANA

Family matters most: My dad, William Marvin Bradshaw
(second from right); my mom—note that contrary to my
reports she has all her teeth—Novis Bradshaw; and their son,
Terry Paxton Bradshaw . . .
COURTESY OF DAVID MOROSKI

. . . with my big little brother, Craig (left) and my older
brother, Gary.
COURTESY OF THE BRADSHAW FAMILY

My father was my first agent. Our negotiating position was definitely weakened by his integrity.
COURTESY OF THE PITTSBURGH STEELERS

And here I am many years later in my ten-gallon hat.
COURTESY OF GOODALL FINE PORTRAITURE

Once I was a spokesman for a toupee company. The company produced lifelike toupees that allowed you to be any type of person you wanted to be. Actually these wigs—not produced by that company—were part of costumes I wore on my talk show, *The Home Team*.

My CBS family
(from left) Greg
Gumbel, me,
Lesley Visser,
and Pat O'Brien.
CBS PHOTO
ARCHIVE

The "Foxes" in their den (from left): James Brown, me,
Howie Long, and Cris Collinsworth.
COURTESY OF FOX SPORTS

My broadcasting career has allowed me to meet an array of celebrities not usually associated with football, among them then–Secretary of Defense William Cohen and his wife, with whom I traveled to the Middle East, and television stars Homer Simpson and his son, Bart, who joined me in an opening segment of the Fox show.

PHOTO BY ROBERT D. WARD / COURTESY OF
THE DEPARTMENT OF DEFENSE
ILLUSTRATION BY MATT GROENING / COURTESY OF TWENTIETH CENTURY FOX FILM CORPORATION

When I hosted my own television talk show, aimed primarily at women, I tried to get in touch with my feminine side—I'm not sure that it worked.

COURTESY OF JEFF KATZ

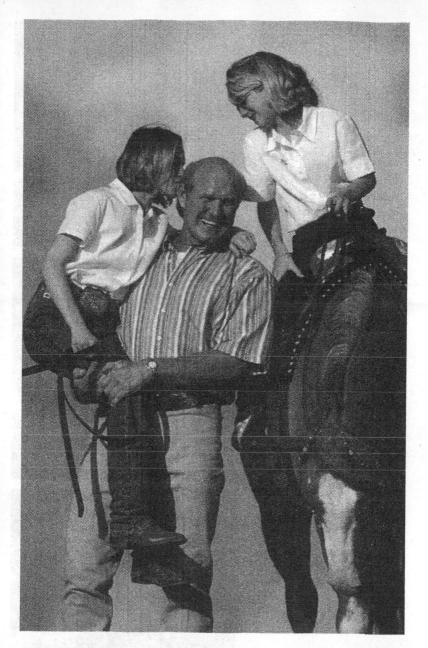

My real family: my beautiful daughters, Erin and Rachel
(on horseback)
COURTESY OF WILLIAM SNYDER

During my rookie season with the Steelers I learned that one of the best means of relaxation was a fast game of cutthroat Go Fish. Here I am doing battle—unsuccessfully—at the old fishing hole with legendary country singer and Go-Fisherman Toby Keith in the semifinals of the annual America Goes Fishin' Tournament held in Las Vegas, Nevada. Either that, or this is a commercial for the MCI discount long-distance service 10-10-220.

ered a good sound bite. I never walked away from a question. I answered every question that I was asked, even if I had to make up the answer. Which I often did. I would sometimes answer the same question asked by three different journalists three different ways. Sometimes my answers even surprised me: Yeah, Jack, I felt really good out there today, I was definitely in the zone. I was? Why didn't I know that? Sometimes I wished that before speaking, my mouth would have checked with the rest of my body.

I just got bored giving the same answers to the same questions over and over. There are only so many times you can discuss the same situation with the same sense of importance. We were playing a game, and I knew it. My answers weren't going to change anybody's life. What possible difference did it make whether or not I read the coverage correctly or just got lucky? So I tried to make my interviews fun. I tried to make them eventful. I wanted to make people smile. Which is why I was considered a good sound bite.

It also attracted the attention of network executives. Well, Mr. Tie, that Bradshaw certainly is outspoken. Why don't we pay him piles of money to be outspoken for our network? Think he will? Oh yeah, I heard he was in the cattle business, he's going to need those piles.

This is how I got into the broadcasting business: One day in the late 1970s the phone rang, and a CBS executive said, "Want five thousand dollars just for talking?"

That is how I got into the broadcasting business.

At first I didn't take it very seriously. I wore my

cowboy hats and talked southern and did silly things. I just tried to have fun. It didn't take me too long to learn that it wasn't all fun: one of the very first—and toughest—interviews I did for television took place after the 1981 NFC Championship game between the Cowboys and the 49ers. I thought it would be pretty easy. By this time I felt comfortable on camera. I had done some football commentary, and as one-half a celebrity couple I had appeared on several talk shows with Jo Jo. And personally I had been interviewed many times after big games and never had any problems—although the fact that we mostly won the big games might have had something to do with that. During my career, postgame interviews were always informal. I never had one of those press-conference-type interviews conducted in the interview room; I was knocked out cold in Super Bowl X, so the only question I answered right after the game was, How many fingers am I holding up? After Super Bowl XIII I leaned against a pole and answered questions for the reporters. Postgame interviews for Super Bowl XIV took place in our locker room. It was never a big scene, never a big deal, and generally the questions were no more complicated than, You just won the Super Bowl, are you happy? When did you know you had the game won? Anything surprise you?

So when the Steelers failed to make the playoffs in 1981, CBS hired me to do postgame interviews from the winning team's locker room after the league championship game. I didn't anticipate any problems. The network also hired Roger Staubach and assigned him to do interviews from the losing team's locker room. I had the easy job. I was ready, I had my questions all set: Are you happy? When did you know you had the game won? Anything surprise you? How do you like your chances in the Super Bowl? This is Terry Bradshaw; back to you, Brent.

The thing that nobody anticipated was the Cowboys losing the football game. In the last minute of the game San Francisco's Dwight Clark made a tremendous catch of Joe Montana's pass into the end zone, and the 49ers won, 28–27. Now, there was no possible way Roger was going to go into the Cowboys' locker room and start asking his former teammates how it felt to lose. No way. So they told me, "Brad, why don't you go ahead on into the Cowboys' locker room and do the interviews?"

Hey, sure, be glad to. You can count on me. How tough can it be?

Tough. Very, very tough. The Cowboys were furious. They were screaming, cussing, throwing helmets, throwing coaches; these were very angry people. And who should saunter into their locker room? Only the man who had beaten them in two previous Super Bowls. Only the human reminder of all the big game defeats they'd suffered. Me. Carrying a microphone.

Ever have the feeling that you were a square peg at a termite's convention? Man, I thought, this is a tough job. And I hadn't even asked my first question yet. This was the first time in my life I'd been in the losing locker room after a championship game; I knew what these guys had put out, but I could only imagine what they were feeling. Even veteran reporters are intimidated by the mood of a losing locker room, but I wasn't a reporter, I was a quarterback playing reporter. I was still an active player. There was a fair chance I would be playing against this team the following season.

I definitely couldn't ask my big question: Are you happy?

Reporters who had never played the game might have felt differently than I did; they may have been able to ask the difficult questions. I imagine if I were to interview a losing politician after an election, I would be able to ask tough questions—but not in that locker room.

Luckily, I got to interview Cowboys coach Tom Landry. Coach Landry was the most gracious, wonderful human being in the world that day. I can't even imagine what he must have been feeling, yet he treated me with all the professionalism and respect that I had yet to earn. He created a situation in which I could comfortably ask the questions that needed to be asked: How devastating is this loss? Regrets? His players followed his example. Anybody ever need a good definition of the word "class," the answer is Tom Landry that afternoon in the losing locker room.

The only real qualification I had for a broadcasting career was four Super Bowl wins. That made me a celebrity, it made me perfect for television. I didn't know enough about broadcasting to be nervous about doing it. Talking? I'd been doing that most of my life. The best advice I got came from Dandy Don Meredith during a golf tournament in Connecticut just before I started my broadcasting career. I was playing in a foursome with Meredith and Frank Gifford—we were all football players, so none of us was good in math—and Meredith told me, "Terry, you just be yourself, and you're going to be fine. Just be yourself. Don't let them change who you are. And have fun."

Be myself? I was good at that. Except that one time at the White House with Nelson Rockefeller, when I was good at being Roger Staubach.

I actually knew I was going to have an opportunity to try broadcasting two or three years before I retired. While we were in Atlanta, a top CBS executive told me that the network wanted to hire me when my career ended. The end of my career? At that point I hadn't even begun thinking about that! What did CBS know that I didn't? I didn't want to talk about my future at that point, as if even discussing it might cause it to happen faster. Like every professional athlete in the middle of his career, I wanted to keep the future as far in the future as possible. But it was comforting to know that I would have the opportunity, even though I doubted very much I would be successful at it.

I figured broadcasting would be a good thing for me to do until I figured out what it was that I really wanted to do. I expected my career would last the same two or three years as most former athletes, just like Sonny Jurgensen and Johnny Unitas, until the network figured out I didn't know what I was doing and the next star quarterback retired. So several years later when it became apparent that I'd caught up to my future, Brent Musburger came down to Louisiana to tell me CBS wanted me. But whatever you do, he said, don't sign with NBC. Meanwhile, NBC contacted me and told me that whatever I do, don't sign with CBS.

CBS offered me a job; NBC offered me an audition. Soon as I heard that, I figured CBS must stand for See Bradshaw Sign.

Fortunately, journalists immediately realized that I would be bringing to the broadcast booth a unique and interesting perspective, and so they treated me with complete respect. Among the first questions I was asked at the press conference held to announce that I'd signed with CBS was whether or not I would wear a hairpiece on camera.

"CBS has a dress code," I responded seriously; "no cowboy hats and no hairpieces." I also revealed my broadcasting philosophy, although I hadn't known I had a philosophy until that moment. "I'm not going to criticize people. That's not my style. Who am I to criticize? . . . I'm not going to be a Goody Two-shoes, but it is hard to say that a guy did something stupid and then try to ask him what's going on the next day. But I will show emotion. If I saw a quarterback on his own ten-yard line throwing a screen pass, my reaction would be, 'My God, you don't do that. Why did he do that?' "

Asked to describe my broadcasting style, I said it probably would be similar to the way I watch football games at home: "I scream and holler and jump up and down."

When I said that, I believed it. Howard Cosell made a reputation for himself and changed TV sports reporting by "telling it like it is." The man deserves credit for that. But he had a lot of imitators. As I learned in my career, it's easy to sit up there safe in that booth and rip people—if you don't have to face them the next week. The easiest way in the world for a broadcaster to make himself seem smart and knowledgeable is to be loudly critical of players, and a lot of broadcasters have done just that. I always thought those people were cowards. Now, that's telling it like it is.

During my playing career I never objected to legitimate criticism of my performance. I knew when I was awful, and I accepted the fact that the people broadcasting our games had a job to do. What I didn't like were those people who said unkind or ridiculous things about me, then didn't have the guts to face me. I had no regard for them. The only two people who came into the locker room to talk with me before a game—except for Bob Griese, who I spoke with once—were Merlin Olsen and Curt Gowdy, and they asked me intelligent questions about our game plan. They wanted to know how we intended to attack, what we perceived to be the strengths and weaknesses of our opponent. They wanted to be prepared for their broadcast. And I would tell them everything. I'd tell more than everything. I'd tell them about the crazy armadillo and the cattle knocking down the fence, I'd tell them about the skunk, I'd tell them . . .

Thank you very much, Terry.

. . . about being shot at when I was teaching Methodists and stealing the pop bottles and . . .

Thanks a lot, Terry, we'll see you later.

So when I signed with CBS, I intended to focus on the game, just like Merlin and Curt. That's what I intended to do. The executive producer of CBS Sports was Terry O'Neill, who told reporters he believed I would be a good broadcaster because "most broadcast ers have a filter between their mouth and their brain. Terry doesn't have that. That's what makes him so distinctive."

Terry O'Neill teamed me with veteran play-by-play announcer Verne Lundquist. He figured Verne Lundquist and I had a lot in common because Verne was a Texan and had been broadcasting Dallas Cowboys games for almost a decade, while I was from Louisiana and had played against the Cowboys for more than a decade. In the inside parlance of the broadcasting business, Verne was what is known as "a sacrificial lamb." He was my mentor. He was facing a big challenge; he had to teach me how to be a broadcaster before I destroyed his entire career.

My very first broadcast was a preseason game in San Diego between the Chargers and the other team. Maybe I didn't get all the details. I didn't have the first clue how to prepare for a broadcast. I really tried; I read everything I could find about the two teams. I read both press guides from front to back, I knew where they played, I knew all about the owners, I knew all the facts, except maybe the players' names, numbers, and positions. When I was playing, I never knew the names of the opposing players or their numbers, so there was no reason I would know them now. Additionally, because this was a preseason game, both the Chargers and the other team—apparently it was the San Francisco 49ers—had greatly expanded rosters that included a lot of rookies no one knew anything about.

I didn't even know a lot of basic strategy. I knew the quarterback's job, but I really didn't know what the linebackers were doing or the safeties or the corners. It hadn't been my job to know about their jobs—that was their job. So I was sort of at a loss to describe their jobs. As a player the big picture was the only thing that mattered to me, but as a broadcaster it was the small frames that made up the big picture. One of the things that has made John Madden a great broadcaster is his understanding of all the smaller aspects that comprised an entire game. But as a coach that was his job.

My greatest fear when I started was that I would say something wrong about football. What I was taught in Pittsburgh was not what people were taught in San Francisco. I understood the Steelers' philosophy, our terminology, our rules, but precisely the same situation might have been handled differently or described differently by other teams. I was worried that players watching my game might hear me say something and wonder, Now what is he talking about? So I tried very hard to keep it simple—block and tackle, run and pass.

So beyond not knowing the players and their assignments, I didn't know when to talk and when to keep quiet, I didn't know what to say, what to look at, how to describe what I was seeing; I didn't know how to get into a replay or out of a replay. When the quarterback went back to pass, for example, my eyes just naturally looked upfield to find the open receivers—and meanwhile I missed the entire play at the line of scrimmage.

And beyond not knowing the players and how to actually work a broadcast, I didn't know many of the rules. I knew the basic penalties: offside—five yards;

pass interference—ball is placed at the point of contact; roughing the passer—a year in solitary confinement at a maximum-security prison. But I didn't know all the intricacies, I didn't know about the rule changes inside the red zone, I didn't know the unusual rules. And truthfully, I still don't know them.

There was so much I didn't know, I didn't even know I didn't know it. That's how much I didn't know. The first few games I broadcast, I was probably more nervous than at any time during my entire playing career. On the field I always felt confident that I knew what was going on; in the booth I was lost. When I started I would always bring two clean shirts with me to the games, because I knew I was going to be so nervous I was going to sweat right through one of them. Maybe I was so nervous because I really cared. I wanted so much to be good, to please the viewers, and it was obvious to me that I didn't really have the knowledge I needed.

I needed a job.

Terry O'Neill tried to help me. One of the tools most broadcasters use to help them identify players is called a spotting board. Basically, it's a piece of cardboard on which each broadcaster writes down in a color code the players' names and numbers in their positions. They showed me a spotting board Dick Vermeil, the former head coach, had made when he was working as a commentator. He had written down very neatly—in seven different colors—all the information he possibly would need during the broadcast. He had every player in his proper position, their backups, everybody's size, weight, age, and college, bits of information about them, their mother's maiden name, credit card numbers, what kind of car they drove, where they bought their socks, their bank balance—I mean, he had covered everything.

Now, the spotting board I prepared was probably a little less complete. I included the players' names and numbers. And by the time the first half was over, mine was in four colors; black ink, brown mustard, red ketchup, and blotchy soda color stains. But my board had something Vermeil's didn't; a big hole in the middle where I'd rolled over it with my chair.

That board was no use to me at all. I didn't know how to use it or when to refer to it, so at the end of the first quarter I just threw it on the floor and forgot all about it. When Verne Lundquist pointed out that for a lot of young players this game would either make or break their careers, I think I identified with them completely when I replied, "A lot of these kids are very close to making it. They've got butterflies. I had butterflies my first night out so . . . I'm nervous and I'm sure they're nervous and they're perspiring heavily and all wondering, hoping, praying, please let me have a great game tonight . . ."

I would not describe my first game as a disaster, mostly because that would be understating how truly bad I was. In about the middle of the first quarter it became obvious to me that in addition to a lack of knowledge combined with a lack of preparation, I had a serious problem: "Verne," I said, "I can't see sh— I swear to you, I can't see a thing down there." It definitely was going to hurt my ability to comment on the game if I couldn't see it. I would have been some great broadcaster: Wow, I could say, I think something great might've just happened down there. But I had never watched a football game from that distance in my life. All I could see was a bunch of people whose numbers I couldn't see running around. It was a new perspective on the game for me. "What's happening is so quick . . . It really seems quick. I can't . . . I'm not . . ."

"Really," Verne said, amazingly calmly, considering the broadcasting partner on whom he was depending for insightful commentary had just announced he was basically useless, "we got to get you binoculars for the next game."

"Oh, man . . . I don't know one player . . . I'm not kidding . . . I'm sweating enough."

To which Verne—wonderful, supportive, lying-through-his-teeth Verne—said, "You're doing super."

"Whew, this is not easy. Take a while . . ." It took me one quarter of broadcasting football to realize it was a whole new ball game. "I'll tell you what, fellas," I continued, "I did not have too much respect . . . I thought these guys had a cakewalk up here. I'm gonna tell ya, I don't see how they do it. Looking at all these names, forget them names. We'll take their names away from them . . ."

Poor Verne. "Call 'em by number," he agreed.

Unfortunately, that wouldn't have helped me either. I admitted, "I can't even see the numbers."

I did have a good time, though. They wanted me to be myself, and I commented on that game as if I were sitting with friends in my living room. "Watch this," I urged, during one of the first replays I did, "just plain old everybody staying in and blocking and . . . Dan stays back and he sees it but he can't get set, here it is, ah, get it! Oooo!

"Let's see what happens, this guy comes down, take 'm on number 52, take him on again, take him on again, Oooo. Fix him, wrassle him down, stay with him down . . ."

Maybe I didn't know exactly what was happening down on the field, but I certainly was excited about it. And every once in a while, if you listened real carefully, I showed just the tiniest little faint glimmer of promise. Once, for example, I was describing a play by the right tackle, "Keep a good eye on the right tackle, number 77, he's trying to get away from the left guard. There's the hit, look at that little spin move. He turned all the way around. Idn't that neat, he spins around, but the guard says oh, no, baby, I been in the league six years, you can spin all you want. Bam! Boy, he bops him again . . . It's just amazing how these big guys, six-five, two-seventy, can move around like a ballerina. You ever do anything like that, Verne?"

"What, pirouette?"

"No. Spin around."

Gradually I got better. Very, very gradually. Very, very, very gradually. It was sort of like watching a worm crawling across the highway, rooting hard for him to hurry on up because there is an eighteen-wheeler bearing down the road. Where I was really lucky was that I had Terry O'Neill, who believed I could do this job well, Verne Lundquist, who worked with me to get better, and a producer named David Michaels, who lived in a little plastic speaker in my ear. Many people don't realize that broadcasters are connected to the production truck by an earpiece and are constantly getting information from people in the truck. At first the earpiece is a little disconcerting. When Brent Musburger was hosting the CBS studio show, he did a live hookup with Ronald Reagan from the Oval Office of the White House. They put an earpiece, it's called an IFB, on Reagan to enable him to talk to the director, Duke Struck. Reagan had once been a sports broadcaster, but back then they had used only the most basic technology, a microphone and a pair of binoculars. While they were preparing, Struck said, "Mr. President?" and Reagan started looking around the room. He turned around and looked behind him, he looked at the ceiling, he just couldn't figure out who was calling him. "No, Mr. President," Struck explained, "the director is in your ear."

David Michaels was always one sentence ahead of me. As the replay began he'd tell me, "Terry, look at the left guard. Watch what happens here."

To which I told the audience with great confidence, "In this play I want you to look at the left guard. Just watch what he does here . . ."

It did take me a little time to get used to that little voice. I might have been talking about a particular player. "This tackle has really had a rough year," I'd say, "right now he's playing with a broken left ankle . . ."

And as I was saying that David would be reminding me, "And don't forgot that his mother is in the hospital right now with pneumonia."

". . . and he's playing on that left ankle, so we want to send our best wishes to his mother right now."

At first, when I heard the producer telling me what to do, I reacted politely. Mrs. Bradshaw did not raise her son to be rude, so I stopped talking to listen to him. I'd be making an incredible salient point, I'd be getting to the very soul of the game, and in the middle of a sentence I would stop talking.

A similar thing happens to me on occasion when I'm making a speech. Pretty much I just speak extemporaneously. I know the areas I intend to cover, I know the themes I'm going to highlight, I know the points I'm going to make, and I know the stories I'm going to use to make them. I just don't know how they're all going to fit together that very night. Often that comes as a delightful surprise to me. I just open my mouth and let it roll on out. But sometimes when I'm speaking, my brain reminds me, Bradshaw, now pay attention to me, boy, don't you forget to go back to point one.

And I start thinking, Okay, yes sir, go back to point one, go ahead.

And my brain, the same brain who started all this trouble, suddenly asks, Uh, what was that point one again?

That's what would happen to me in the booth, until I learned the trick of talking and listening at the same time. What surprised me most about broadcasting was how much preparation it took to make it seem as if there had been no preparation. It was hard to make it look easy. As I admitted, I hadn't really appreciated that talking football is a job. It's a good job, it's definitely better than working the pipeline or shoveling behind the outhouse, but it is a job. And like throwing the football, the more I worked at it, the better I got at it.

It definitely took some time, and I made a lot of mistakes. Sometimes I got so excited I said the wrong thing. Once, I remember, Verne and I were doing a Cardinals game, and quarterback Neil Lomax was moving his team down the field by throwing simple, short hook passes. He completed three, four, five, six in a row. "Verne," I said, "the way he's going it's just like pissing and catching."

Verne ignored me completely, until we broke for a commercial. Then he could barely contain his laughter, "Pissing and catching?" he said.

Pissing and catching? Then I got it. "Is that what I said?" That was what I said. "Oh my, I meant pitching and catching. Pitch-ing and catching."

During another game while the cameras focused on the Swashbucklers, Tampa Bay's cheerleaders, I casually mentioned how attractive they were, then added that I had never dated anybody but "real dogs."

Now folks, that was intended to be a joke. It was a joke when I said it, it was a joke when I wrote it. I know it's a joke, and if anyone does not, I cannot be responsible for their lack of a sense of humor. My goodness, that would be a terrible thing to say. Obviously not every woman I ever dated was a dog.

That's a joke! I mean, look at me. Who am I to be criticizing anyone else's appearance? I'm the guy that when people tell me I have to face facts, I tell 'em, Not with this face.

But as soon as I said that, I knew I was going to receive some pretty angry letters. So I told reporters after the game, "I'm glad I've had so few dates. 'Cause I'd really hear from a lot of women if I had had more."

I continually got players' names wrong. At times even when I knew a player's name, I would mispronounce it. I rooted for players with easy names; man, I used to have nightmares about those little kickers from Eastern Europe who were so poor that they'd sold the vowels in their names. I never saw so many *j*'s and *g*'s in one name in my life. Why didn't they bring in kickers from places like Ireland, I wondered, O'Brien, that I could pronounce? When they started drafting these huge linemen from Hawaii, I had no chance. When I tried to pronounce their names, I got letters from my old teammates congratulating me on finally learning how to speak in tongues. Sometimes it got so bad I'd even make up names or use my friends' names. Nobody ever noticed.

Initially I got what I would consider mixed reviews. One week I didn't even know there was such a thing as a TV sports critic, the next week I was really concerned about what they were writing. While none of these journalists raved about my work, none of them suggested people should sell their television sets and flee the country either. The worst review I ever got was actually delivered while I was on the air, just about the time I was beginning to feel comfortable in the booth. For example, I'd learned that while doing a replay, "Boy, look at that, willya," is not considered adequate commentary. And I found myself really getting into the games, really getting excited. When I knew the inside reasons a play succeeded or failed, I couldn't wait to tell the audience. This one afternoon

I was really doing a good job, I was into that game, and suddenly there was a knock on the door to the booth and a messenger handed a mail-o-gram to the security guard. The guard handed it to Verne who handed it to me. I opened it up, and it was from a fan, and I can quote it exactly. "Shut the $%$##%! up," it read.

I took a moment to analyze the deeper meaning of that note. Basically, I decided, it meant I should shut the $%$##%! up. As this was the voice of the fan watching at home, I did exactly that. For the last few minutes of the game I barely said a word.

Almost immediately Verne noticed something was wrong, much the same way you notice the eerie quiet when a car alarm that has been blaring for forty minutes suddenly goes silent. At the first break he asked me, "What's the matter? What's wrong?" I showed him the note, and he started laughing again. I'd learned years earlier to ignore the criticism of my play on the field; now I had to learn how to ignore it off the field. Eventually I began to put the whole thing in perspective. There are 300 million people in this country and, at most, I had 10 million of them watching. That means there were 290 million people doing something else, saying that they had more important things to do with their lives. I figured at least a million of them were washing dirty dishes rather than watching my game. The realization that I was competing with dirty dishes was kind of humbling, and a good dose of reality.

At one point I decided if I was going to be serious about a broadcasting career I should have a real agent, so I invited this big-time TV agent down to Shreveport, Louisiana, to discuss my future. He flew all the way down from New York City, we met for a big dinner, and we finally got around to talking about my career. I asked him if he could help me get to the next level.

No.

No?

No. As he explained, my career was riding the down escalator. My elevator was going to the basement. I was mining coal. He'd heard my work. His suggestion was that I find a real job. Ever think about a career in the cosmetics business? he asked. He had absolutely no interest in representing me.

It was only after I realized that the quality of my broadcast really mattered to just two people—me and the man who finally agreed to represent me, Mr. David Gershenson—that I began to relax and have fun.

The network made my apprenticeship as easy as possible for me. When my first season began, Verne and I were assigned the Tampa Bay Buccaneers opener. I didn't mind that at all—that game was broadcast regionally, and because the Bucs weren't doing well we probably only had less than a million viewers. It gave me a chance to break in my game slowly. The second week I checked my schedule, and—what a coincidence—Tampa Bay again. The third week, I must have been attracting some viewers—Tampa Bay again. The fourth week . . . the fifth week . . . The fifth week we finally got our big break, the New Orleans Saints game. The network decided people in the Deep South would understand me.

Maybe it wasn't quite that extreme, but it did

seem to me that CBS was trying to hide me. As the network's newest broadcasting team we were assigned to the . . . smaller markets. Basically a Sam's Warehouse and a bunch of 7-Elevens. Let me put it a little more diplomatically: if the CBS television network was depending on people seeing my broadcasts to stay in business, they would have been better off selling frozen chickens off the back of a truck. When a CBS representative was asked about that, he pointed out, "Madden didn't go on the number-one team until he worked here a couple of years," and explained that I wouldn't be heard in the larger broadcast markets like New York, Los Angeles, Chicago, Boston, Washington . . . About a week later he was still listing places I wouldn't be heard. CBS had made a big investment in me as a broadcaster; and to protect that investment they were making certain that nobody heard me broadcasting.

But given the opportunity in private to develop, Verne and I developed a rapport. Verne could have treated me very differently. He was a professional who had worked his way practically to the top of his profession; I was an athlete handed the job with little experience or preparation. I got most of the attention, most of the publicity. Some veteran broadcasters might have resented that, but Verne was as supportive as it was possible to be. He taught me, he encouraged me, he knew I was struggling and he was patient with me, and when I needed a friend he hugged on me. He made it possible for me to be Terry Bradshaw.

When necessary he played the straight man. During the Saints–49ers game we had a shot of Joe Montana talking on the telephone, and I suggested that perhaps he was speaking with his stockbroker. We got onto the subject of salaries, particularly players who were earning millions and still wanted more. "I don't understand that," I said. "I was happy to play for $17,500 my last season."

Verne recognized a cue when it hit him head-on. "You played for $17,500?" he asked.

"That's right, Verne, $17,500 . . . per quarter."

And when necessary he played the bent-over man. This is how a roll of toilet paper contributed to my success: normally a television broadcasting team is paid to be heard and not seen. The job is to present the game in an entertaining manner, not become the focal point. Well, I had never sat down through an entire game in my life, and I had a difficult time just sitting in my seat. And sometimes when I had some information or analysis I wanted to share with my audience, I got so excited I couldn't sit down. One time, I remember, we were doing a 49ers game and Joe Montana fumbled the snap, killing a long drive. I knew that the 49er fans were furious. Sure, the man won four Super Bowls, but he fumbled the snap, for darn sake. The snap is the simplest play in football, how in the world can you mess up a snap? Well, I knew the answer, and I couldn't wait to explain it. It was my high-butted center story.

Explaining the reason for the fumble wouldn't make nearly as much sense to viewers as demonstrating it. But to do that I needed a football, and I didn't have a football. So I went to the men's room and got myself a roll of toilet paper. I used the roll of toilet paper as my football. Now please, ladies and gentlemen, do not try this at home. "Oh Vernnnne," I said politely, handing him the roll of toilet paper, "would you bend down please?

"There are two kinds of great center butts . . . Now Verne, bend down there real low." I shook my head with disdain. "Now this is not a good butt." Sorry, Verne. "You've got a low butt here. It makes it tough for someone as big and tall as Montana to get in there and take the ball. Now raise up there a bit." While Verne played the butt of the illustration, I played Joe Montana. "Look at this butt. See how high it is. Now look and see how tall Montana can stand under the sun." My point was made.

CBS's number-one greatest announcing team in the universe was John Madden and Pat Summerall. They were number one, everybody else was tied for a distant number two. One of the gimmicks that had helped John Madden gain the recognition he deserved was the Telestrator, sort of a high-tech electronic blackboard that allowed him to draw diagrams right on the screen. So John could draw arrows as he explained, "Now you got this guy going over here, but this guy way over here can't get there, so . . ." We were only one of several number twos, we didn't get a Telestrator—so I asked for a real blackboard. I figured they could afford that. A blackboard? Nobody used blackboards. It was so . . . no-tech.

Which made it perfect for me. We put "Terry's blackboard" in the booth, and I'd draw up my plays and explain to viewers exactly what was going on down on the field, then they would show a replay. It worked extremely well, and we never once had to re-place the batteries in my chalk.

What surprised me most when I became a broad-caster was how much preparation was required to do the job. Verne and I would do as many as eight inter-views before a game. We'd meet with coaches and co-ordinators and players. Generally they would be pretty candid with us. I'd look at a team's stat sheets and no-tice that a veteran receiver just wasn't catching a lot of passes, so I might ask the coach, "You're not throwing a lot over here, Coach, there a reason for that?"

"Damn right," I've had more than one coach tell me, "the sucker can't get open. But don't use that."

I would never use that quote, but I would use that information if the situation demanded it. If that player dropped a pass during the game, I'd say, "The reason they haven't been throwing to him is that he's having difficulty getting open. But it might also be because he's having trouble holding on to the ball. That's why you're probably going to see number 83, Biondo, the rookie out of Villanova, playing more in the second half."

We weren't as interested in the X's and O's as much as helpful bits of inside information. We wanted to add insight to our telecasts. For example, Giants quarterback Phil Simms explained to me that when the wind was blowing in Giants Stadium, to maintain con-trol he had to hold the ball differently. And I broke the big news about Tampa Bay quarterback Vinny Tes-taverde being colorblind.

Hey, in football that constituted big news. Of course, I didn't even know it was news; Testaverde mentioned it casually during our pregame interview, and I happened to mention it casually during the broadcast. I didn't make a big deal out of it—I didn't say, Boy, that was some great pass for a colorblind quarterback, or It's a great tribute to the fortitude of Vinny Testaverde that he has managed to overcome the handicap of colorblindness to become so successful. But the local press immediately picked it up. I told them, "I wasn't trying to dig up something controversial." Controversial? Revealing that he was colorblind?

Testaverde told reporters that to compensate for this problem he had requested that Tampa Bay wear white jerseys at home because they would be easier for him to pick up in the bright sun.

I agreed, explaining, "On a bright day, I would much rather throw against dark-colored uniforms than to dark-colored uniforms." Of course, I was only nearsighted, not colorblind, so maybe what I really would have needed was bigger uniforms.

Initially, if I had an interesting piece of information I would try to find a place to use it rather than waiting for the proper situation to occur. I had to learn to work within the game, rather than broadcasting over it.

The one thing I promised myself when I accepted the job was that I would be honest with the fans. I was determined to tell it like it is allowed to be told by the network lawyers. In one of the first games we worked, Verne asked me why a particular player was struggling. He wondered if it might be that he didn't really fit into the offensive system, or if the blocking for him was poor . . . I stopped him and said flatly, "Verne, that guy really isn't any good."

Well, that certainly answered that question. I think it was that outspoken honesty that caused Terry O'Neill to stick with me when the critics began ganging up.

It took me a while to learn my strengths and weaknesses as a broadcaster. As it turned out, my strengths and weaknesses turned out to be the same thing: me. Initially I was trying too hard to be natural—to be me, multiplied. Just as on the football field, I figured if I kept throwing, I'd complete a few; I just kept throwing out lines, hoping that a few of them would connect. Viewers seemed to enjoy my broadcasting style, but I think that sometimes it got to be a bit too much. It was a little too down-home, even though I was mostly talking to the people down home. And when I did a game seen up North, a lot of people had no idea what I was talking about. Martha, what did that young man say? Something about farm animals, dear. Perhaps you should consider changing the channel?

I had to low-key my approach, figure out what irritated viewers and stop doing it. On occasion I got real silly, and there were a lot of fans who didn't appreciate it. I knew I had to be myself, but at times that proved to be a bit scary. I spent several seasons searching for the same elusive balance I've spent my whole life trying to find.

There were some bumps on the old county road. For a while the critics thought that CBS stood for Can Bradshaw Survive? I would not have without the support of Terry O'Neill, and after him, Ted Shaker. O'Neill made me his project. He paid no attention to the critics. He was a Pittsburgh boy, and he did everything possible to make sure that I made it. Of course, two years after hiring me he left for NBC.

Ted Shaker was very honest with me. He told me straight ahead what I had to do if I wanted to be successful in this world. And I did want to be successful, so I listened. I changed.

Well, I didn't change every little thing. After I had worked with Verne for two seasons, the network teamed me with Tim Ryan and began assigning me to games played north of Louisiana. Adjusting to Tim Ryan was difficult for me because his style was so different from Verne's. Verne would describe the play and then quiet down. That silence made me nervous, and I filled it up. Some people thought I was rambling, but on many occasions I actually did speak about football. Tim was different. He was from up North, way up North—he was from Canada. Since it was always too hot in Louisiana, we spoke slooooow and easy so as not to get tired; being from Canada, Tim spokefasttokeepwarm. There were no silences, and I had to learn to pick my speaking spots.

During a Washington–Green Bay game, for example, I said so little that after the game my friends called up, worried that I was sick. They hadn't seen me so quiet since Mom lost the Monster Truck finals.

Tim Ryan was tougher on me than Verne had been. Eventually I completely cut out my Huck Finn good-old-southern-boy routine and began looking at the game from a gambler's point of view; what would I want to know about this game from a gambler's point of view: what would I want to know about this game if I had my last $100 riding on it?

I also worked with Dick Stockton and finally was teamed again with good old Verne. I'll never forget Verne's reaction when he was asked by Ted Shaker to work with me again: Does anyone have Dr. Kevorkian's phone number?

Actually, Verne and I got along so well that when I was inducted into the Football Hall of Fame I asked him to be my presenter. I was criticized for not inviting someone from the Steelers, but the man I most respected from Pittsburgh, Art Rooney, had died, and I wasn't really in contact with my old teammates. I felt Verne deserved some sort of award for pulling me through, and I was proud to invite him to my induction ceremony.

I learned from each of the people I worked with. And I could see that I was improving every season. By the end of my fifth year I was finally comfortable behind the microphone.

So, naturally, I made myself *un*comfortable.

SIX

After my fourth season as a broadcaster *Sports Illustrated* wrote, "Bradshaw . . . has put away his cowboy
hats and stopped forcing his down home humor. . . .
His twang can be grating, but he's honest and enthusiastic and dispenses well-reasoned criticism. It has taken
him four years to come into his own as an analyst."
Verne Lundquist was graded a B, and I received a B-
minus. I wasn't upset about that—it was a whole lot
better than I ever did at Tech, and John Madden only
got an A-minus.

Naturally, now that I was getting comfortable, I
was beginning to feel uncomfortable. Ol' Verne and I
were pretty much established as the number-one CBS
broadcasting team among all the number twos. The
only team ahead of us was Pat Summerall and John
Madden, which is like saying the only thing standing
between me and the top of Mount Everest is the biggest
mountain in the whole entire world. At CBS there was
really only one analyst, John Madden. The rest of us

were just moppin' up. I'd done my time shoveling behind the outhouse, so for me moppin' up was a promotion. The problem was, I was stuck there. Admittedly I
was probably a little bit jealous of John's career and the
attention he received. I didn't begrudge him his success
at all—I love John Madden, and he had earned his position. He created the role of the knowledgeable, humorous, enthusiastic analyst. He was the original, but I
was a competitor, and I was stuck in a situation where I
wasn't allowed to compete. It was like being at a wedding where the bride refuses to throw the bouquet. I
don't like being second at anything. It was definitely
rankling me.

Once again, it was the Super Bowl that changed
everything for me. In 1990 I was in New Orleans for
Super Bowl . . . let's see, that's X plus X, take away the I
because it's in front of the V . . . XXIV, Super Bowl 24.
Joe Montana's San Francisco 49ers were playing John
Elway's Denver Broncos. I was doing a promotion for
Budweiser Beer's Bud Bowl. Imagine that: two decades
earlier I had refused to attend Baylor University because
I saw an old teammate drinking beer and now I was
doing commercials for Anheuser-Busch. It's amazing
how much that company had changed.

At this press conference I was asked to compare
Montana and Elway. To me, at that time in their careers, there was no comparison. "Get serious," I
began. "What's John Elway ever won? Look at this year,
John didn't have a great season. He had one great game.
One game doesn't cut it with me. I mean, John Elway's
very good, but he's not great. He's inconsistent."

I suppose if I would have stopped there, it might

have been okay. But I was just getting started. I continued, "And if he wins this Super Bowl? So what? Good for him. That's one Super Bowl. Jim McMahon won a Super Bowl. Is *he* great? Would you call *him* great?"

Had I even stopped there, my comments wouldn't have created such a controversy. Maybe Elway wouldn't have spoken to me for only two years instead of four. But did I stop there? I did not stop there. "I think things bother John a lot more than they bother Joe. You hear all these things that John was upset about, the fans suffocating him, the press suffocating him—hey, you make $2 million a year, you'd better expect some attention, boy! Wait'll you have to go out there and get a real job."

Did I mention that I had a real job once?

I was on a roll and not about to stop, "You know what John's problem is: he's been babied all his life. He was babied by his city until this year, and he's been babied by his coaches at least a little bit. I think John Elway needs to get tougher emotionally."

Finished with Elway, I dared to predict the outcome of the Super Bowl: "The game, as I see it, is a total mismatch, no contest." You do understand that the purpose of this press conference was to hype the game to the public. But I was being honest. "I don't see any way in the world the 49ers won't win this football game.

"Now, I know everybody, including the people I work for, would like me to use all sorts of 'ifs and buts' when I say something like this, but why should a man not say what he really thinks? And I think anybody who thinks Denver has a chance is probably not being very realistic . . . If [the 49ers] play the way I think they'll play, this sucker could be as bad as 55–3, believe me."

I said quite a bit more, but those were the highlights. Afterward I went on back home, not aware that my comments were making headlines. When reporters quoted my remarks to Elway, he responded, "He's been bashing me since I got in the league. He didn't like the money I made then, and he still doesn't like the money I make. He can stick it in his ear."

Broncos head coach Dan Reeves was also upset. After he found out I was at a Budweiser press party, he said, "That was a good place for him to have said that. He must have had a lot of Budweisers in him when he said it. . . . Those TV commentators, they're not as smart as they're given credit for."

Now that last remark was simply untrue. As far as I could determine, there was nobody out there giving me credit for being smart! I really was surprised that my remarks created such a stir. Usually I know when I've said something I shouldn't have said—the gasps from network executives give it away—or something that is going to make the papers. But in this instance it never occurred to me that anything was wrong.

It did occur to me when I read Elway's response that maybe he wasn't completely wrong. Maybe I was a little jealous. He had done something I hadn't had the guts to do: originally he had been drafted by Baltimore, and he had decided he wouldn't play there. He refused to report to the Colts and ended up in Denver. Part of me cheered him for that, wondering why he should be forced to play where he didn't want to play. But the smarter part of me responded, Hey, I had to go and play in Pittsburgh my whole career, and I sure didn't want to do that. Those were the rules, and I played by them.

I did try to contact Elway to speak with him. Not to apologize—I said what I believed—but rather to explain that this was my professional opinion, there was nothing personal about it. But John wouldn't talk to me. He just thought I hated his guts, which was not true at all.

Admittedly, I was wrong in my prediction that the 49ers would win 55–3. They won 55–10.

My remarks and the resulting controversy were the turning point in my career. After that I got the reputation that if you wanted to know the truth, call Bradshaw. He'll give it to you. He won't be able to stop himself from giving it to you.

After one more season in the booth I decided I had been there long enough. I did something I'd never done before in my life. I quit. Bye-bye. Adios. I called Ted Shaker and told him that I appreciated everything CBS had done, blah, blah, blah, blah, blah.

"Blah?" Shaker replied. He didn't believe I was serious. "You're just tired," he said. Tired? Of sitting in a booth saying, That was a great play, Verne. He asked me to wait a few months before making a final decision.

On April 1 David Gershenson called and told me. CBS had just fired Brent Musburger, the anchor of the Sunday-afternoon pregame show *The NFL Today.* I didn't believe him. I assumed this was an April Fools joke. You'd be perfect for that show, Gershenson insisted.

When I pointed out that I was the complete opposite of the smooth, serious Musburger, he said, "They're going to clean house. When the big engine goes, all of the little cabooses follow."

Cabooses? Engine? I thought we were talking pregame show here. But Gershenson was absolutely right. CBS eventually offered me the job as cohost with Greg Gumbel of the *The NFL Today*. I don't think I'll ever forget Shaker's words, "a four-year contract at double your present salary."

I was really excited about appearing regularly on the studio show, even if I had absolutely no idea what I was going to do on it. At the first of the many lunches and dinners we were to share, I asked Greg Gumbel, "What is it exactly that we're going to do?"

"We're going to work together," Greg told me, then said emphatically, "and we're going to have fun."

"Okay, but what if they tell us to vamp?" Vamp is an inside television word that means make up something to fill time.

"Then we'll vamp," Greg said.

I liked him immediately. Sometimes he made as little sense as I did, but he sure sounded smart doing it. "Well, what'll we talk about?"

"Football," he said flatly. He was decisive too.

I wondered, "Well, what if I don't know what I'm talking about?"

"Look, number one, you won four Super Bowls. Who the hell is going to argue with you? Number two, if you start off everything with, 'Here's what I think,' then nobody can argue with you. And third, I don't think you're ever wrong."

I could see we were going to get along extremely well.

The object of the studio show is to weave together all of the games being played that day. It's a conglomeration of previews, updates, features, news reports, commentary, some discussion, and maybe a little inside football. Brent Musburger had anchored the CBS show for a decade and had been really successful. CBS's studio show had been on the air for twenty-eight years. It had been the number-one program in its time slot for the last fourteen years, longer than any other program on TV. When I was hired to do the show, CBS made it clear they wanted me to do anything I wanted to do. First they would tell me exactly what I wanted to do, then I would do it.

I wanted to be free. Management wanted to restrain me. I was continually getting notes telling me to tone down a little. I just wanted to have fun, to make viewers feel good. I kept reminding management that it was only a game; management reminded me that it was a very profitable television program. Once, I remember, we were showing viewers the protective covering that fits over the top of the helmet and is held in place by Velcro. So I took this shell top and put it on my head. I looked ridiculous; I looked like a Chinese coolie from a bad B movie. Everybody in the studio was laughing. But as soon as we went to a commercial, the red phone on my desk started ringing. Oh, Terry, we don't think that was a good idea, so please take it off your head.

After the first season Ted Shaker left the show, and we stayed. I always felt that was sort of like the mouse running over the cat, but the situation never really changed. The network continued to insist that we include at least some football on the show.

I have to admit, though, that before the first show I was nervous. There had been a tremendous amount of publicity about the fact that Greg and I were hosting it. Brent Musburger had a lot of fans who might not take kindly to him being replaced. I was being billed as "unpredictable," and funny. With Bradshaw, an executive told reporters, expect the unexpected. So there was a lot of pressure on me. What if I *don't* make a fool of myself, I wondered? Would viewers be disappointed?

I was ready to do the show. I kept reminding myself to forget all about being nervous. And then, about three minutes before we went on the air, I got hammered by a heavy boom microphone. It smacked me right upside the head and nearly knocked me out. It really hurt. I got dizzy, sick to my stomach, there was a ringing in my ears, and the whole side of my head was sore.

I had never realized that being a studio analyst was such a tough job. I felt like I was right back in the game. But in some strange way, that hit in the head relaxed me. Being in the studio was brand-new to me, but I could relate to a pain in my head. During my playing career there had been many games when I had to play hurt, but as a reporter wrote, this was the first time I had to talk hurt. "If it had happened to Greg or reporter Lesley Visser," producer Eric Mann said, "I would have been worried. Fortunately, it happened to Terry. He's used to getting hit."

Fortunately? Fortunately? Eventually, I got even with everybody. Gumbel first. We developed a couple of rituals, things we did for good luck. Before each game, for example, we'd do this jive handshake; sort of a grasp, wrap, twist, tap, turn, pull ceremony that ended with us snapping our fingers and pointing to each other. The same kind of thing I'm sure Tom Brokaw does each night before his newscast. Also, at the end of the morning production meeting Eric Mann would ask, "Is that it?" We'd reply it was, get up off the couch, and high-five each other. Bam! Smack those hands! Go! We're gonna do it! Let's make magic! Give 'em a great show!

Except one Sunday morning we stood up and I went to slap his hand—and missed. Smacked him right in the eye. His eye swelled up like a balloon and began turning interesting colors. Eric Mann was stunned. He could see the headlines: "Gumbel and Bradshaw Brawl before Show!" "Ice!" he screamed. "Get ice!" Greg walked around the studio for the next two hours and fifteen minutes with an ice bag covering his eye. The swelling actually went down, then they just covered his eye with makeup.

I really felt bad for Greg. How was he going to explain to people what had happened? We missed a high-five?

Naturally I couldn't let it end right there. After finishing the half-hour pregame show, we stayed around the studio the rest of the day to do a halftime report and give updates on other games being played. While we were waiting to do the halftime segment, I sort of moseyed on out of the studio. About ten minutes later I came back in a wheelchair, my head almost completely wrapped in gauze, screaming in pain,

"Ooohhhh, ohhhhhh, Greg hit me back! Greg hit me back!"

Or course that was almost nothing compared to the unfortunate barbecue incident. Well, unfortunate for everybody working on the show, I mean—except me. I will tell you flatly that the best barbecued ribs in the whole entire world, and I do mean the whoooooole world, come from the great State of Texas. There is none better. Amen to that, Brother. And on occasion, as my way of telling the people with whom I worked how much I appreciated every single thing they did to make me the suave, sophisticated commentator that I appeared to be, I would host a barbecue in the studio.

During our second season, I believe it was, I had 175 pounds of those fine Texas ribs shipped in dry ice to the studio kitchen. The plan was that workers in the kitchen would heat them up while we were on the air, and when the pregame show ended, we'd eat them. The problem was that when the ribs arrived, no one unpacked them, so some of the meat on top thawed and spoiled. When all the meat was cooked the next day, the delicious Texas ribs were mixed up with the bad meat.

But as this was a television crew and the meal was free, it went real fast. Television crews are generally not known for their good taste. Basically, they will eat anything: So how'd you like that box lunch? Oh, best cardboard I ever ate. You gonna eat that little box?

The show was based in New York City, and this was the first time I'd spent a lot of time there. I'd heard the restaurants were among the best in the world, but these people didn't even notice that some of the meat they were eating was rotten. I took a bite or two of the spoiled meat and immediately threw it out. I felt fine.

The first hint we had that something was wrong came from Eric Mann. "I never saw anything like this," he said. "Everybody's getting sick. Two people went home, and I've got two technicians lying on the floor in the hallway."

Hmm, I wondered, what could that be? Right about then I looked at Greg as reality began dawning on him. Well, I call it reality, but it was really nature. All of a sudden his eyes opened wide and he was . . . *fffftttttthhh* . . . out of his chair and gone.

That was about the time people started dropping fast. I was just sitting there, watching them whizzing by me on their way to the rest room. I'll say this for Greg, the man had staying power. He kept coming back to the set, then turning around and going back to the rest room.

The men's room looked like an emergency ward. We ran out of toilet paper real fast. Lines of people were waiting to get in there. We lost half our research department early. But these people were professionals. When we had to go on the air, everybody was in position and did their job. At least for a little while. My buddy Greg finally had to leave the premises, and I had to finish the show myself. I never said a word about it. Exactly how would I explain what happened to a national television audience? As for everybody else, the second, the half-second, we went off the air you could have gotten windburn just standing there as people ran past. The amazing thing was that the audience never knew anything was wrong, except for the fact that Greg Gumbel seemed to disappear.

Later he asked me why I hadn't gotten sick. I told him, "I got a plate, and when I ate into bad meat, I thought, this is bad meat, and I threw it away. When I got to the good meat, I ate it."

He said, "Well, obviously we didn't know the difference."

I remembered the scene. It was sort of like *MASH* comes to *NFL Today*. "Obviously," I agreed.

After that those people were always very nice to me. They definitely were more careful with that boom mike. From the very first week the show proved successful. The fact that CBS carried NFC games, which were much more popular than NBC's AFC games, contributed to our success in the ratings. But we were also a critical success. Just as John Madden and Pat Summerall changed the way football games were broadcast, I believe we changed the structure of studio shows. Cris Collinsworth has said that when he joined J.B., Howie, and myself at Fox, "We were actually still doing a glimmer of football." Maybe, but that was a few years ago, and we pretty much eliminated that. The real change in the nature of the studio show began at CBS.

The NFL Today was only a half-hour program, which presented a problem to me. I was never real good about hurrying up. I don't walk fast, I don't talk fast, it takes me two minutes to cook a one-minute egg. The most difficult thing for me to do on a football field was run the two-minute drill. I need to have options; I loved first down because I had all the options available to me. A half-hour program didn't give me any options. There was no time to really talk football. If there were three possible reasons a play failed, for example, I only had time to discuss one of them. People were probably saying, That Bradshaw, no wonder he didn't win that fifth Super Bowl, the man doesn't understand the game. I had to try to squeeze 1 percent of my football knowledge into eight seconds. It just couldn't be done.

It was impossible to do a real inside football show, including previews, features, updates, and highlights, in a half hour. Initially the producers wanted to do a scripted show, but I couldn't do that. I wanted to have fun, to say whatever came into my head. So instead of a script I wrote down a few points I might want to make and then pretty much ignored what I had written down. I never read from the TelePrompTer. To me, football was supposed to be fun. Football is only a game. That was the attitude I brought with me into the studio. If CBS had wanted a real serious Mr. Football Guy in the studio, they would not have hired me. The only thing I could bring into the studio that nobody else could bring was my personality. As a future ex-wife once admitted, "I get very nervous when I watch him on TV, because he is so much himself."

I don't know exactly when it was that we became an entertainment program disguised as a football studio show, but that's what we were. We weren't quite doing *The Three Stooges Go to Church,* but we did try to have a lot of fun in a setting that up until then had been treated very seriously. Typical of the features we did was a piece in which I played Young Bradshawstein, a mad scientist who created the perfect quarterback. Notice you never heard of Young Musbergerstein! Interspersed with clips from Mel Brooks's *Young Frankenstein,* my quartercreature consisted of the body of Troy Aikman, the legs of Randall Cunningham, Dan Marino's wrist, John Elway's arm, the eyes of Bernie Kosar, the heart of Phil Simms, the daredevil nature of Jim Kelly, and the mind of Joe Montana. The only thing we forgot was the perfect quarterback's salary demands.

Commenting on my thespian abilities, Greg Gumbel looked directly into the camera and admitted, "For me, it's like working with Olivier."

CBS encouraged me to be honest. But I'm not sure they expected me to be quite as honest as I was. I doubt, for example, that the network really expected me to state on its football pregame television show that there are too many football games on television and that the game is boring. In my mind, as I said that, I could almost see the president of the network watching our show and saying, This is great, this is honesty, this is truth, this is . . . what did he say? Bradshaw really didn't just say what I thought he said. Boring? Did he say boring?

As much as I loved football, I didn't like the way it had been changed to satisfy television's belief that viewers wanted higher-scoring games. The game was built on high scoring. The excitement of the game was built through brute force. The American public loved the big hit. Many people claim that it's cruel and dangerous—and that's why they watch it every week. That's what made players like Dick Butkus and Jack Lambert so popular. So on the show I created the BFL, the Bradshaw Fun League.

In the BFL we would not allow team meetings, we would have a two-point conversion after every touchdown, in the final two minutes of the game the clock would stop after every play, field goals made from inside the twenty would count for only 1 point, between the twenty and thirty 2 points, and 3 points for everything beyond that—but if the defense blocked a field goal attempt, it would get 1 point—officials would be paid $200,000 a year, but if an official inadvertently blew his whistle, we'd take it away from him. There's more: BFL coaches would have to sit in the stands during games, and each team would have to bring in college bands and cheerleaders. Each player would be able to pick the music he wanted the band to play when he scored. Just imagine the beautiful *Barry Sanders Symphony* or the thrilling *Franco's Theme*. There would be no penalty for roughing the passer, and quarterbacks would have to call their own plays—did I happen to mention that I called my own plays?—on first and second down. Zone defense would be prohibited, the bump-and-run would be allowed, the ground could cause a fumble. In case of offsetting penalties, the most severe penalty would count. In the BFL we'd have limited substitutions; players would have to stay on the field for four downs or until possession of the ball changed. End-zone celebrations would definitely be encouraged—if the defense is offended by them, the defense should do a better job stopping them—although a line would have to be drawn between jubilation and taunting. I love special teams, so all kickoffs would have to be returned. And there would be absolutely no instant replay. Instant replay would be dead and buried, and we'll give all the instant replay machines to third world countries—

. . . Boring? Bradshaw said boring? We pay half a billion dollars for rights to the games, and he says it's boring. . . .

Whether they wanted it or not, CBS had Bradshawstein. While we had fun with aspects of the game, we never made fun of it, and never made fun of the players. Well, there was one exception—it was my fault, and I apologized for it.

We had some tape of Eagles great Jerome Brown lumbering down the sideline trying to catch a ball carrier. Jerome was a big man and I thought he looked pretty funny clumping on down the field with all the grace of a truck. I said so, and I embarrassed him. As my luck would have it, the next week I was in Philadelphia. When I walked my ass out on the Eagles practice field, those people were all over me worse than negligence lawyers on a train wreck. I didn't want to be there, but I had to do it. Jerome was really angry—and he should have been angry. Maybe I was wrong, I was getting personal, and I apologized to him for my remarks and we went on about our business. That wasn't an easy thing to do, I didn't like doing it, but I did it.

If a player made a mistake and I pointed it out, all I was doing was telling the truth. When I stated an opinion like, That boy has no heart, he shows no character, I was going too far. How could I know what was in his heart? How much could I know about his character from a few plays? I couldn't—but unfortunately that didn't always stop me.

I'm a very emotional person; I'll cry if the bus is late in the morning. And admittedly, on occasion, once in a while, from time to time, there have been a very few occasions when I've allowed my emotions to overcome my good sense. During a Falcons–49ers game, for example, Deion Sanders made a great play to intercept a pass and had an open field all the way to the end zone. Instead of just running it in with class, he teased and taunted his former Atlanta teammates, doing his high-stepping hey-everybody-look-at-me-aren't-I-wonderful act. All way down the field. I didn't like it at all. The 49ers were blowing out the Falcons, and I thought his actions were cruel and mean-spirited and said so. In fact, what I said was, "I'd love to see a guy pull a hamstring when he's doing something like that."

I had not been a fan of Deion Sanders's act for a long time. A couple of years before this, when someone was raving about him, I said, "He's primarily a return specialist. He's not a good tackler. People who haven't seen him play judge him on his press clippings." But did I really want him to pull a hamstring? Of course I did. At that moment that's exactly what I felt he deserved.

A little while later Sanders pulled a groin muscle and missed the second half of the game. Now, if I did have the ability to make wishes come true, I guarantee you I wouldn't be wasting them on Deion Sanders's groin muscle. The fact that he did get hurt magnified my remarks. I received a lot of criticism for them, and on the air a few weeks later I apologized, explaining, "In this business I do emotionally get caught up in games and things that happen. I react to them spontaneously, and then I go, Uh-oh." I admitted I'd made a mistake, and added that I certainly did not wish harm or injury to any player.

Of course, then I was criticized by some reporters for apologizing.

I never hesitated to criticize players for their play or coaches for their decisions. That was my job. So when head coach Ray Perkins down in Tampa Bay benched Vinny Testaverde, I didn't hesitate to suggest, "Get Perkins out of there and get Testaverde back in." Or when the Cincinnati Bengals started rookie Dave Klingler at quarterback against the Steelers, then prohibited him from changing plays at the line of scrimmage, I pointed out, "That's like sending him to war without any bullets." Klingler was sacked ten times. I liked the Oakland Raiders owner, Al Davis; when I retired, Davis called and told me that if I ever needed anything, all I had to do was call him, but that didn't stop me from describing the Raiders' decision to bench quarterback Jay Schroeder as "stupid" and "gutless."

. . . Please, tell me he really didn't say boring? Daring! Maybe he said "daring"? . . .

There are broadcasters who won't criticize players or coaches because they know eventually they'll have to face them. They might even need them at some point for an interview. But when I became a broadcaster, after seriously considering the ramifications of this problem and its potential to impact upon my career, the conclusion that I reached can best be described as . . . screw 'em. I've been sprayed by a skunk, shot at by a recluse, dragged by a horse, sacked by a Butkus, and beaten centsless by divorce lawyers: do I really care if John Elway is mad at me?

During my playing career I longed for the time when people could ask me a question and I could tell them the complete truth. It always bothered me that I couldn't tell people what I felt, but I couldn't because I knew it would cause problems, it would make some people mad. When I started doing the studio show, I finally got that opportunity. I never mean to offend people, but if I'm going to be honest, people's feelings are going to be hurt. Trust me, it is not easy to stick a microphone in front of a man like former Falcons coach Jerry Glanville and ask, "What's your response to being a phony?"

Doing my job properly requires talking to a lot of people during the week. And I do talk to everybody; players, coaches, team executives, the official turf consultants, parking lot attendants, beer salespeople. I even quoted the coach's wife once; I called Cowboys coach Dave Campo and he wasn't home, but his wife said, "How about our defense? We're playing better than ever. We're going to stuff these guys on Sunday."

I got her permission to quote her, and when we were on the air I said, "I tried to call Dave Campo and couldn't get him, but I got the next best thing, his lovely wife. She told me their defense is playing better than ever and they're going to stuff 'em today. And who knows better than the coach's wife!"

I've always had a great rapport with players. Eventually I even became friendly with Deion. The word has gotten around that Bradshaw isn't out to burn anybody. I don't have interviews as much as conversations.

I've spoken with many players—and coaches—who get so comfortable that they tell me things they later regret. I'm sitting there listening, and I don't believe what I'm hearing. A lot of players tell me about other players who are not performing or coaches who are not doing their job. I imagine that a few hours later they're driving in their cars or sitting at home when suddenly they realize: I told *what* to Bradshaw? I said *who* can't play? I called the coach a *what?*

I've had coaches tell me about star players, "If that son of a bitch doesn't play well in the first half, Terry, I don't give a hoot who he is, he's out of there in the second half. But that's just between us." I had a coach tell me, "Our left guard broke his foot in practice, but we didn't turn it into the league. So don't tell anybody." Once a team executive in Buffalo told me the team had shoes specially made for the turf and asked me to keep it quiet. I've been told that coaches were going to be fired before management told the coach. I know for sure I saved at least one coach's job—which was my intention—by complimenting the job he was doing on the show.

On many occasions I've had players or team media directors call me and ask me not to use certain information or to edit certain comments out of a taped interview. And I do it. I'm not going to let anybody else make a fool of himself on my show—that's my job. I'm not trying to create news or controversy, I'm trying to let viewers see these people close up, to get to know a little more about them. If I ever write a book, I just might include some of that material.

There are players I've just loved interviewing. Dan

Marino was great, Reggie White was awesome, Brett Favre, terrific. But there were also players who have looked me right in the face and lied to me. You lie straight out to me, you are going to get caught—unless, of course, we're married. There is nothing that makes me angrier. Jeff George, for example, Jeff George makes me angry. My experience has been that he is about as honest as pro wrestling. All people talk about is his talent; all he talks about is his talent. But I don't believe Jeff George is a team player. I believe there is a good reason he has played on five teams. There definitely is a flaw there somewhere. When he finally got settled in Minnesota, he said, I don't want to go anywhere. I want to finish my career right here in Minnesota. It's not about the money.

Brothers and sisters, an athlete saying it's not about the money is like a politician saying it's for the good of the people. Say Amen and hold tight to your wallet. I didn't believe Jeff George at all. Now, I had always been very critical of him, especially when he was with the Raiders. When he was with the Raiders, I just wore him out. Quarterbacking in the NFL is more than throwing a football better than anyone else in the league. It's leadership, it's generalship—and the fact that he had moved from Indianapolis to Atlanta to Oakland to Minnesota indicated to me that he lacked those qualities. But when he got to Minnesota, I finally interviewed him. I sat right opposite and quoted several of the negative things I had said about him. A situation like that is never comfortable, but as the saying almost goes, if you're going to talk the talk, you better be able to walk the plank. I remember using words like "selfish," "not a leader," and "overrated."

"I know," he responded, "people told me. Terry, you're entitled to your opinion."

I was surprised. Jeff George turned out to be the nicest person in the world. Could not have been nicer. Said he liked my work too. We had a nice conversation, and when it ended, I thought maybe I was wrong about him. Maybe, like some quarterbacks I knew, it just took him a while to mature.

And then, as soon as he got a good offer he left Minnesota and signed with the Redskins. When I'm wrong, I'm willing to admit it, and I admit that I was completely wrong in thinking I might have been wrong about Jeff George. The man fooled me real good.

Randall Cunningham was another player that I said some less than flattering things about, stating that he was a lot more interested in personal accomplishments than the success of the team. "I listen to him, I watch him, and I come away with the impression that this guy is more impressed with himself than I am. Consequently, he won't speak with me either."

Apparently Cunningham was so upset about my remarks that he complained to a higher authority—his agent. His agent called Greg to tell him that his client didn't much like me—but added that he did like Greg. Naturally my close friend Greg was protective of me. "Oh, thank you very much," he said, "I'll make sure to tell ol' what's-his-name."

Well, maybe not. In the Old West arguments would be settled with six-shooters at high noon. The weapon used most today is the TV microphone. Cunningham agreed to appear on our show. Not wanting to exploit this potentially volatile confrontation, CBS did everything except advertise in skywriting. Cunningham and I sat facing each other with Greg between us.

The fact is that this made for great TV. Until Greg and I began hosting the pregame show, it had been a serious program previewing the games played that day. We were bringing the element of the unexpected to it—danger. Nobody had ever watched the studio show just to see if Brent Musburger would get hit.

During the conversation Cunningham said that some of his teammates thought a remark I'd made the previous season, in which I'd referred to him as a great athlete rather than a quarterback, was racist. In the past coaches had used that excuse as a reason for switching black quarterbacks coming out of college to other positions. But all I meant by it was that Cunningham was a gifted athlete. I'm not smart enough to have those dipsy-double meanings.

The fact that Greg Gumbel is also a black man made it easier for him to interrupt and ask Cunningham if *he* thought that was a racist remark. He didn't think so, he said, he understood that I had a job to do.

I still thought he was a great athlete. And toward the end of his career we actually got pretty friendly.

Eventually I even sat down face-to-face with John Elway. After four years Elway was the only NFL quarterback I hadn't interviewed on the show. And in those four years he had proved himself to be a great player. The fact that the week before I was scheduled to fly to Denver to meet him I selected him as the league's Most Valuable Player so far that season had nothing to do with the interview. And believe me, the fact that the day before I did the interview, I predicted Elway would be elected to the Football Hall of Fame, "perhaps on the first ballot," was not an attempt to mollify him.

I didn't think anybody even remembered what I'd said four years earlier. Four years! Since then we'd elected a new president, fought the Gulf War, East and West Germany had been unified and the Berlin Wall had come down, and the Soviet Union had been dismantled. Who could possibly remember or even care what an old quarterback had said so many years earlier?

That's what I thought too. But while I was driving over to the Broncos headquarters with my video crew, we got lost. When I saw a police officer, I pulled over and asked for directions. The officer looked at me and sort of did a double take. It was a look I knew well. From the show, from the commercials I'd done, from my appearances on Leno and Letterman, I had become very recognizable. I was used to people seeing me and smiling and asking for an autograph, telling me how much they enjoy my work—even if they couldn't exactly figure out what it was I did. And, naturally, I would give it to them. Kind of got to like it a little, meeting the public. So I could tell that this police officer recognized me. "Aren't you Terry Bradshaw?" he asked.

"Yeah," I said sort of shyly, "yeah, I sure am."

The smile disappeared. "Well then, why should I help you after all those horrible things you said about John?"

Well, that's it, I thought, no autograph for him! I rolled up my window and took off. I mean, who did that man think he was to talk to me like that, Chuck Noll?

My interview with Elway was brief and pleasant. When Elway came out, he claimed, "It was fine. I won a ten-round decision."

"We buried the hatchet," I said. "Now, that doesn't mean we're best friends. That doesn't mean we'll play golf together, but I do respect him." And ladies and gentlemen, let me point out that I respected him even before he led the Broncos to back-to-back Super Bowl championships.

Probably the strangest interview Greg and I ever did took place when we served as studio hosts for a Super Bowl. We had a live conversation with astronauts speaking to us from the space shuttle. One of the astronauts was a woman, and she kind of balled herself up, and the men started spinning her. We watched with fascination for a moment, until Greg said in awe, "Wow, that gives a whole new wrinkle to heads or tails, doesn't it?"

Considering all the interviews I've done in almost two decades of broadcasting, about the most surprising thing is that I've never received an angry phone call from a player. Not one. In fact, the only person who called me to complain about something I'd said was Redskins owner Daniel Snyder. I'd revealed that Snyder had told his team not to be concerned about the coaching staff, a pretty strong hint that the coaching staff would be fired after the season. We spent an hour on the phone as he tried to smart-talk me into supporting him. I forgave him for that. He was relatively new to the league, so he didn't know that smart-talking wouldn't work with me. Didn't he know I got a 15 on my college entrance exam?

What made the show work is that we were serious about having fun. Only nine years after I announced my retirement, the Steelers finally got around to officially releasing their rights to me, making me a free agent. I was free to sign with any other football team that wanted me. Of course, the operative clause in that sentence is "that wanted me." I got approximately no calls, give or take none, which cut down drastically on my ability to use those three beautiful words, "big signing bonus." Several coaches expressed a certain degree of interest in signing me. The Lions' Wayne Fontes, for example, told reporters, "Maybe we could get him in here and use him in a trade." After complimenting my ability, the Bears' Mike Ditka said he might consider giving me a tryout—"But first of all, we'd have to get him a hairpiece."

Everyone in sports had heard about "bonus babies"; this was my chance to be football's first "bonus geriatric!" "Boomer" Esiason was still playing; why not "Baby Boomer" Bradshaw? So we decided it would be fun to do a piece about my comeback attempt. And what team would be most appropriate for me to try to hook on with? The team that we had beaten in two Super Bowls, the Dallas Cowboys. I thought the Cowboys would be the perfect team for me: I can't hear very well, so I wouldn't be bothered by their fans booing me; I lived real close, so I could drive in to work; and their quarterbacks, Troy Aikman and Steve Beuerlein, were so young they could come out to my ranch and play with my kids. So the producers contacted the Cowboys and arranged a tryout for me.

As Dallas head coach Jimmy Johnson and quarterback Troy Aikman watched, I began my tryout by running a forty-yard dash. Maybe "dash" is not the most accurate word here. Then I threw passes to the Cowboys' tight end, Alfredo Roberts. Aikman, who was four years old when I had been drafted by the Steelers, was impressed. "He looked as good as he did when he stopped playing," he said—although he didn't mention that I had stopped playing when my arm was so sore I couldn't lift it above my knee—"except that he's lost a few hairs here and there."

I thought I got along real well with Coach Johnson until I reminded him that I had called my own plays for fourteen seasons and expected to keep doing it. I don't think he liked that at all. I suspect he thought I was some sort of troublemaker. Finally he turned me down, telling me the Cowboys still had Roger Staubach on their reserve-inactive list. That actually surprised me; the Steelers had released me only nine years after I'd retired, but the Cowboys still retained the rights to Staubach twelve years after he'd retired. Not that I was being competitive, but I wondered why Staubach was that much more valuable not playing than I was—he didn't even call his own plays!

My tryout, the last breath of my career, made a really nice piece for the show—although it still didn't get me any job offers.

I think viewers enjoyed our show because they never knew what to expect next. Here's a secret: neither did we. The show was very loosely scripted—I use the word loosely, much as I used "dash." Basically, the producers let us follow our instincts.

We probably had as much fun off the air as we

did while live. We often had live guests in the studio, and honestly, there were occasions when we were not as kind to them as we might have been. Basically, every week. Usually before we went on the air, Greg and I would spend time with our guests just talking football. And most of the time they would tell us things in complete confidence—meaning that we would not tell anyone else, and certainly not several million anyone elses. Phil Simms, for example, had broken his foot and couldn't play, so he came into the studio for an interview. While we were talking before the show, he told us that he was having some problems with Giants head coach Bill Parcells and that he had received some feelers about finishing his career with another team. It was nothing monumental, just football gossip.

His on-air interview was very nice: he hoped to return soon, even with him being injured the Giants still had a great shot at the Super Bowl, he hoped blah, blah, blah. When we finished, Simms started to get up, but our producer, Eric Mann, signaled him to stay seated, telling him, "We're having some technical problems in Chicago. Stand by. We're coming back to the studio."

Minutes later our theme music began playing, the cameras swung around, and we were back on the air. Well, at least as far as Phil Simms was concerned, we were back on the air. Everybody else in the studio knew what was going on. Greg did the introductions, "Greg Gumbel back with Terry Bradshaw and Phil Simms. While we get things straightened out with our feed to Chicago, we're going to continue our discussion here."

Then Greg turned to Phil and said pleasantly, "Phil, while we were off the air, you made it sound like you might be ready for a change of scenery."

Phil Simms's head snapped back, and his eyes opened in terror.

"That's right, Phil," I agreed. "You were saying you might want to leave the Giants and go play someplace else?"

Simms couldn't believe what was happening to him. "Oh, no, Terry," he said. "I love New York, I mean, I love playing for the Giants."

"Well, then, you were saying something about Bill Parcells, how y'all didn't get along and you wanted to be traded. What was that all about?"

"No, no, no, that's not true at all." The man was sweating bombs. "I . . . I . . . I love playing for Bill Parcells . . ."

"Well, how about that drug problem on the Giants you were telling us about. How bad is it, really?"

"What? What drug problem? I . . . I mean, I never said anything . . . no, that's not true . . ."

"So then it really isn't true that one of your star players is using cocaine?"

The man's mouth was moving, but the only thing coming out of it were gasping sounds. Finally, neither Greg nor I could talk a straight line. We both started laughing. Simms jumped up and started throwing magazines at us.

We did that same kind of thing to most of our guests. When Matt Millen was sitting there, we came back from our weekly technical difficulties and started asking him about his steroid use. This is one of the biggest, strongest men you'll ever meet. I thought he was going to faint.

I always suspected someone tipped off Bo Jackson before he appeared on the show. When we had our technical difficulty, the first question Greg asked him was, "How does your hip replacement affect you in normal life?"

"No problem," he said, "it's fine."

"Well, then," I asked in my most serious broadcaster voice, "how 'bout with sex? Do you find it affects your movement?"

Bo shook his head, "No, Terry," he responded just as seriously, "I'm still swinging from the chandelier."

Bo knew practical jokes, too.

Man, I laughed at those guys. How could they fall for something so obvious? I knew nothing like that could ever happen to me because I was too . . . sophisticated. Except that a few years later I was substituting for James Brown as host of *NFL Sunday*. Being the host of the show was going to be more difficult for me than for J.B. because I wouldn't have the luxury that he did of throwing it to me! All I had was Howie Long, and I wasn't available to save myself. Generally the opening of the Fox show lasts about seven minutes and requires a lot of moving around from person to person. While the movements are scripted, making it all happen smoothly is tough, and J.B. does an incredible job.

Usually we do it live, but because this was my first time serving as host and I'd have to read from a TelePrompTer, we decided to tape it. It took us three takes to get it right, but the third take was acceptable. I was feeling pretty good about myself; I'd begun to realize all that stuff J.B. had been telling us about him being the glue holding the show together, the oil that makes it run so smoothly, the engine that keeps it going, wasn't quite as true as we'd been led to believe. A Bradshaw could do it.

Then our director Scott Ackerson accidentally switched on the speaker system, and we heard him say, "What do you mean, you didn't get it? How is that possible? Guys, we taped this three times, and you recorded over it! I don't . . . what are you guys thinking in there? I don't know, with Brad doing this . . ."

What? What did he say?

Then Ackerson addressed us in a calm, reassuring voice. "Hey, guys, listen. We've had a little screwup here. We didn't get a tape of that last take. I don't know how to tell you this, but we're going to have to do it live. We've got . . . Lemme see, we've got two minutes thirty-five and counting. Let's do it."

Do it? Do it live! People were running all over the set. Technicians who had left the studio came racing back inside. Headphones went on, mikes were adjusted. "Sound check!" And the whole time I'm thinking, Live? I'm supposed to do this live? That's probably when I started sweating. "One minute, places everyone." Oh, man, the sweat was pouring down my shirt. I was the Hoover Dam of studio show hosts. I never used the Prompter, I could barely see it.

"Ten seconds . . . nine . . . eight . . . seven . . . six . . . five . . . music up . . ." Our theme music came on; I straightened my shoulders, took a deep breath, and looked straight into the camera. And just then Scott Ackerson said, "Gotcha."

Music down, headphones off, the technicians just walked off the set, laughing. I think that was probably the afternoon I figured it was time for another Texas barbecue.

During the four years that Greg Gumbel and I hosted the show, we became close friends. I'd fly into New York Friday night, and we would pretty much spend the weekend together. We had the kind of kidding relationship you just can't write about in books. I wouldn't want anyone to know that Greg would kid me about my intelligence. When I sign an autograph, for example, I take my time. I've never understood the value of an autograph nobody can read: Look everybody, look whose autograph I got. It's either . . . Abe Lincoln or Evel Knievel. So when I started to sign my name, Greg would lean over my shoulder and say slowly, "That's B . . . r . . . a . . ."

And I certainly would never write about the racial humor we shared, because some people might not understand it. Suppose it was revealed that when Greg called me at home, as soon as I heard his voice, I would say politely, "Thank you for calling, but I don't need the north-forty fencing repaired today."

And I do like to leave kind of strange messages on his answering machine, like "Mr. Gum-bel. I'm just calling about that cat you done sold my neighbor. He say about that cat that that cat ain't got but one testicle and he wanted to use him for a breeding cat. That man ain't found that cat's missing testicle yet. He wants all his money back, and he want's him a new cat. That's all I got to say. You'll be hearing from my lawyer soons he get his sorry ass out of law school. 'Bye."

I can't write about that or the shooting at the China Club or . . . well, we did have good times together, and I think that was reflected in the quality of the work we did together. I always said that Greg Gumbel and I would remain close friends forever, or until the show ended, whichever came first.

Me and what's-his-name were really shaken up when CBS lost the TV rights to NFL football. CBS's contract with the NFL expired at the end of the 1993 season. The value of pro football to a network is incalculable—but every few years they have to calculate it. The new Fox network had been trying to buy a slice of the broadcast package for several years, but nobody really took them seriously. CBS had played an important role in making the NFL the most valuable sports programming on TV. CBS carried the NFC games, which included most of the teams from before the merger with the American Football League, and almost always drew more viewers than NBC's AFC games. CBS was John Madden and Pat Summerall, Gumbel and me. CBS and the NFL went together like trains and tracks, like crawfish and butter, like the two inseparable lovers in *Titanic*.

Remember the guy floating in the water at the end of *Titanic?* That was CBS.

We had heard rumors that Fox was going all-out to get NFL football, but most people assumed they were going after the NBC package. I don't think anybody really believed CBS would lose the NFL. That was a relationship that had benefited both parties for more than a quarter century. There was no reason to end it. Personally, I felt that out of loyalty the NFL had an obligation to CBS.

One Friday night in late December I got a call in my hotel room in New York from a radio sports reporter in Alabama asking me how I felt about Fox outbidding CBS for rights to broadcast the NFC games. I told him he was nuts and hung up on him, that's how I felt. CBS lose football? My goodness, next thing you know, Sonny and Cher are going to break up.

Given the circumstances I think I made the best decision possible; I went down to the bar. A couple of hours later Greg walked in, looking like he had lost his best job. When I saw him I got all emotional; I started to cry. The word spread really fast: Fox had won the rights to broadcast NFC games with a bid of $1.6 billion for four years. That's billion. I know I had said there were too many pro football games being broadcast and that some of them were boring, but this was a remedy I had never expected. I had been with CBS for ten years. It was my home, those people were my family. They had stuck with me during my rough beginning, and I felt like I owed them my career. I was angry at the NFL for sacrificing loyalty for a few hundred million bucks. The fact that Neil Pilson, head of sports at CBS, had promised me we'd sit down and work out a new contract soon as negotiations with the NFL were done had nothing to do with it.

The next day Greg and I did the show, but we were both still in shock. That night we went out for dinner, and people kept asking us how we felt. How did we feel? How did we feel? Unemployed is how we felt. "How should we feel?" I responded. "We got fired."

Greg kept correcting me, "Terry, we didn't get fired. I've never been fired in my life."

"Oh, yeah, that's right," I said, "they fired the whole damn network!"

I was truly depressed that night. Once again, I had no job. I had no income. I remember in the middle of my depression I looked right at Greg, and after everything we'd been through together, I said to him, "Greg, I think this check is yours."

Everybody kept telling me not to worry, I would get a job. But I noticed the people who told me were people who already had a job. I truly was very nervous about finding another job. A lot of people don't believe that; but anybody who has been unemployed knows exactly how I felt. I figured they had probably filled my spot at the cosmetics company, so that was out.

Almost immediately Dick Ebersol of NBC contacted me. I flew down to Florida for an all-night meeting with him. We talked football and television through the night, and Ebersol made it clear that there was a job for me at NBC. I suddenly remembered that next to CBS, NBC had always been my favorite network. I admired their peacock. So for a time it looked like I was going to work there—and then Fox made me an offer.

Starting right about at the moment they made their offer, Fox had always been my favorite network. I liked Fox even before it was a network. The more we talked, the longer I had liked them. The head of Fox Sports was David Hill, an Australian who had been producing NFL telecasts there since 1979. It was surprising how much David Hill and I had in common; he used expressions like "Down under"; I said things like, "Down yonder." He said, "We'll pay you a lot more than NBC"; I said, "What's NBC?"

Fox really was the perfect place for me. To break up the three-network monopoly, they had to break with tradition; so they tried to be original, they tried to go a little further than the competition. Fox was the network that introduced Bart Simpson, the Bundy's of *Married with Children*, and the new, improved Terry Bradshaw.

Our last day at CBS was pretty emotional. I had signed a new contract with Fox for a substantial raise, but I hadn't told anyone. Greg would soon be reaching an agreement with NBC. While I was excited, it was also a very sad day. It wasn't exactly like I was leaving home, it was more like I had gone out for a cup of coffee, and when I came back, the house was gone. Without pro football, as far as I was concerned CBS was a vacant lot. On our last show, previewing the 1994 NFC Championship game in Dallas, Greg and I tried to act as normal as possible. We talked just a bit about how much fun we had had working together—although I did notice that he didn't mention the barbecue—and signed off. Usually, when the show ended, people would run around the studio putting equipment away, trying to get out of there as fast as possible. But when we went off the air this time, everybody just stood around. Nobody knew what to do. Nobody had ever done the last show before. Finally, Greg and I just got up and hugged each other. There were more than a few tears shed that day.

I was going to work for a network that had never televised a single football game, run by an Australian. Hill and Fox president Ed Goren told me they intended to build the studio show around me, although when they told me that, Fox didn't even have a studio. I believed them when they told me Fox was going to change the way football had been broadcast, although at that point I didn't know exactly what they meant. I do have to admit, though, that I did get a little nervous when one of the first questions they asked me was how well I rode a horse.

SEVEN

This is how valuable I was to Fox: in addition to my work on the Sunday football show, I was going to broadcast from ringside at a bull-riding competition. Actually, rather than bull riding, a better name for that event would have been the holding-on-to-a-bull-for-a-few-seconds-so-as-not-to-get-killed competition. My job was to interview competitors after their brief ride, then throw it back up to Bubba Ray in the booth.

To promote this show they brought the world's greatest bucking bull, Bodacious, to the Fort Worth stockyards. Bodacious is the only bull in the entire history of the Professional Rodeo Association to be banned because he was too vicious. Bodacious had mastered this little trick: he would throw his flanks up to slam the rider forward, then throw back his own head to smash the head of the rider. He was so dangerous that he was retired early.

My assignment was to stand next to Bodacious and do the promo.

The producer of the spot had been given strict orders by Fox that I was not to be allowed to sit on Bodacious. Do not let Bradshaw sit on that bull, he was told, because he will get hurt and we do not want him hurt. That's how valuable I was to Fox. "You can stand next to the gate," the producer told me; "you can stand over him in the pen, but you can't sit on him."

Can't? Well, naturally, that meant I really wanted to sit on him. "Why can't I sit on him?" I began arguing. "The bull is in the pen. He ain't goin' nowhere."

"Terry, this is probably the most vicious bull in the world. He's gonna squeeze you or lean on your leg, and you're gonna get hurt."

I spoke to a bull rider who told me that Bodacious might throw his head back, but as long as he was in the pen—unless I fell off—I wasn't going to get hurt.

But the producer was adamant: Terry, you cannot ride this bull. That made me mad. And the more I thought about it, the angrier I got. What am I, I thought, some kind of wimp? I was in the cattle business. I was in the horse business. I wore cowboy hats and cowboy shirts, and I had real cowboy boots on. What was I, afraid to sit on the back of a bull locked in a pen?

We shot the promo. Bodacious just stood still in his chute. Just stood there. He didn't budge. The producer was moving the camera for the next setup. As he did, I looked around—no one was watching me, so I gently lowered myself onto Bodacious's back. Well, now, I thought, look at this. I'm sitting on the greatest bull in the whole history of professional rodeo. This is pretty neat. There are not too many men who sat on Bodacious and got sacked by Butkus!

And he liked me! I leaned forward just a bit and started petting him. Nice bull. I started scratching his big, thick muscular neck. He still hadn't moved a muscle. This isn't so tough, I thought. Just got to be gentle with him. I started getting comfortable, sort of leaned back and tried to put my hand on his butt to support myself—and as I did I accidentally touched his flank.

While flying through the air, I realized that touching his flank was probably not a smart idea. I guess what surprised me most was how high I went. I landed in the next pen. But on my way down to the ground, I banged off railings like the ball in a pinball machine. The whole left side of my body was banged up, I was black and blue on the inside. Man, I hurt. But I had done it, I'd sat on Bodacious, the world's greatest bucking bull.

Unfortunately, nobody saw me. Nobody. And like the Baptist preacher who secretly played golf on Sunday and shot a hole in one, I couldn't tell anybody about it. The absolute last thing the producer wanted anybody at Fox to know was that he'd let me sit on the bull and I'd been thrown into the next county.

That didn't make much sense to me. When David Hill hired me, he told me specifically he wanted me to be me. Now, ladies and gentlemen, let us be honest here: would anyone who knows me really believe that I *wasn't* going to ride that bull?

Fox really did build its football preview show around me. I was the first hire. Some people felt that was sort of like hiring Ray Charles to drive your limousine—you definitely know it's going to be an interesting ride. Hill and Ed Goren wanted to create a new kind of studio show. They wanted to entertain the mass audience, not worry about the opinion of the critics. The objective was to have fun with your basic football; information with a smile. CBS was always trying to tone me down because they were afraid the audience was going to lose its respect for me. Now *that* is a straight line.

Ed Goren once pointed out that until I joined the CBS studio show, no one had ever seen the legs of an NFL pregame analyst. Traditionally they sat behind a desk talking serious football for a half hour. Greg and I were probably the first people to get up from behind that desk to demonstrate a little inside football. It wasn't particularly exciting, but at least we brought something new to the format. So when Fox was designing the set for *NFL Sunday,* Goren said he wanted to build a stadium for me. Bradshaw Field. Maybe Bradshaw Stadium. Or maybe, dum-da-da-dum . . . the Bradshaw Dome. Well, the finished set wasn't exactly a stadium, it was more like the Bradshaw Piece of Astroturf, but it served as a place for us to do our demonstrations.

Goren modeled our show on the original *NFL Today* with Brent Musburger, the wonderful Miss Phyllis George, Irv Cross, and Jimmy the Greek. That show managed in a half-hour weekly to create four clearly defined national personalities. His goal was to create an hour show featuring an ensemble of four personalities— led by me—who would become nationally known. In other words, an hour-long lite beer commercial.

We did a lot of auditions. The first person Fox hired to join me was . . . Mr. Howard M. Long. Howie Long is just maybe the best-looking human being on the planet. He is our matinee idol, our movie star. Just imagine how tough it is for me to have to look across our desk and see that handsome, square-jawed face looking back at me. I'm the kind of guy whose wife left me and kept the dogs. Cris Collinsworth described Howie as "the fifth face on Mount Rushmore."

Howie Long was a Hall of Fame defensive end with the Oakland Raiders, one of the most tenacious defensive players in the history of football. He was known for being just as strong and tough on the last play of the game as on the first play. Howie took the game seriously, I mean seriously, my friends, and he brought that attitude with him into the studio. Basically, he was the kind of intelligent, sensitive human being who would instantly analyze a situation, determine the proper response, and then just crush it. After he was hired, we did a considerable amount of time traveling around the country greeting potential sponsors and promoting the show. At one point Howie admitted, "This is really a change for me. I'm just not accustomed to smiling at this many people and being this nice."

Howie and I never played against each other—his career began as mine was ending—although he claims that when he was growing up, I was one of his heroes. He told me that he had desperately wanted to be a Pittsburgh Steeler, that he had begged the Steelers to draft him and even wore number 75 with the Raiders because Mean Joe Greene had worn that number.

How can you not love a fine young man like that?

Howie and I did not get along too well initially, though. We did not have too much in common. I'm from Louisiana, he's from Boston; I went to Louisiana Tech, he went to Villanova. I was a quarterback, he was a defensive end. I didn't take too much very seriously, he took everything seriously. I'm bald and craggy-looking, and he . . . isn't.

Howie would be the first to admit that he has a short fuse. And as soon as I realized that, well, naturally I wanted to ride that bull. I didn't understand him at first. I think we probably had a bit of an ego clash; maybe we were both a little insecure. Howie had never watched the CBS show, so he didn't understand my role, and I did not understand what his role was going to be. We did have some words early on, definitely. One time on the show we were talking football, and he was telling me what he would have done to me on the field. "How would you do that?" I asked him. "You couldn't get by my guy."

Howie is one of those people whose anger becomes visible. His eyes narrow, and he glares at you. In this case it looked to me like he had flames in his eyes. So I pushed him a little more. "Just what do you think you would have done to me?"

Howie did not smile as he told me, "I would take your head off."

I felt there was only one adequate response to that. "Now let me tell you something," I said, waving my warning finger at him. "If you hit me, I swear to goodness, if you *ever* hit me, I would bleed all over you like you have never seen before!"

That time he laughed. But I meant it! I was just trying to find out how far I could push him, what buttons to stay away from. Howie is an extremely bright, insightful man, but in the beginning he was just so serious on the show, and I wanted him to loosen up. Sometimes I didn't go about it in the best possible way. One Sunday afternoon I was teasing him about something, and I embarrassed him. I didn't do it on purpose, Mom, I promise. Howie does not like to be embarrassed, and he called me at home to talk about it. We talked it through, and learned about each other. That marked the beginning of what has become a very strong, loving friendship.

Howie describes me as the older brother he was glad he never had. And then he emphasizes the "older." I tell him if that's true, then how come he got all the looks in the family?

While our personalities are very different, together we create a wonderful chemistry. The truth about Howie is that when he makes a commitment, he is serious about it. He was committed to the success of the show. I mean com-mit-ted! About the only thing more important to him was his family. Let me tell the truth, of the three people I work with at the desk, Howie is my best friend.

The third person Fox hired was the former Dallas Cowboys coach Jimmy Johnson. Let me say this about Jimmy Johnson: that man had the best hair of any man on the show. Maybe the best hair on television. You could ski off my old bald head, Howie's flattop was so smooth you could land a plane on it, and Jimmy's was so thick you could get lost in it. One writer claimed that Jimmy's "liberal use of hairspray constituted a permanent threat to the ozone layer." Jimmy was hired to provide the coach's perspective, but I think it became obvious pretty quickly that he had no-mit-ment. Jimmy loved coaching; he had left the Cowboys because of a personality conflict with owner Jerry Jones after winning two Super Bowls. Like several other coaches before him, he felt the television job was just a way for him to keep busy until he accepted another head coaching job, I believed.

A month before he went on the air for the first time, the cast and crew spent a week together in California to plan and rehearse, and Jimmy didn't show up. When we were asked by the media where he was, Howie Long told them, "He's in the Witness Protection Program."

Actually David Hill had excused him to fulfill other commitments, but I felt he should have been there. To me it indicated that the show wasn't too important to him. "I'm not going to ride Jimmy all year long," I said, "because I don't think he's going to be on the set all year long."

To which Jimmy replied, when reporters found him, "Terry talks before he thinks, but I don't think it would make any difference if he thought first."

Jimmy Johnson is a smart man; he was certainly capable of becoming a national television personality. But I knew that if he intended to coach again, he wasn't about to say anything controversial—not only wasn't he going to burn any bridges, he was going to stay at the speed limit and stop to pay the toll.

He was never really a comfortable fit on the show. With Jimmy it seemed like there were limits to how far we could go; we just couldn't have as much fun with him as we did with everyone else. But during his two years at Fox Jimmy and I did do one thing that had never been done on television before.

It was the end of the regular season, and Fox was broadcasting a meaningless game between San Diego and Arizona. This was the kind of game best used as punishment; I'm warning you, Gary, you hit Terry with that stick one more time, I'm gonna make you watch the whole Chargers–Cardinals game! Normally, the ratings for this game would have been south of a *Gilligan's Island* repeat, but Fox came up with an interesting idea: Jimmy and I would broadcast the game without a play-by-play announcer.

Years earlier NBC had done a game without any broadcasters at all and had been really criticized for it. So basically, someone figured out that Jimmy and I were better than nothing. I hadn't been in the booth for six seasons, Jimmy had never done a game. Jimmy and I were supposed to talk about the game without giving details like the score, who carried the ball, and who caught the pass. The theory was that this was going to be just like sitting in your living room watching the game with me and Jimmy. Fox called it an experiment; but then again, so did Dr. Frankenstein.

The best review we got said, "It's nice to know that clunky headsets still can do no damage to the most perfect hair in the history of football." That was Jimmy Johnson they were writing about. The best thing I can say about doing the game was that it was not as terrible as I was afraid it was going to be. It actually was hard to sit there and not talk about every play. If we had been watching at home, we would have been saying things like, "Look at that, look at that, you ever see anything that stupid before?" and "What the %$^% was he thinking?" and "Pass me over another one of those, please."

For his first time in the booth, Jimmy did a nice job. And I think he thought so too. Because there was one time when I went to pat him on the back, but his hand got in the way.

The last hire was Mr. James Brown, a graduate of Haaaavard University, who had been doing play-by-play at CBS. Originally Hill and Goren planned to have only three people at the desk. I was going to serve as the host, but I wasn't real comfortable with that, and we decided we needed a straight man. Ed Goren wanted to hire James Brown, but Hill resisted. After hiring Madden, Summerall, Matt Millen, and me, Hill was concerned that viewers were going to think of Fox football coverage as CBS West and didn't want to bring in anybody else from that network. So we auditioned probably twenty different people for this role. The problem was that Howie and I were so strong that we just rolled over these people. Meanwhile Ed Goren kept telling David Hill, "J.B. is the man. He can do the job."

"There must be somebody who's just perfect for the job," Hill said.

"J.B., James Brown," Goren said.

"Wait a second," Hill said, real excited, "I just got a great idea. How about James Brown?"

"Oh, man," Goren said, "why didn't I think of that? You're absolutely right, boss."

And believe me, I would tell that story the same way even if David Hill didn't sign my paycheck! But however it happened, J.B. became the fourth member of our team. Of us all, J.B. is by far the most well rounded. I kid him about that a lot, but he has tried everything to lose that stomach. A lot of people don't understand J.B.'s role. They ask me exactly what it is that he does, and I tell them, "He went to Harvard. He can read the Prompter better than the rest of us." Actually, J.B. probably has the toughest job of all—he has to keep the rest of us under control. He's the host, the traffic cop, the point man, the teacher, the director, the emcee, the man who makes sure we cover those subjects we need to cover and still get in all the commercials. The man has an extremely complex job, which he does smooth as silk. His role is to stay out of the back-and-forth, set the stage, and then bring in the clowns.

From the very beginning I sat next to him because I knew he would have the right answers, and if I asked him real nice, he'd let me copy off him. Now, Howie also would have the right answers and probably would let me cheat off him. But not Cris Collinsworth, who joined us after Jimmy Johnson left and Ronnie Lott, who replaced him, also left. Cris would never let me copy his answers. Cris might even tell the teacher, Terry's trying to read my paper. In fact, Cris definitely would be the one who would tell the teacher, Terry threw that at Howie.

But J.B. would feel sorry for me, and against his better judgment he'd let me see his answers. He'd sigh about it, but he would move his paper around so I could see it. J.B. is just a big old teddy bear, a sweet, sweet man. He is the nicest person in the world—of course, on our show that also makes him the biggest target. I'm bad, I know it, but sometimes I just can't help myself. For example, J.B. prides himself on remembering everybody's name. He works at it. So one day a man we all knew came on the set. J.B. couldn't remember his name. "T.B.," he whispered to me, "T.B., who is that? What's his name?"

I whispered right back, "Rex."

"Thanks," he said, loud, "Hey, Rex, how you doing?"

"Phil," the man said. "It's Phil."

"J.B.," I said, "don't you remember Phil?" J.B. never asked me again.

Over time J.B. became my closest friend on the show. We hug and kiss on each other, and he often turns to me for advice. He had been dating a lovely woman for several years and was thinking about marrying her, for example. We talked about it a lot, and I gave him the benefit of my own experience. Are you out of your mind? I asked him. That was the benefit of my experience.

Being a Harvard graduate, though, J.B. understood the value of my advice. So one Sunday he showed up at the studio wearing a wedding ring. Now, J.B. has also helped me when I need a little advice: he introduced me to his mother, Ma Brown. I love Ma Brown, she is a wonderful Christian woman. Before one of our early telecasts he was on the phone with her, and he said to me in a serious tone, "T.B., I've got my mother on the phone, and she'd like to say hello. She really loves you. Now please, be gentle with her. She has diabetes and she just had a couple of toes amputated and she's home recuperating right now."

That was tough, and I was my usual somber, sympathetic self. "Ma Brown," I shouted, "how you doing, baby?"

This stunned look appeared on J.B.'s face.

"God bless you, my boy," Ma Brown answered me, "you are so funny. You light up my day, I just love you."

"Well, thank you. Now how you doing today?"

Maybe I expected to hear a little bit of self-sorrow, with her diabetes and the loss of a toe, but this was before I had gotten to know her. "God is blessing me so much," she told me, "all of these nice people are calling and checking on me—"

"Well, look," I said, "I've got to go, but I want you to understand one thing. There's a silver lining in every cloud, and there are good things about losing that toe. Look at it like this, you have to buy a lot less toenail paint now, don't you?"

Poor J.B. He grabbed the phone back from me. "Ma? Ma? You all right?" He looked at me and shook his head. "You have to buy less toenail paint," he repeated.

"She all right with that?" I asked.

"I can't believe it," he replied. "She's laughing her butt off."

After that Ma Brown and I became close telephone friends. She even told J.B. that he had to stop calling me "a lovable redneck." When I finally met her, she was everything I thought she would be, just hugging and kissing and making a fuss. When I was particularly sad about my last marriage breaking up, I felt I needed some spiritual solace and called on her. Ma Brown has seen life, she's experienced it. When I get on an airplane, I'm a lot more comfortable if the pilot has got some gray hairs on his head. If I want to learn how to be successful in business, I don't go to someone who's gone bankrupt; I go to someone on the Fortune 500. Ma Brown has been there, nothing excites her. She knew how to provide the support I needed. We talked for about an hour. She quoted Scripture to me, and then we prayed together. She helped me get through a difficult time in my life.

Now of course, while J.B. is the ringleader, he has also become the butt of my jokes—a job for which he has the perfect build. J.B. is a big man, and there have been times when I've commented on his weight. Like when I told him that I had seen the posters for his new movie—*The Nutty Professor.*

After two seasons Jimmy Johnson went back to coaching and was replaced by Ronnie Lott. Ronnie Lott was fun to work with; if Ronnie was in class with us and Cris wouldn't give him the answers, Ronnie would probably beat him up. But it never would have come to that, because Ronnie wouldn't have time to take tests, he'd be too busy passing out business cards, making deals, and slipping people Cuban cigars. In fact, Ronnie would have gotten the contract from the teacher to print the tests. Ronnie was involved in more deals than Hershey's got kisses. He was a principal in a venture capital company, he had a car dealership, he was making movies and commercials, he had fitness clubs and was part owner of a company that made magnets to improve your health, and he was involved in all kinds of charitable activities—including his own golf tournament. It was always HiRonnieByeRonnie. Ronnie was also with us in the studio for two years, then he went back into the broadcasting booth. I was really sorry to see him go, because in that brief time he had become my best friend on the show.

J.B., Howie, and I were hoping they didn't hire anybody to replace him. We thought we could do fine by ourselves. Sometimes four people having a lot to say made that hour pretty thin. So I figured it out: divide three people into one hour instead of four, and you get about . . . a lot of extra time. But then Fox told us they could get Cris Collinsworth. Cris had been doing analysis at NBC for almost ten years. He filled a need we didn't know we had at the time. J.B. was the warden, Howie was happy doing the X's and O's, the strategy, and I just wanted to have a good time. The element Cris could bring to the show was real hard-line football commentary, which neither Howie nor I wanted to do. Cris did his reporting and did not hesitate to speak his mind. Not only did he burn some bridges, he blew them to smithereens.

As Cris has said, the only reason he left NBC was because he was fired. Cris said that, I didn't.

Cris and I played against each other at the beginning of his career. He remembered, "I came out on the field early just to watch the Steelers warm up. I just stood there in awe. There was Bradshaw and Jack Ham and Jack Lambert, Mel Blount, and Rocky Bleier, Lynn Swann, and John Stallworth, Franco. These were my heroes, this was a team of John Waynes to me. I felt like I was on a movie set or something."

How can you not love a fine upstanding young man like that?

It was my privilege to introduce Cris to the top executives of all the Fox stations at the annual affiliates meeting. "We got this new guy on our show this year," I told them, "but you don't have to worry about him. I know he's not much to look at right now, but we are going to have the boy dewormed and we think we can fatten him up a little bit and make something out of him. A lot of people didn't want to work with Cris Collinsworth because they said the boy was two-faced, but my God, ladies and gentlemen, if the boy had another face, don't you think he'd use it?"

Then I handed him the microphone, and that young man looked out at those people, and he said to me, "Are you finished? Because I was going to say something very nice about you. I was going to tell these people what a real honor it is to be able to work with someone who is living proof that Hooked on Phonics really works."

Admittedly we didn't do a whole lot to make him feel real welcome at first. Jimmy Johnson had lasted only two years, Ronnie Lott had lasted two years, so it probably didn't do a lot for Cris's confidence when he came into the studio and caught us taking bets on the over-under how long he would last.

I have to admit that, as smart as Cris Collinsworth is—the man does have a law degree—at first he didn't quite understand the type of show we were doing. He claimed that when he was at NBC, after they had finished taping their show, they would flip the channel to our show to see what we were doing, but he still came into the Fox studio that first week fully prepared. Cris was all pumped up, he was ready to go, the man was psyched. He had been working four months, no, six months, on his opening, he had filled seventeen yellow legal pads with notes. Anything anybody wanted to know about the National Football League, he had written on those pads.

I looked at J.B. This was definitely something we could not permit on our show. I would estimate that we allowed him to go on with his report for at least one minute. "And here's another thing that I learned about their defensive strategy—" he was saying or something like that, when I started rolling my eyes. Maybe I started shaking my head a little too.

He tried to continue, "Their, um . . . coach told me . . . just ah . . ."

Then Howie interrupted him, "Cris, what's that black thing you got between your teeth?"

". . . they . . . last week . . ."

I leaned forward to see that black thing Howie was talking about. "I don't see it, Howie."

Cris Collinsworth never did have a chance. To his credit, when he joined the program he had a great attitude. He told me right from the very beginning that he could take whatever Howie and I wanted to throw at him and that we shouldn't hesitate. "Don't worry what you say about me," he said.

Well, what in the world would make him even think we would worry about that? Howie and I took it upon ourselves to make his life a holy hell. At NBC the show had been taped, and Cris worked from a script;

most of our show is done live. So when we interrupted Cris, he didn't know how to react. One time, I remember, Howie interrupted him in the middle of some long speech, and he completely lost his train of thought. When he finally started again, I sighed and said to Howie, "I can't believe you did that, you ought to be ashamed. Let the man finish what he's got to say. Now you go on, Cris, don't let him bother you again. My goodness."

And as soon as Cris started again, Howie interrupted again, "Now that's not fair, Terry, you interrupted him first . . ."

By the end of the show that boy was stumped. On almost every TV show when the producer tells you, "Wrap," it means you finish as quickly as possible. Every show except ours. I was speaking, and Scott Ackerson told me to "wrap," and about a minute later I finally got quiet. Then Howie made his final comments, and Ackerson told him to wrap, and two minutes later he did that. Finally it was Cris's turn, and we are short on time, and Ackerson is telling him, "Wrap, wrap, wrap," and Cris was so confused he just sat there looking straight into the camera and never said a word.

Finally I had to prod him, "Are you going to say anything or what?"

He looked at me and smiled. It was a strange smile; mostly it reminded me of Jack Nicholson in *The Shining*.

It took Cris a few weeks to fully understand the way we worked. On the Saturday night before the show we would all go out to a local deli to go over what we wanted to talk about the next day. That session usually lasted about an hour and a half. In the studio the next morning we would do a full rehearsal of the show. Now Cris made a mistake of believing that what we talked about Saturday night or what we rehearsed Sunday morning had something to do with the show we were going to do. I could see how he might have had that impression. But as he discovered, the real purpose of these meetings was to provide ammunition to rip him to shreds.

I think it's unfair to place all the blame on me and Howie for everything that was done to Cris at the beginning; some of the blame also has to go to me and J.B. It is a known true fact that Cris Collinsworth has the longest neck of any person in the United States. The first time I saw him, I wanted to hire him to sit in the rear seat of my car facing out the back window so people would think I had one of those bobbers. But J.B. and I used to play a little game: after we'd finished the pregame show, production assistants would bring out the food. I would turn my back on Cris until he had something to eat. Then J.B. would tell me to turn around. My challenge was to watch it going down his throat and tell J.B. exactly what he was eating. Turned out I was gifted at this task. I got so good I could identify the brand of cream cheese on his bagel!

Eventually Howie and I got called into the office by the principal. The principal told us that we were being naughty, and that enough was enough. It was strongly suggested that we ease up on him a little. So we did. Basically, we stopped teasing him completely.

Poor Cris. He thought the fact that we had stopped kidding with him meant that we didn't like him. He called me to find out if there was a problem between us. I told him that we'd had our hands slapped and couldn't tease him anymore.

"Sure you can," he said, "go ahead. C'mon, do it." Cris had learned a very important lesson. At times he had found himself wondering, did I go too far this week? And he had learned that on our show there is no such thing as too far. That's why I can admit that of the three people I work with, Cris has become my best friend.

Now, we didn't stop teasing him completely, we just spread it around a little more. The strong ratings of our program prove that viewers enjoy what they see on camera. So they would probably really love to see what goes on off camera. My friends, we do not make it easy for each other. At times various among us have been known to make faces at that person who is speaking or whisper conspiratorially with the person sitting next to us while looking directly at the speaker. What bothers Cris most of all is that whenever he makes a mistake, I make note of it by putting a little check mark on the paper in front of me—which means I'm keeping track of his mistakes—and that almost inevitably flusters him, causing him to stutter or hesitate. And when he does that, I just make another check mark.

From the very beginning my role on the show was to be the sit-down comedian. I'm not a journalist, I'm a former football player. I don't use a lot of big words. There are some broadcasters who love to use those big words, and I listen to those blatherskites and wonder, why? Are they trying to impress people with their intelligence? Or speaking for the critics? If I began talking like that, my people would run to pray for me. Poor Terry, the boy got hisself possessed by the ghost of some English teacher. When people watch me, I believe they think they're probably smarter than me, and that brings a certain comfort level to them.

The fact is that a lot of them are smarter than me. They must be, they've got real jobs.

I consider myself a TV personality, a football entertainer. My role on the show is to be not serious. People do not want to hear me speak football. If I started saying things like "That's the old 66 Inside Release. Watch how the weak safety will pick him up and . . . ," people would suspect I had a DNA transplant. They expect to hear me explain, "The Giants are having a bad offensive day, and they've got to make some changes. It's like when I went fishing with my dad last week and we were catching a lot of fish and all of a sudden we couldn't catch mud. Nothing. Then my daddy said to me, 'Son, either these fish got real bright right all of a sudden or they're not interested in these lures. We got to change lures.' So we went to a different lure, and them fish started biting again. When the defense isn't biting, you've got to change your offense at half time. You got to change lures." That's what people want to hear from me.

David Hill made it possible for me to emphasize that aspect of my personality. I don't think people realize it, but two of the most important people in the whole history of professional football were Howard Cosell and Dandy Don Meredith. Cosell didn't know much about football. He didn't understand the nuts-and-bolts strategy. He did know the lore of the league, and he loved the players, but what he most understood was that football is an entertainment medium, and he fancied himself an entertainer. Dandy Don knew the game and had a sense of humor about it. Frank Gifford did the play-by-play between them and deserves a lot of credit for somehow managing to maintain a semblance of order. But for the first time viewers turned on the football game as much to listen to Cosell and Meredith as to watch the game. People who knew nothing about football would tune in just to see what everybody else was talking about. It was entertainment.

Entertainment first was what David Hill had in mind when he created our show. His objective from the very beginning has been to create a comfortable mix of football and fun. The football was there—we all knew football—but when I signed on, even I didn't have any idea how far they were willing to go for the entertainment, least not until I found myself in the huddle with those cows.

To promote the show before we went on the air, we did a bunch of commercials. In one of them I was in the middle of my field calling my cows into a huddle. It's well known that cows do not make good football players. To begin with they have very poor lateral movement. The tag line of the spot was "Same game. Different attitude."

We knew that the opening of our first shoe would set the tone. So we wanted to do something unusual. I don't know where the horse idea came from. But our first show opened with me riding a horse down Sunset Boulevard dressed as a cowboy, tying up my horse, and walking into the studio, where I took a deep breath and admitted, "Nobody tole me it was so far from Pittsburgh to L.A."

Well, that certainly did impress Jimmy Johnson, who claimed, "I didn't know which end to look at."

There is a story that J.B. tells people about that first show. Now listen up: J.B. tells this, I don't. I never would tell this story because some people might take it wrong. But about two minutes before we went on the air, we were all sitting behind the desk, loosening up. For Howie and Jimmy, this was the first time they'd ever done a studio, and I wondered if maybe they were a little nervous. So I took a little tube of Vaseline out of my pocket and said, "Look here, Jimmy, gimme your finger. Rub a little of this on your lips, so if you get dry mouth your lips won't stick to your teeth." So I squeezed a little onto Jimmy's finger, and he rubbed it on his lips.

Then I turned to Howie, "Big boy, come here. Everything's gonna be okay. Just put a little of this on your lips, and you'll be fine." I squeezed a bit onto his finger. Then I put some on my own finger, rubbed it on my lips, and put the tube back in my pocket.

"Redneck," J.B. said—now this is the story James Brown tells—"How come you didn't offer the Brother any of that?"

I took the small tube out of my pocket and looked at it, then I looked at J.B.'s mouth, and then I looked at the tube again—and sighed, "Well, you know what, J.B., I don't think this tube is big enough."

Ten seconds later we were on the air. Laughing. Pretty much we've been laughing ever since.

For several years Howie and I opened the show every week with a two-minute filmed comedy bit. One week, for example, we were in an old-fashioned barbershop talking football with the customers—and when I got up after they'd been fussin' with my hair, it was revealed that I had a Jimmy Johnson wig on. In another segment we were in an art museum with J.B., who was trying to culturize us, and the piece of art I said I liked best was two push brooms leaning against a wall that "showed a certain whimsy"—least they did till the janitor came and carried them away. In one bit Howie and I were cruising in a convertible when we got pulled over by a California highway patrolman, who turned out to be Erik Estrada; I told Howie not to worry, the officer will know who I am—I think Estrada's words were something like, "Wow, I had no idea who was in this car. Howie Long! What a thrill." We even had a brief piece costarring Homer Simpson. What surprised me most about that one is that Homer is actually shorter in real life than he appears to be on his show.

Not every critic liked our show. Or liked me. There are people who take their football real seriously. As one man wrote in the *Washington Post,* "Let's have Terry Bradshaw and his faithful four-legged companion just ride off into the sunset, leave the western motif to John Wayne and give us football, nothing but football. . . ."

Another critic wrote that I was loquacious. Loquacious? Me? Loquacious? Let me tell you something, I have been called a lot of different things in my life, from the time I was just beginning my career through all my years with the Steelers, you just can't imagine some of the things people said—and that doesn't even include the things that I've heard when I am speaking to groups or during my acting career or when I had my radio show or my television. Loquacious? I could go on for a long time proving that just about the last thing in the world I am is loquacious.

Of course, there are occasional times when I do go on a bit too long.

But most critics and viewers liked what we were doing. Not only did the viewers come back for more, other networks began revamping their shows to be more like *NFL Sunday*. Every one of the other shows has to have their funny commentator. They have funny openings, funny commercials. We started all that.

And it wasn't just the pregame show that Fox changed. The network's game coverage utilized more cameras, videotape machines, and super slow-motion cameras than ever before and even put special microphones right down on the field. But the biggest change in the presentation of the game was the Fox Box, a little scoreboard in the upper left corner of the screen that included the score and the game clock. Anytime a viewer wanted to know the score of the game or how much time was left, it was right there on the screen. Anytime. It's difficult to believe that giving the viewer the most important statistics about the game on a continuous basis could be controversial, but a lot of people seemed to have strong opinions about it. It was too big, too small, too intrusive. People just weren't used to it: Homer, what's that thing up there in the corner of my TV pitcher? G'wan and hit it with the newspaper before it gets away. It's the score of the game, Daddy.

Well, dang it, what's it doing on my TV set? Those overpaid announcers getting too lazy to tell me the score now?

By the end of the first season viewers had become used to it. Most of the other networks now include it in all their sports coverage.

Initially just about everything new we tried received some criticism, particularly the inside football segment on our field. Because this segment has to be carefully choreographed, it is planned as long as— thirty, forty seconds in advance. The fact is that there are weeks that we don't even know what we're going to talk about till we're standing right there. What do you want to talk about this week, Howie? I don't know, Terry, what do you want to talk about? If we have a guest on the show, we definitely want him. The one guest I do remember very well was the late Ray Nitschke, the Hall of Fame middle linebacker from Vince Lombardi's Green Bay Packers. Nitschke had established himself as one of the toughest players in football when Mean Joe Greene was still just sort of cranky. Nitschke was so tough when he played that one of his own teammates used to complain that in practice, "he was just liable to make you try to eat a bone." Lombardi used to watch practice from a raised wooden tower; one day the tower fell over and hit Nitschke in the head, driving a bolt into his helmet. Supposedly when Lombardi found out who had been hit, he sighed in relief and ordered everybody back to practice.

On our little field we decided Ray should demonstrate how he would break through the offensive line to get to the quarterback. I lined up at quarterback, and I believe my close friend Jeff Quinn, a former pro football player who is our permanent stand-in, was the center. As we were lining up, I mentioned casually to Nitschke, "Be honest about it, Ray, you couldn't play effectively in today's game, could you?" Next to suggesting to my soon-to-be-ex wife that we go parasailing, this was truly one of the sillier things I ever said. We were on national television, and I was telling a man known for his pride that he wasn't a good enough player.

"What are you talking about?" he asked.

"Well, seriously now, the players are bigger and faster now than they were when you were playing, right? It's a whole different game."

Ray smiled. "Come on, I'll show you what I would do."

Least, I thought he was smiling. So we lined up. "Down," I yelled.

"Hold it a second," Ray said standing up, "hold on and let me take my glasses off." So he took off his glasses and handed them to a crew member.

"Set," I said. That's good, I thought, he's going along with my little joke.

"Whoa, whoa," Ray interrupted, "just lemme take my coat off right now." So he took off his coat and handed it to the stagehand.

It was probably right about then that I began to wonder if both of us knew that I had been joking. It was like a switch had turned on in him. His eyes were cold, and he was locked on me. "Hut one," I said.

"Wait now," Ray said, "just let me put my watch

over here. And then I'm going to tear your head off."
He took off his watch.

"Hut one," I repeated. I looked over at him. It
looked to me like he was serious. Was I really going to
let him intimidate me on national television? You bet I
was. "Time out," I said, making a T-sign with my two
hands, "we're gonna pause right here for a commercial."

A few feet away I could hear J.B. laughing. He
knew that I'd made up the commercial break—he's the
one who is supposed to take us into the commercials.
Was Nitschke really serious? The man had a tower fall
on his head and got up. It wasn't really necessary for
me to find out.

But the thing for which we have received the most
criticism is our humorous approach to the dissemina-
tion of football information. There are people who
complain we don't show enough respect to the game,
that we don't provide enough information. To those
people who protest that we're not serious enough, I
have only one thing to say: *Pffffftttttttt!* Maybe our
package isn't wrapped so pretty, but we do our homework, we understand the intricacies of the game, and
we let people know what's going on. We rarely just say,
Wow, lookee here at this great catch isn't it beautiful
let's look at it again this time in slow motion. What we
will tell you is which defensive back left his assignment
too soon, allowing the receiver to get free. We also provide information I know, I absolutely know, viewers
just are not going to be able to get anywhere else. We
work the phones. One time I was speaking with an Eagles coach a few days before Philadelphia was flying to

Dallas to play the Cowboys. Texas was suffering through a major heat wave, and I asked him how the Eagles were preparing for the weather. He told me confidentially that they were bringing down jars of pickle juice—let me repeat that, pickle juice—because it supposedly helped prevent muscle cramping. Pickle juice! A Bradshaw exclusive! Nobody else would have that information. Pickle juice was definitely worth digging for. I couldn't wait to casually mention it in the middle of our show, although admittedly pickle juice is a tough subject to casually bring up. When I finally broke the story on the air, Howie looked at me as if wondering if this was true or just an introduction to another one of my farm stories, Cris looked frustrated because he didn't get that information, and J.B. had a look somewhere between pure awe and satisfaction that he still had a job.

It turned out to be a pretty big story. A week after I broke it on the air, a major pickle company signed a lucrative endorsement deal with the Eagles. And I wasn't the slightest bit upset I didn't get a slice of the deal—although some people might call that sour pickles!

In addition to me and J.B., Howie, and Cris, Fox has added several regular segments to our program. Supposedly to attract the younger male audience they forced upon us a comedian named Jimmy Kimmel, who each week attempts to pick the winners of several games. Jimmy does a little taped comedy spot ending with his selections for that day. CBS had Jimmy the Greek to pick games; we got Jimmy the Cable Comedian. Jimmy had been doing his particular type of humor on cable TV before Fox came along and rescued his career from the certain oblivion toward which it was most definitely headed. When Jimmy first started doing his comedy spot on our show, it lacked a certain element—like being funny, for example. Those people on the Weather Channel were funnier. Now, the truth is that Jimmy can be . . . amusing. The problem was that he did not relate to us at all. His segment seemed separate from the rest of the show. At a production meeting after the show one week we discussed it, and we all agreed the problem wasn't Jimmy—the poor boy was doing the best job he could—but rather the fact that there was no interplay between us. So the next week we began reacting to his spot, and my friends I must admit, that reaction was not a pretty thing to see. Jimmy wasn't just an easy target, he was the thirty-foot fire hydrant at the Westminster Dog Show of targets.

To his credit, he fired right back. Several times a year, for example, we broadcast the show from other cities—we like to give Howie's fans a chance to swoon in person—and one time when we were in Detroit Kimmel did his segment from our vacant set. And he did it naked. Apparently, though we could not see below the desk—and my friends, trust me, I guarantee you that we would not have wanted to see below the desk—he was completely naked. This was sort of a new definition of the phrase "comic strip." None of us had ever seen anything like it before, which definitely was the good news for us. To me, taking off your clothes on national television does not seem to require substantial talent; after seeing this piece it clearly also does not require a decent body. But if Jimmy Kimmel felt he needed to be naked to reveal his picks, we just sort of shook our heads and accepted it. At least we did until Cris Collinsworth pointed out to me, "Terry, that boy is naked in your chair."

The magnitude of that remark did take a moment to reveal its full self to me. But there was no avoiding the truth of it: Jimmy Kimmel was sitting in my chair. Butt naked—among other parts. A feeling washed over me not unlike the day my brother and I hit that skunk.

This was certainly a full frontal assault—about as full frontal as it's possible to get. There wasn't much I could do about it; somehow just getting rid of the chair in which he'd sat naked didn't seem enough. But Fox really insisted on keeping the studio. The more I've gotten to know Jimmy Kimmel, the easier it is for me to say that Jimmy Kimmel is definitely not my best friend on the show.

I will say this about Jimmy Kimmel; he is the only one on the show who has gone too far. We like to think that on our show there are no rules, but then he went ahead and broke them. To promote the show Fox actually produced and distributed dolls that looked just like Howie, Cris, J.B., and myself. 'Least, they were supposed to look like us. Howie believes the chin on his doll is exaggerated, claiming if you hooked it up to the front bumper of a pickup, you could plow a driveway with it. J.B.'s doll has his arm outstretched and one finger pointing, and J.B. wants to know why his doll is the only one that looks like it's holding up a bank. Cris's doll looks just like him, except it's a lot smaller and fatter. And my doll is truly unfortunate; it looks just like me. They wouldn't even bother painting on hair. I sent one to my parents, and I suspect they didn't like it very much—they sent two of them back to me.

They didn't bother making a Jimmy Kimmel doll. So Jimmy Kimmel made one himself, even going so far as gluing on to it his own body hair. Truthfully, it looked pretty much like a potato with hair glued on it. Then at the end of his taped segment Jimmy took his doll in one hand and my doll in the other hand and . . . and that's the material they wouldn't let Jimmy use on the show.

The other addition to the show is our weather report, hosted by our weatherperson, a young woman named Jillian Barberie. This is also an attempt by our producers to appeal to younger male football fans, who seem to be real interested in knowing what the weather is going to be around the league. Now I have to admit, I did not believe that so many men in this country were interested in the weather before we included this segment. As real football fans know, weather can affect the outcome of games, and we've found from the response to this segment that apparently young men of all ages watch this report very closely.

Jillian Barberie is not a professional meteorologist, but she most definitely brings other important credentials to the job. For example, one reporter wrote that she wears clothes so tight that he could see the outline of her tattoos. She's a lovely person; a nice, funny lady. And she is so good at playing the role of an attractive woman that even though there are four of us and only one of her, she definitely has us outnumbered. I would say that it accurately sums up my success with women since my last divorce to point out that the person who chose to sit naked in my chair was Jimmy Kimmel.

But even including the addition of Kimmel, I do dearly love doing the show. I am one of the fortunate people who just can't wait to get up in the morning and go to work. Everything good that has happened to me in my life is a direct result of my faith in the Lord and my passion for football. I never do forget that. I loved the game of football when I was a little kid bouncing footballs off the ceiling of my room in Shreveport, and I never did find a reason to stop loving it. And if I should ever forget how much I owe the game, I've got five herniated disks, permanent ligament damage in my right arm, and a fused wrist to remind me.

NFL Sunday has allowed me the privilege of staying around the game, and I try and repay that by being honest and truthful. So in addition to the jokes and the silliness, the audience gets that too. I've never held back an honest opinion. For example, I believe that professional football just after the turn of the twenty-first century ranks right up there with the very worst professional football we have ever seen played. There are too many teams and not enough great players. The owners seem to be more interested in competing about which one of them can agree to overpay the biggest and dumbest contract than the Super Bowl; I have never seen people so desperately trying to give away their money. And the players are certainly smart enough to demand it, even if they never earn it.

Oh, I certainly have my opinions, and the show gives me an opportunity to state them. The good news is that I just need to be loud and firm, I don't even need to be right. But I never mind admitting it when I'm wrong. I remember very well that one time in 1995 I was wrong. "I don't give the 49ers any hope at all of winning this game," I said before they played the Cowboys. At halftime the 49ers were leading 31–7, en route to a 38–20 victory. When I walked out of the studio that Sunday night, I said to my stats man, Jeff Quinn, "If I ever talk like that again, just reach over and slap me."

More than anything, though, I believe that what makes the show really work is the fact that J.B., Howie, Cris, and I really do like each other a whole lot, and we work with such a fine crew of people. I love my bosses there at Fox. They act just like they know what they're doing. I love my producer and director. I love the set, I love the camerapeople, I love the stagehands, I love the people who open the doors in the morning, I love the wonderful makeup people, I love the caterers and the people from the cleaning crew, I love the technicians. Love 'em all; in fact, that's why I am so proud to be able to say that the entire crew is my best friend on the show.

EIGHT

I couldn't even get *out* of the cattle business easy. I had decided that the quality of my life would be much improved when I got rid of everything that moos. So I loaded up my remaining cattle and hauled them off to the auction house in Mansfield, Louisiana. The morning after we got there, three of them made a break for it. They went out through a gate and took off into town. Seconds later I took off after them.

The cows did have a good head start—but they had the definite disadvantage of being cows. Believe me, it does not take much expertise to track a cow. Particularly through a nice little town. Right away they headed through backyards, trampling through gardens, ripping down clotheslines, knocking down fences. They went into tall grass so I couldn't see them, but it was possible to hear them knocking down things from oh, maybe a mile away.

I was as relentless in my pursuit of these cows as Buck Buchanan had been chasing me. People were standing on their front porches pointing me in the right direction. I can now verify from my own personal experience that it is nearly impossible to maintain your dignity when you're chasing cows. Oh, look, Ma, there's Terry Bradshaw chasing that big old bossy cow. Terry Bradshaw the football player? My my, didn't know ol' Terry was so slow. As I went running through one backyard a huge St. Bernard tied to a clothesline took a leap at me, but I was too quick for him.

Along the way I picked up some help. A drunk man wearing a white suit and a white hat started running with me. Where we running? he asked. Cow chasing, I told him. He seemed to think that was acceptable. Some kids joined the great cow chase, and some dogs. But no police—I notice there never seems to be a policeman around when you need one to chase a few cows. Finally those cows got tuckered out and turned around, and ran right back through the same backyards, across the same roads, right back through the same gate into the auction house.

We closed the gate. For me, the cattle business was done. But I always did wonder what happened to that man in the white suit when he got home that night and had to explain to his wife how his suit got ruined. Now, sweetheart darling, you're not gonna believe this, he probably told her, but I was just walking along minding my own business when all of a sudden Terry Bradshaw came tearing down the street chasing these three cows . . .

But as soon as I got out of the cattle business, I had to find something else to do to fill that time. One job was just never enough for me. Maybe because of my attention deficit disorder I always had to be doing several different jobs at the same time. I never have been able to be satisfied with just being satisfied. I've always had to keep busy, do more, keep moving all the time. Fortunately for me, you win four Super Bowls, you qualify for a lot of other jobs that don't involve heavy lifting. There is a fine tradition in this country that if you are a successful athlete or actor, people supposedly will want to eat the same peanut butter that you do, drink the same beer, or wear the same hairpiece.

At first, it was surprising to me that people might want to use a product just because I said I used it. Growing up, even my very own brothers didn't want to use the same things I did—and they could do it for free. The first product I was ever hired to endorse were pants. Now, there have been many things in my life for which I have received recognition, but none of them involve sartorial splendor. Just after I was drafted by the Steelers, I was hired by a company out of Monroe, Louisiana, to appear at their booth at the Apparel Mart in Dallas for two days, for which I was paid $100 a day and all the slacks I could carry in my car. I got some seriously funny-looking slacks for me and all my friends. Trust me, we were the best-dressed young men wearing striped bell-bottoms in Louisiana.

Many years later I starred in the pilot for a TV series entitled *Game Night*, in which I played a football broadcaster named Terry Bradley. In this first episode I had to work with an egomaniacal football player I detested. At one point I watched a ridiculous television commercial he had done and asked him, "How can you stand up there and let them make a fool of you?"

To which he replied, "Did I mention the fifteen million dollars?"

Did I mention the $100 a day plus all the pants I could carry? Just for standing at their booth and shaking hands with people? Come meet Terry Bradshaw. He wears pants! To me, this was the greatest deal of all time. It had only been a few months since I'd been stealing pop bottles for the deposit, and suddenly people were paying me to wear clothes.

But the thing I remember most was that I had the opportunity to meet Mickey Mantle. He was waiting for Billy Martin. It was the first time in my life I ever asked anyone for an autograph. I was really embarrassed, but Mickey was great. As I had just been drafted, he had no idea who I was, but he was kind and polite to me. Billy Martin wasn't; he didn't want to be bothered. One thing I noticed right off about Mickey Mantle: he definitely was not wearing striped bell-bottoms.

The first few years of my playing career I pretty much accepted every opportunity I was offered—except alcoholic beverages; my mother and dad frowned on that, so I wouldn't do it. I did a lot of commercials in Pittsburgh for regional companies like Kuppenheimer Men's Wear, Furr's Bishop's Cafeterias and Dick's Clothing and Sporting Goods. As I became more successful and a little better known, I did spots for national companies like Tony Lama's great cowboy boots and Red Man Chewing Tobacco.

I even did commercials for products most people don't know exist. In recent years, for example, the star of the Super Bowl gets paid a lot of money to smile at the camera and tell the world, "Now I'm going to Disneyland." I never have been invited to Disneyland—there were years I was barely welcome in Pittsburgh—but I can claim with some confidence that I am the only Super Bowl MVP ever to do a commercial for TBZ, the finest cattle dewormer in existence. Folks, trust me on this one, if you happen to need a good cattle dewormer, TBZ is the product for you.

In my career I have made literally hundreds of commercials for some of the best-known and finest products in the world. I've worked with the best directors and the best advertising agencies. I've done commercials with budgets so big they even went out and hired a hairstylist to do my hair—now that is definitely a no-show job. Normally when we're making a commercial the director is very precise in what he wants: Terry, the way you read that line was absolutely perfect, it could not possibly be better, so now let's try it another way. Or, that was just beautiful, Terry, just beautiful, now let's shoot it again—this time with you facing the camera.

On commercial shoots the representative of the client always has his or her own ideas, but they rarely talk directly to me, the protocol is that they speak only to the director. I could be standing two feet away from the director, and the client would ask the director, "You know what would be great? If you could have Terry do it all over again but let's try it with a British accent."

But the best commercial I ever made was for TBZ. There was no script, no storyboard, basically no plan. A film crew just came out to my ranch to shoot footage of me and my dad, my uncle Bobby, my dog Goldie, and a couple of my friends from the local fire department riding around on horses trying to pen some cattle. We ad-libbed the whole thing, but so did the cattle. Everything we did stayed in the commercial. The highlight was my dad stepping on Goldie's tail, which caused the dog to squeal, which scared the cattle, which banged into my uncle Bobby's horse, which started turning around. Think of it as *The Three Stooges Go West.*

This was basically a do-it-yourself commercial. It was hysterical. Even the horses were laughing, and horses have no sense of humor at all. Now, if it had been a big-time commercial, it would have been very different. Just imagine hearing the client tell the director, "Could you please ask the cattle to try to look a little happier?"

There is absolutely no question about the very worst product endorsement I ever did. My friends— and I feel you are my friends—in each of our lives there happen things for which we can offer no sensible explanation, things for which we shall always bear the scars of regret and even shame, things that make us tingle with embarrassment at the mere memory of them, things even more ridiculous than my first marriage. My friends, I willingly became the spokesman and model for a toupee company.

Did I mention the $15 million? If I had had even a little bit of good sense or pride, I would not have done this, but they just offered me so much money, I couldn't turn it down. I admit that I knew what I was doing and why I was doing it. But it just never dawned on me that people would make fun of me or that I would look so stupid until the day I saw my head looking back at me from a box.

The basic concept of the campaign was that if a he-man football player like Terry Bradshaw was not embarrassed to wear a toupee, no one else should be; and that if Bradshaw believed a toupee made him look better and more appealing, then naturally other men would believe it too. To show potential customers how good I looked with hair, the company made and distributed to salons all over the country a plastic model of my head. These salons would then stick a toupee on my head and put it on the counter or in the front window so everybody could see it.

They made the mold for my head at a Holiday Inn at Shreveport Airport. I laid down on a bed, and they covered my entire head with this plaster, then they stuck straws up my nose so I could breathe. I promise you, every Sunday I look at Howie Long's hair, and I am reminded that he will never know what it feels like to have his whole head covered with plaster and be breathing through two straws stuck up his nose.

Unfortunately, the people making the mold were not experts at this. The plaster began drying too quickly, and they couldn't get it off my head. I was having real difficulty breathing. There are a lot of bad ways to die, but being suffocated by a plaster mold in a Holiday Inn while getting your head duplicated for a toupee display is high among them.

Eventually they mass-produced my head. Truthfully, it looked just like me. These people were so proud of this plastic bust that they sent one in the mail to my dad. They didn't tell him it was coming; I don't even think I told my parents I was doing this thing. So this big box arrived at their house, and my father opened it up and was absolutely shocked to see me looking right back at him. Novis, he yelled to my mother, you better get in here. They sent us Terry's head in a box.

My dad didn't know what this thing was. My mother thought it was nice; she didn't know what it was either, but she still thought it was nice. My dad finally decided that maybe this was some terrible reverse of nature. To him it appeared that I'd been shot and had my head stuffed. They didn't know what to do with this thing: it was a little too bizarre to just set it up on the mantelpiece, where it would be a conversation piece. Ah yes, we got Terry's head in the mail just last week. And how's your son doing these days? On the other hand, they couldn't exactly give it away as a gift. We couldn't figure out what to get you for your anniversary, so we thought you might like Terry's head. Eventually it scared my mother too much, so they put it back in the box and packed the box away up in the attic.

I also filmed several commercials. In one, for example, I had to swim with a hairpiece on as an announcer explained, "You too can have a full robust life with our toupee. Look, Terry's in the pool swimming. Look how natural it looks. . . ." Then I surfaced with what looked like synthetic roadkill stuck to my head. The last thing in the world this thing looked was natural. Ray Charles would have known I was wearing a hairpiece. It was completely obvious.

Maybe the worst thing about the whole situation

was that in my contract I agreed to wear a toupee whenever I appeared in public. I wasn't supposed to leave the house without it. Now this was a fine company, a lot of very nice people worked there. My mother actually liked the way I looked in this toupee, but I thought everything about it was terrible. It was made of some synthetic material and had a pretty dense silicone base, so my body heat would escape through my scalp and get trapped under the wig, causing me to start sweating. So everywhere I went, I'd be sweating just something terrible. One night I remember I was going back to my apartment in Pittsburgh in the middle of a snowstorm when I met a couple I knew, and we started talking. Sweat just started pouring down my face, I wiped it off in buckets. It was just so obvious what was happening, but these people didn't want to embarrass me, so they never mentioned the fact that Niagara Falls was rolling down my face. Normally I wear a size $7\frac{3}{8}$ hat. I'm sure if I'd continued wearing this toupee, my head would have shrunk to about a 5.

At first they attached it to my head with little clips that made it easy to clip it on or take it off. At home I'd take it off and put it on my dachshund. I'd take a rubber band and wrap it around her neck. Made her look like a collie.

But the clips were so uncomfortable the manufacturer eventually knotted the toupee to my real hair, which made it just about impossible to take it off. One time, I remember, when I was just beginning my country singing career, I was performing at a club in New Mexico. I was with my brand-new road manager, my right guard Moon Mullins. We made a perfect team:

Moon didn't know any more about road managing than I knew about singing. When we finished in New Mexico we had a week off, so we flew to Miami and went fishing in the Florida Keys with the great broadcaster Curt Gowdy. We were out in the sun catching fish. We were flat out catching fish. We stayed out in the scorching sun for at least eight hours. Normally that would have sunburned my head, but I had this toupee on to protect me, so I didn't even need a hat.

When we came back in, Moon and I decided to have a beer, and maybe meet some girls. We didn't even bother going back to our hotel, we went straight to the bar. Almost immediately we started talking to some nice young ladies. I felt like I was covered with salt, so I went to the men's room to wash off some of it. I looked into the mirror, and I scared myself.

I always tell people, When you look like me you learn how to shave real fast; if I looked like Howie Long, I swear it would take me an hour every day to shave. But when I looked in the mirror this time, I looked even worse than normal. My real hair was lying down flat along the sides, but the synthetic hair was standing straight up. I looked as if I'd stuck my finger in an electric socket. I looked like Don King on a bad hair day. It was spooky. I was so embarrassed I took out my pocket knife and cut eight big gaps in my head where the wig was tied to my hair. I cut off this toupee, stuck it in my back pocket, where it hung out like a squirrel's tail, put my hand on top of my head as if I was rubbing it, and went out to the bar. Within minutes I'd conned some guy out of a cap. I put the cap on my head, and about a year later I took it off.

But that's not what got me fired. What got me fired was that I was playing in a pro-am golf tournament on a real hot day. I was out in the sun, and once again sweat was rolling out from under the wig; my head looked like a pot with a lid on it, overflowing. Finally I just couldn't take it anymore; I went behind a tree and ripped off the hairpiece, then shoved it into my back pocket. What I did not realize was that I had I cut myself when I took it off, so my scalp was bleeding. I spent the rest of the gold tournament walking around with blood running down my face and the hairpiece sticking out of my back pocket. For some reason the company decided I was not a proper spokesman for their toupees and fired me. I had to hand in my hair.

I never did find out what happened to all those heads. The salons were supposed to return them when my contract ended, but evidently they did not, because I still hear from people telling me they saw my head in a window with an animal sitting on top of it. I don't have one of my heads, but if I did, I know exactly what I would do with it. I'd put it down by the front gate of my ranch, and if people came calling when I wasn't home, my head would pop right up and say to them, "Welcome to Terry Bradshaw's. I'm not home right now, but please leave your name and phone number in the mailbox."

For the early part of my life I was known as "the Blond Bomber." I had really nice blond hair. But when I was about thirty, it started falling out. I attribute that to a popular hair tonic. I'd put gops of this stuff on my head to keep my hair in place, but it dried out your hair something terrible. So I'd run my hand through my hair—and end up with a handful of hair. Under the circumstances I think my response was quite reasonable—absolute, total panic. Compared to the way I felt about losing my hair, a letter from the IRS announcing an audit would be considered good news. I knew that someday I would lose my hair, I just hadn't expected that day to come for another, say, seventy, eighty years. It really stressed me out—and when I found out that stress makes hair fall out faster, the stress got even worse. Worrying about the fact that I was worrying too much was causing more hair to fall out, which made me worry some more.

I tried about everything short of glue, but eventually I just had to accept the fact that bald men are more virile than men with Jimmy Johnson hair. However, I did try pretty much everything that came along—which is how I turned a horse shampoo into a national hair-growing craze.

At one time I had 135 quarter horses on my ranch. And we were just going through gallons of a horse shampoo and conditioner named Mane 'n Tail. While it certainly made the horses' coats look better, I was spending a lot of money making my horses look fancy considering the fact that they weren't even dating. Then I heard that some men had found that this horse shampoo apparently would grow hair on their own heads. So I went on the David Letterman show and admitted that my sister-in-law had given me a tub of this stuff. She told me that a friend of my brother's had been using it on his head, and hair had started growing. "I've been using the shampoo and conditioner for six months," I said, "and some of the people around Fox said they can see my hair growing. And the best part is you can buy it at seed and feed stores."

It seemed to work great, I said, adding that there were a few mild side effects: "I seem to be eating a hell of a lot of oats, I have this craving for alfalfa, and lately I have this desire to sleep in the barn."

I wasn't being paid to tell that story. I had no contact with the manufacturer. But the publicity I generated for Mane 'n Tail was enormous. The newspapers loved the story: Terry Bradshaw rubbing horse shampoo on his head to grow hair. One paper even ran the manufacturers' instructions for use: Add 1 oz. per gallon of warm water into a bucket. Pre-wet the coat with just water to remove excess, loose dirt. Apply shampoo with a sponge . . .

It turned out that a lot of people were putting this stuff on their heads. Kmart and Wal-Mart were selling it. The company started marketing additional products, like the Hoofmaker, a skin moisturizer that is also used as a fingernail strengthener. Sales literally doubled. One day I was at Fox when producer Scott Ackerson asked me to come into his office, saying, "There's some stuff in there that came for you." I walked in and there were cases and cases of Mane 'n Tail. It was piled high. "You know what this is all about?" he asked.

I admitted that maybe I had briefly mentioned on some late-night TV show that on occasion I had put this horse shampoo on my head—and hair had started popping out. Scott looked at me like I was crazy, and maybe I was— but I got several dozen cases of this extraordinary product that I have always respected and loved, just in the event that the manufacturer is reading this.

When Jimmy Kimmel was a guest on my Los Angeles radio show, he said a makeup lady at Fox had told him I was using this horse shampoo, so he'd gone out and bought it himself. "I used it for months and months," he said, "and I was checking my head every few days to see if maybe there was one hair that was growing. Terry uses this stuff, I kept telling myself—and then it dawned on me: Terry Bradshaw's bald! What kind of endorsement is that?"

You can't slip anything by that Jimmy Kimmel. I admitted to Jimmy—and all the listeners to my show—that I'd told the story on Letterman because I was spending too much money on this stuff for my horses, and "do you realize how many cases of this stuff just showed up?"

Kimmel was astonished. "So you tricked America," he said.

"Well," I admitted kindly, "I certainly tricked you."

Mane 'n Tail never did grow a single strand of hair on my head. But I have come to the conclusion that being bald doesn't matter; what matters is how you feel about being bald. To me, bald is cool. It is definitely cool. I have received more letters from women telling me they would like to run their fingers through my scalp, that bald is sexy, than I ever would have imagined possible. So I don't wear a toupee, I don't use Mane 'n Tail or any other hair-growing solution, I don't comb the few long strands of hair I've got on the side of my head over the top and pretend it just naturally grew that way. And believe me, since my divorce I have had just as much success with women as I had when I was the Blond Bomber!

Unfortunately.

Most of the commercials or endorsements I've done started when an advertising agency or company approached me, but one time I wanted to be the spokesperson for a company: Red Man Tobacco. My grandfather chewed Red Man Tobacco, my father chewed Red Man Tobacco, so I chewed Red Man Tobacco. I wanted to do a commercial for that company because I believed in their product, but I had to hustle them.

Early in my career the NFL allowed cameras on the sidelines to come right up into your face during the game. Most players used that opportunity to say, "Hi, Mom!" Not me, my mom really didn't need a national spokesman—but this was my only chance to get that Red Man spot. Now, there is no greater tribute to a football player—especially a quarterback—than to be taken out of the game when your team is well ahead with a few minutes left to play. It is the acknowledgment of the coaching staff that they need to preserve you to fight another day. We were a fine football team, and there were many Sundays when I got pulled out near the end of the game. For me, that was always the ultimate. I'd jog humbly off the field, pretending I didn't hear the cheers. I knew that soon as I got to the sideline and took off my helmet, that camera would be in my face.

I went right to the trainer's supplies, where I'd put my Red Man pouch, and just stuck a big plug in my cheek. Then I looked at the camera and gave them that big old smile, making real sure my Red Man pouch was highly visible. Hi, Red Man!

It definitely did work. I became their spokesman for four or five years. During that period I actually created a product for them. We were filming a spot for plug tobacco in the Cotton Bowl in Dallas, Texas. The problem with plug tobacco was that it came wrapped in cellophane, and once the package was opened, it couldn't be resealed. Eventually it dried out. So I sat down and designed a foil pouch for plug tobacco that could be resealed, keeping the tobacco moist. I showed it to the executive I worked with, Ralph Lane, and he agreed it was a fine idea. They went ahead and did it. To show their appreciation for my contribution, they flew me all the way to Owensboro, Kentucky, and gave me a huge silver belt buckle with the Red Man logo on it.

Owensboro, Kentucky, is a lovely little city—but nobody ever said after winning a Super Bowl, "Now I'm going to Owensboro, Kentucky!" They didn't pay me a Red Man cent for the idea either.

This all happened before people realized the dangers of chewing tobacco. As my little girls got bigger, they asked me to stop chewing. Finally Rachel, who was maybe seven years old, offered me a deal. "If I quit sucking my thumb," she said, "will you quit chewing tobacco?"

We shook on it. It took me a bit, but eventually I managed to quit. Unfortunately, now I suck my thumb.

I also smoke cigars. Hi, Romeo y Julieta. Rachel wants me to stop smoking cigars, but we're negotiating. "If you quit smoking cigars . . . ," she said.

I finished it for her, "What are you going to quit doing that I don't know about?" So for a little while, at least, I've got her stymied.

In addition to creating plug tobacco packaging I once had my very own product, Terry's Peanut Butter. Actually, those two products probably didn't go very well together. If you're eating peanut butter, don't chew tobacco. But that wasn't necessary. Some friends of mine in the food business believed I was so popular in Pittsburgh my name on a product would be enough to sell it. Now, it probably isn't fair to judge my popularity based on peanut butter sales, but they were convinced it would work. Before deciding on peanut butter we did some market testing and analysis. What would you prefer, Mrs. Consumer, Terry's Peanut Butter or Terry's Fish Soup?

Our tests showed that there was no clear favorite among Pittsburgh's peanut butters.

The only thing that was wrong with our product was its taste. Apparently people didn't seem to like the taste very much. One newspaper arranged a taste test conducted by a panel of young people, and we won the top award for Least Desirable. Other than that it was a fine peanut butter. It had a real nice label.

I am often asked if there are products I would not endorse or do commercials for, to which I reply, I'm a divorced man. I am very much available, and not nearly as expensive as you might think. I can be very flexible, particularly around the first of the month, when that alimony check needs to be written.

Actually, that's a little less true than it once was; I do have to believe that the product I'm endorsing by my presence does exactly what I'm supposed to say it does. If that car isn't safe, I'm not going to stand behind it! I have turned down a lot of offers. I still don't do commercials for alcoholic beverages, for example, or anything associated with gambling, and I've never done anything political.

Well, except for that one commercial for Miller Beer, but technically it wasn't for the beer, it was for the Miller Beer Adjustable Inflatable Super Bowl Cheer Chair. Truly, I am one of the few people who did a chair commercial for a beer company. It was actually a plastic blow-up chair. I did one commercial with James Brown. The two of us were sitting in front of the television in our Miller Beer Adjustable Inflatable Super Bowl Cheer Chairs, and I kept making . . . flatulence sounds. I mean these were . . . flatulence sounds like never heard before on network television. J.B. shook his head and looked disgusted. It was the look appropriate for a Harvaaaad graduate caught in the middle of a . . . flatulence joke. Finally he asked me what I was doing. By this point it was pretty obvious to viewers what he was supposed to think I was doing, wink, wink. So I told him, J.B., I'm letting the air out of my chair! And then I did it again. Longer, with more flat.

That was the classier of the Miller Beer Adjustable Inflatable Super Bowl Cheer Chair commercials. I did a second one with a cute little poodle, a little fluffy thing. I was sitting in my Miller Beer chair watching a football game when this poodle made it clear to me she needed to go outside. She had her leash in her mouth, and she was dancing around the room. The more I told her I was watching the football game, the more desperate she got. Finally the tough little poodle pulled the plug on me, releasing a jet stream of air from the chair and sending me whizzing around just as if someone had released air from a balloon. As the poodle watched I bounced off the walls, the ceiling—and finally right through the wall. The desperate poodle jumped outside through the hole I supposedly made in the wall. And as I disappeared high into the sky, the dog happily lifted her leg on a tree.

I admit that I get a lot of satisfaction out of the fact that I've turned the reputation that once really bothered me—that I was so dumb that I couldn't spell *cat* if they spotted me the . . . the . . . most of the letters—into a comic character. In just about all the commercials I do I play a lovable dunce, the man so dumb he can't properly pronounce the Japanese word for raw fish, the man so dumb that when he gets together with his high-roller friends they play a tough game of Go Fish. But when I first started doing commercials—I only found this out several years later—that reputation cost me a lot of opportunities. Financial institutions—banks, mortgage companies, credit card companies—didn't want anything to do with me because I was supposed to be dumb. They were afraid people might think, Be as dumb as Terry Bradshaw, give us your money! Or maybe, We're so dumb that we hired Terry Bradshaw as our representative, give us your money.

So instead of banks I got cattle dewormers, toupees, and peanut butter. It took a long time, but eventually people began to understand that I was playing a role, a character. That it wasn't really me. Hee Haw, Howie called this character, the guy whose mother drives a truck and has only one tooth— which she uses to chaw her initials into an ear of corn. The guy who could do a commercial with Howie Long for Lay's potato chips in which we host a "show" called *Cooking with Terry and Howie*—and I get to tell the audience, "Today's recipe is one bag of Lay's potato chips, pour into bowl, let stand. Here, here's one I prepared earlier."

Now Howie has established a character too; Howie's character is the real handsome, sophisticated, perfectly dressed leading man. That's why Howie's character gets to costar with a beautiful woman named Teri Hatcher for Radio Shack, while my guy gets to costar in a series of commercials for Wendy's hamburgers with a monkey.

I enjoy playing my character, it's easy for me to be not me. I know going in that the joke is going to be on me; if something bad is going to happen to someone, it's going to happen to me. The audience knows it too, and seems to enjoy seeing it happen to me.

Eventually even some of those financial service companies hired me. I suspect their message was something like, If Terry Bradshaw is smart enough to be associated with our company, how come you're not? I did a series of commercials for the Associates, a Texas home equity loan company, in which they even let me sing a little country-western home equity loan music.

And easily the most memorable commercial I've done was with Dick Butkus for the Visa credit card people to publicize their relationship with the NFL Hall of Fame. I sang in this one too. There is this sweet song from the musical *Gigi* called "I Remember It

Well," in which an elderly man and woman recall the beginning of their relationship—and he gets every single detail wrong. Butkus and I sang a specially written version of that song in which we remembered the games we played against each other. The idea was that Butkus had hit me so often and so hard that I was too shell-sacked to get a single detail right. I sang, "You crushed my knee," to which he responded, "It was your toe"; I sang, "You broke my ribs," and he answered, "It was your nose"; and I finished, "Ah yes . . . I remember it welllllll. . . ."

"You sacked me once," I sang to begin the second verse.

"I sacked you twice," Butkus corrected.

"In pouring rain . . ."

"No, it was nice . . ."

"Ah yes, I remember it well . . ."

We filmed it at the Hall of Fame in Canton, Ohio. We started shooting at six-thirty in the evening, after the Hall of Fame closed, and went until maybe five o'clock the next morning. We were supposed to do a little soft-shoe dance, but they eventually had to give up that idea because Mr. Butkus only did a hard-shoe.

It was a long night, and both of us got tired. There isn't too much you can do about that. People mess up. And mess up, and mess up. People forget their lines or do a poor reading or blink at the key moment or can't get it exactly the way the director or the client wants it.

We did all that. We just did it over and over through the night. We were hot and tired and aggravated, but we kept going. The real truth is that after a while Dick was really tired and messing up. But way late in the evening, while we were pausing to let them reset the lights, Butkus leaned over to me— to me!— and growled, "You better not screw up your lines!"

Me? Screw up my lines? What was he gonna do, hit me?

We were hot and tired and irritable, so that definitely was a possibility. "I'll do my best, Mr. Butkus," I told him.

I love the end of the commercial. After I'd spent the whole time claiming I remember every hit so well, I walked away and as I did I said pleasantly to him, "See you, Nitschke."

The commercial was very popular. I know a lot of people stopped me to tell me how much they enjoyed it. But one day I was passing through the Oklahoma City airport when I saw Butkus standing in the middle of the baggage claim area speaking with two people. The man looked like the Rhinestone Cowboy. He was wearing black lizard cowboy boots that went up almost to his knees with his black jeans tucked into them, a big round silver belt buckle and a black hat about three feet wide and a foot high with a crease down the middle. So I went over to him and asked him about his outfit. "Ever since we did that commercial," he confided in me, "people got to recognizing me wherever I go. I don't want to be recognized. I want to be left alone."

I took one step back to admire his outfit. I remember it well. The black boots, black jeans, shining silver belt buckle and big black hat. "Real good plan, Dick," I said admiringly, "no one's going to notice you dressed in this outfit."

The commercials I've most enjoyed doing were for the discount long distance telephone company 10-10-220, because they let me be my other self. These were the spots in which I proudly called raw fish su-che instead of sushi and was playing cutthroat Go Fish. After doing the spots the way they were written by the copywriter, they allowed me to have some fun with the words. I think what continues to amaze me is that I'm probably known to more people for these commercials than for my playing career or even the Fox show.

Maybe the best thing about the 10-10-220 commercials is that I've never gotten injured while making them—although unfortunately I did end up hurting somebody else. This was almost the most expensive commercial in the whole wonderful history of commercials. I was making the commercial on a golf course with Mets catcher Mike Piazza and a third person, a real actor. The nice part about making these commercials is that the client allows us to create our own endings, our own punchlines—although in this case it was a headline.

As we did this commercial, it became obvious that it was too serious. There was no humor in it. So I thought it would be funny if I had a golf club on my shoulder, as I turned to watch Mike's drive I accidentally turned the club, hitting the actor in the back of the head and knocking him down. This actor was a trouper! I mean a trouper! We did it several times, and I kept successfully conking him in the head. You okay? I asked. I'm okay, he said. Okay, I said. I'd heard about actors hitting their marks, but I'm not really an actor.

We rehearsed it three or four times. I'm okay, the

actor said. Then, a little less convincingly, I'mmmm okayy. Then, Imokay. Finally, Mmmooooo. He wasn't about to admit it hurt; this was a national commercial with Mike Piazza and Terry Bradshaw, this was the rent-payer. But it was pretty obvious he was taking a beating. The director was ready to film it. Piazza hit his drive, and I turned to watch it, but as my golf club came around this time the actor anticipated getting hit and involuntarily ducked; my club glanced off the top of his head and hit Piazza right on his cheekbone, just a hair under his eyelid.

I cut his eyelid right open. Blood started flowing pretty fast. My first thought was a simple one: I have ended the playing career of a future Hall-of-Famer. The side of his face swelled up like it was being inflated. I would describe what happened on the set as controlled panic—meaning nobody yelled "Fire!" But people were pretty intense for a few minutes there. Mike kept telling people he was fine. We were lucky—just a smidgeon more, and I would have hit him square in the eye with the club. Who knows what kind of damage that would have caused. I definitely was sincerely apologetic. I'd heard about dying for your art, but never ending your career for a commercial.

While some of my Steelers teammates will claim my acting career began with my Oscar-caliber performances as an injured quarterback, it was actually Burt Reynolds who gave me my first movie role.

Burt Reynolds and I became friends after he apologized for making jokes about my intelligence, and in 1977 he offered me a part in a movie he was making named *Hooper*. It was a story about competition between stuntmen, as the young buck tries to take over for the old veteran—*All About Eve* with car crashes.

I didn't know anything about acting. I didn't have to; my big scene consisted of me being thrown out of a bar. Right through the front window. This was a stuntman movie. A stunt coordinator taught me how to movie fight and how to fly through the window. It was not a dangerous stunt; instead of glass in the window there was a kind of clear sugar substance, and on the other side of the window, out of camera range, was a pile of garbage bags filled with foam to cushion my landing.

I was psyched. Psyched! This was my motion picture debut. I was going to be on the silver screen! Fifty feet high! This was the beginning of my acting career, and who knew where it might lead. Well, initially I knew it led through that window. But I was determined to be thrown through that window like nobody had ever been thrown through a window before. The director was Hal Needham, who had started his own career as one of the great stuntmen. The scene began with me striding over to the table where Burt Reynolds was sitting with Sally Field and telling him, "Hey, buddy, I put fifty cents in that jukebox and all I can hear is your lips flappin'."

I was definitely going through that window. The fight started; Pow! Bam! I spit out a couple of stunt teeth. Then it was time for me to go through that window. The way it's done is you run and dive through the window and after editing it looks like you got tossed through it. But in my eagerness to please Hal Needham I hit my mark—the takeoff point—at full speed. I went sailing through the window—and right over the pile of garbage bags, landing on the asphalt. I landed smack dab on my elbow. I shattered something called the bursa, but I was in the movies, and the cameras were rolling, so I had to keep going. I leaped up and just kept running.

I played the whole next season with restricted movement in my elbow. I think I must be one of very few people whose movie-making injury affected his professional football career. After that season they went in, drained blood out of it, and cleaned it out. While *Hooper* received nice reviews, no one even mentioned my cinematic debut. But at least I was an official actor.

Hal Needham and Burt Reynolds must have liked the way I went flying through that window, because a couple of years later they cast me in *Cannonball Run*, a story based on an illegal cross-country race on public roads. This was one of the strangest casts in movie history. In addition to Burt and me, it included Farrah Fawcett, Jackie Chan, Bianca Jagger, Molly Picon from the Yiddish theater, Dean Martin, and Sammy Davis Jr. I was partnered with the great country songwriter and performer Mel Tillis. Needham must have respected my acting ability because he cast us as country bumpkins. It was the whole hog. It was *Hee Haw* time. I had been a fan of Mel Tillis just about forever, so it was exciting to be acting with him. Now, it is a known fact that Mel Tillis stutters—except for when he is singing. When he sings, he pronounces his words perfectly. So in one scene in the movie we were supposed to be looking for a short cut and got lost. Mel was supposed to say, "I cain't see a damn thing, can you?" Over and over he tried to say that line, but every time he opened his mouth he stuttered. The harder he tried, the worse he stuttered. We'd done it a lot of times, and it was getting pretty late. Finally, in desperation, he sang his line, "I can't see #%$#, can you?"

It was perfect. And in response, I sang my line too, "No problem, son, no problem."

About halfway through the race we were eliminated when we drove our car into a swimming pool. Unlike diving through the window, I didn't actually have to drive the car into the pool—although several years later I did shoot some ducks that landed in my swimming pool. But that scene eliminated us from the race and the rest of the movie.

People laughed at me when I acted. Turned out that was a good thing. Hal Needham told me I was a natural-born comedy actor, that all I had to do was open my mouth and people started laughing. Apparently some television executives thought that Mel Tillis and I worked well together, because in 1981 they created a half-hour sitcom called *The Stockers* around the characters we played in the movie. Basically, *The Stockers* was a less sophisticated *Dukes of Hazzard*. I played a character named J. J. Spangler, a stock car driver running dirt tracks in the South, and Mel Tillis played my mechanic and best friend.

This was a real TV series. The show was going to be done by Johnny Carson's production company, produced by Al Ruddy, who had produced *The Godfather*, and directed by Hal Needham. The problem was that if the series was successful, I would have to retire from football. I'd have to accept a lot more money than I was making with the Steelers to have fun making TV shows with Mel Tillis in Hollywood, and I'd have to give up the opportunity to have people chasing me around trying to hurt me.

I considered my options for, I don't know, three or four seconds. Maybe less. If the two-hour pilot film was successful, and NBC decided to make it into a weekly series, I would retire. When I announced my decision to the media, there were a lot of people who supported me, among them Cliff Stoudt, my backup, who would never take over at quarterback, and the entire cities of Houston and Dallas.

Making the show was not as easy as I had expected it to be. In the other pictures I'd done, I was very much a secondary character. Secondary? At best I was ninthary. But this time I was the costar. My name went right up at the top. The show would succeed or fail based on my ability. Admittedly, I was really nervous when we started. And I learned something very quickly; it's not easy playing opposite an actor who stutters. I'd be all ready for him to finish his line, and he'd be stuttering, and I'd be waiting, and he'd be stuttering, I was all ready to respond, just waiting, waiting a little more, he'd be stuttering, maybe I'd lean against a car as I was waiting, and then I'd sit down, Mel was trying, then I'd go have some lunch, I was all ready . . . As Hal Needham said, "We did have to cut some of the stuttering because it was only a half-hour show."

Needham was just as complimentary about my work. "In my life I have only seen one athlete who took to acting better," he said, "Merlin Olsen." That included Alex Karras, whose main claim to acting fame was a scene in which he punched out a horse. If that wasn't compliment enough, Hal went on to say that while I had started a little rough in the acting business, by the end of the week, "he looked like a white hog in a fresh mud puddle on a windy morning."

Gosh, those Hollywood folks sure knew how to flatter a guy.

I couldn't tell if the show was any good or not. But the professional people around us kept telling us that it was going great, sweetheart. We were continually assured that NBC wanted to put the show on its schedule. A "90 percent chance," the head of Carson Productions told us; they had eleven more scripts written. Good-bye NFL, hello I'd like to thank the Academy for this honor.

Finally, *The Stockers* was broadcast. The Steelers had been very interested in seeing it before the annual college draft; if the show was picked up by NBC, I would have to retire and they might decide to draft a young quarterback. After seeing it the Steelers drafted defensive linemen. Even the entire cities of Houston and Dallas couldn't make it a hit. The movie was embarrassing. Terrible. After watching it, my very own mother found it necessary to reassure me that she still loved me. The only thing that could have saved it, I decided, was to have Oral Roberts himself put his hands upon it and heal it. I admitted to reporters that it wasn't canceled, it had a heart attack. The great *New York Times* sportswriter Red Smith decided that "*The Stockers* pilot was witless, its comedy lamentable, its dialogue wooden and its plot nonexistent." And those were the highlights of his review. He particularly didn't like the scene "in which Terry, eager to attract a young woman, sorts through a stock of toupees until he finds a rug to suit the occasion."

Good-bye three-picture deal, hello Jack Tatum.

Of course I wasn't an actor, I was just acting like one. And obviously I wasn't very good at it. But I definitely did enjoy it. Like most other things in my life other than family, football, and my ranch, I didn't really take it very seriously. The opportunity was offered to me because of my football popularity, and I accepted it. I wasn't prepared for it, though, and as much as I hoped to succeed, I didn't really do much to make that happen. I didn't take a single acting lesson; when the director screamed "Action," I just did my part.

I never did let the fact that I didn't know what I was doing stop me from doing it. Over and over again. I was continually offered small guest star roles on weekly series, mostly playing myself. On the sitcom *Blossom,* for example, I was a high school baseball coach who explained, "My job is to teach boys that professional sports is not just a game, but it's a game where they pay you money!"

On *Married with Children* they were going to name the high school football field after me rather than the loser main character, Al Bundy. That surprised me because, as I told Al's not-so-bright daughter, Kelly Bundy, "I only went there two months and never put on a football uniform."

Which caused her to wonder, "You mean you played naked?"

I appeared in a lot of episodes of TV series—*Sin-*

bad; *Hardcastle and McCormick;* two episodes of Burt
Reynolds's hit show *Evening Shade; The Jeff Foxwor-
thy Show; Everybody Loves Raymond*—and if I didn't
play myself, I played someone who could have been
mistaken for myself. Except for my role in *The Adven-
tures of Brisco County Jr.,* in which I played a villain-
ous cavalry officer, Colonel Forest March, trying to kill
bounty hunter Brisco County and assassinate the president of the United States. In the acting business, that is
known as "playing against type."

I had never played the bad guy before—trust me,
friends, quarterbacks are never the bad guy—and I enjoyed it quite a bit. This was definitely the hardest part
I ever played because I really had to act. In the show I
hired three men for my posse to track down that mav-
erick Brisco County; former linebacker Carl Banks,
former quarterback Jim Harbaugh, and Ken Norton Jr.
Reviewing my performance, the great *Chicago Sun-
Times* wrote, "Bradshaw proves he's a better actor than
Jim Harbaugh."

Professionally, a lot of good things continued to
happen in my life. I never stopped to ask why. I never
slowed down to try to figure it out. I was smart enough
to know that it wasn't because I was smarter than
everybody else, and it definitely was not because of my
good looks. I do often claim that one reason for my
popularity is that I don't intimidate anybody. There are
not a lot of people who believe I'm a lot smarter than
they are, and even fewer people who think I'm better
looking than they are. I think they figure, Look, if that
guy can make it with what he has going for him, then
there's even hope for me. I've always been pretty open

about my life, about my failures as well as my successes, and I think that has allowed people to relate to me. I'm just ol' Terry, I'm Brad, Hee-Haw, a guy it would be fun to sit with in front of the TV chugging down a couple of cold ones.

But I am smart enough to believe that there is more to my success than just being available. Not to name-drop any really, really big Name, but I do thank You-Know-Who for all of it every single day. For a man whose best talent was throwing an inflated ellipsoid a long way, I've been very fortunate. I am not saying that the good Lord has presented me with these opportunities because I believe in Him, but rather that by following my beliefs, I have become a certain type of person. And other people seem to enjoy my electronic company. A lot of people seem to find pleasure watching me try to survive. Hey, Marge, look, there's old Terr playing a cavalry officer. Good thing they put that big hat on that old bald head a his.

But for whatever reason, things have always just seemed to happen to me. There are a lot of actors who have made a failed TV show, but my friends, there are very few people who aren't actors who have starred in *three* failed TV programs, two of them series and my very own talk show. Proving once again that the Lord does work in mysterious ways, more than a decade after the complete failure of *The Stockers,* I made the pilot for the half-hour sitcom *Game Night.*

Game Night was created, developed, and produced by Witt-Thomas. Witt-Thomas are big-time producers, one of the most successful production companies in television. They made *Soap, Blossom, Golden Girls,*

Empty Nest, Benson . . . and Game Night. Our pilot was directed by Robby Benson. I played Terry "Bradley"—Terry Bradley, Terry Bradshaw, get it? I was really supposed to be me playing me—a former football player who had become a broadcaster on Sunday-night football. Man I don't know how they continue to come up with these creative ideas.

This was definitely the only situation comedy pilot in TV history that began with a discussion of all the possible deadly plagues that could be brought into the United States. Football? I thought you said kill us all! Ba-dum-bump! So we immediately hooked all those viewers who thought deadly plagues were pretty funny. As one character told my character, Terry "Bradley"— not me, my character—"There are five billion germs on the head of a pin."

Terry Bradley was not supposed to be real smart. When I told the beautiful female reporter in the office, "I got to write that down," she responded, "Good, I'll get you a stick and some dirt!" Ba-dum-bump.

Game Night did not get picked up by ABC to become a series.

The third show, *The Home Team* with Terry Bradshaw, actually did get on the air for a few months. On this show I got to do things like sing with rock bands, cook with well-known chefs, interview children, and let a giant tarantula walk on my head. *The Home Team* was my very own daytime talk show.

My real talent turned out to be just being myself. I knew all my lines. I just opened my mouth, and they came out. Starting while I was still playing, I've made appearances on every kind of TV show you can imagine; I've done Super Bowl specials, *Hee Haw, Larry King Live, Later with Bob Costas, Country Kitchen, Nashville Now;* in 1990 I was the host of CBS's *New Year's Eve* program; I've done golf shows, fishing shows, cooking shows, even the Home Shopping Network shows. I cohosted *The National Cheerleading Competition* with Joe Namath and Lynn Swann. The first thing CBS did after I signed with them was send me as far away as possible to do the sled-by-sled for the Iditarod, the dogsled race across Alaska. When I had signed with CBS, some people said I was going to the dogs—this definitely proved them right. I've appeared everywhere; if they put a TV camera in the storefront so people could see themselves on TV as they walked by, I did that too. Name a show. Mike Douglas? Jo Jo and I did his show several times. Merv Griffin? He was great. Oprah? Oprah and I fell in love and eloped, but we been trying to keep it a secret. David Letterman?

I'm real comfortable with David Letterman, though it didn't start out that way. The first time I did his show was a hoot. I did not know how sensitive he was about his neck. Evidently he'd been in a car wreck and had a bad neck. He did not want anybody touching it—particularly a football player. Well, he made some off-the-wall comment, which he is so capable of doing, and I reached over and—me being a he-man football player and all—popped him gently on the face. 'Least I thought it was gentle. His head didn't spin or anything. This wasn't like hitting Mike Piazza in the head with a golf club, it was just a little . . . pop, but he exploded into a rage. He's some actor, I thought. At the time I didn't know it was for real. I didn't know he was really worried about being injured. He jumped out of his chair and ran behind his desk for protection.

Oh, I thought, he wants to play! That's a funny idea. I'll just chase him. So I took off after him. He backed away from me, pleading no, no, no . . .

Yeah, yeah, yeah. The show went to a commercial, and I was out of there. I disappeared faster than a turkey in November. Clearly we didn't understand each other; I thought we were having a great time, he was fearful about his life.

I found out later what had happened, and that David Letterman did not want me back on his show no how no way. That's not good, I thought, I wouldn't hurt him knowingly. But eventually, Letterman decided to bring me back. David immediately began talking about my last visit, saying, "There has been some talk out there that you and I didn't get along last time you were here." And then he ran the tape of me slapping him . . . in slow motion. Instant replay. "Now there," he said, "see that vicious hit you gave me?"

"You think that little love tap's a hit?" I asked. Then they ran a tape of me getting smacked, slammed, and sacked, including getting turned upside down and jackhammered into the ground by Turkey Jones. "Now that's a hit, you wimp!"

After that I went on regularly, once even wearing a bathing suit. A one-piece. I'm not like many of his guests; usually I don't go on there to promote something, we just talk about life. One time he asked me about being in the cattle business, which led me to the story about the time I fought the bull. I used to go up to the feed store in the morning, I explained, and drank some coffee with all the farmers. I was there one morning with my father when a dairyman showed up delivering his milk. He had a little trailer hooked onto the back of his old dairy truck, and in the trailer was a big old bull someone had given him to settle a debt. "I don't know what I'm a-gonna do with him," the dairyman said, "he ain't worth but a hunnred dollars."

"Lemme take a look at him," I said. We went outside, and I decided to buy the bull for $100. We made the deal, and I started herding the bull into a holding pen—but this was a bull, and bulls do not like to be told what to do. So he put his head down and came charging right at me. I turned and took off running faster than Letterman running from Bradshaw. This might have been a cheap bull, but he had horns, and coming right at me they looked pretty sharp. My dad tried to distract the bull, but that bull was of one mind. I reached the fence, and just as I put my foot up on the fence to hoist myself up, that bull nailed me in the back. He sacked me, knocking all the wind right out of me. As I started sliding down the rails, he decided to rake my ribs with his horns. My father was on the other side of the fence, and he grabbed me and dragged me under the rail to safety. But I was hurting big-time.

David Letterman was truly captivated by my true story, so I continued.

When I finally got my senses about me, I was pretty damn mad. That bull might not have realized it, but I had been trying to do him a big favor. If that dairyman couldn't have sold him, he was going straight to the meat locker. So I decided I was going to hasten that journey. I went over to my truck and got my .357 magnum. I walked back over to the pen. He was looking straight at me, I was looking right back at him. I cocked that hammer and shot him right between the eyes, dropped him on the spot graveyard dead.

I went and got my tractor and brought him home. Then I gutted him, skinned him, quartered him, and took it all to the meat locker plant, where they cut him up to eat. So, David, I finished, you best not mess with me.

Letterman was stunned. The bandleader, Paul Shaffer, was some kind of animal activist, and he was outraged. He was looking at me like *I* was some kind of animal. Well, I didn't try to butt my sorry ass. I was just trying to help this animal. I knew that people watching at home were either agreeing, Hell yeah, he oughta have shot his ass off, or out organizing protests against me. Letterman did not know if I was serious, so he asked me. I am completely serious, I told him, that story is one hundred percent true.

Except for that part about killing him.

Jay Leno? I'm real comfortable with Jay Leno. I'm always surprised to hear what I have to say when I go on Leno. Unfortunately, so is my family. I always sweat a lot more on Leno than on Letterman, number one because his studio is much warmer, and number two because I know I'm embarrassing the family name. I know that because they tell me. Jay Leno always asks me questions about how my family's doing back there in the woods, and I tell him all about braiding that hair on my mother's back or what happened to her at her welding job or the problems she had with her tooth.

My mom actually asked them to say a special prayer for me at Sunday school. A fellow walked up to her after I'd been on Leno and said, "I didn't know you weld," and she just tsk-tsked him and said, "Oh, that's just Terry."

I've always believed if you can't make fun of your very own family, who can you make fun of?

On Letterman I can just sit and talk; Jay Leno's people often have something for me to do. The year I opened up our first pregame show at Fox by riding a horse down Sunset Boulevard, for example, I came from behind the curtain on Leno riding a horse. I will say this for Jay, the man noticed it right away; no matter what people may say about Jay, you have to get up pretty early in the afternoon to put something over on him. Another time he led me into a conversation about baseball—knowing that I do not like the game of baseball. If I think playing the game of baseball is boring, just imagine how much I enjoy talking about it. Discussing compost heaps is more interesting. So I challenged Jay, tell me what is so interesting about a perfect game. No runs, no hits. You're watching nothing happening, and the more nothing happens, the more excited people get. Oh, look, it's nothing! This is so exciting. Explain that to me.

My desire whenever I appeared on a television show was simply to bring pleasure to people. I like to make people happy, and sometimes I may go just a bit too far. I may have even been embarrassed by some of the things I've said on television. For example, I do sincerely regret talking about my ex-wife and all the millions of dollars I had to give her and her new husband.

And I regret mentioning that even though we're divorced she uses my last name professionally. I regret mentioning that. I regret acting like an idiot on occasion. It is embarrassing, but it is me. The difficulty for me is that I have to live with me. That is me; sometimes I truly wish it wasn't, but it surely is. Trust me when I admit this, but there is a large part of me who wishes that I wasn't who I am personality-wise. If I were a little more subdued, I believe I would get more respect from people and maybe even be admired as an athlete who accomplished quite a lot. Sometimes I think, I wish I was more like Howie, I wish I was more like J.B. Not like Cris, though, not unless he has his neck shortened. I wish I could be like Bob Costas. But I can't, that's not how God made me. Then I realize that it is okay to be goofy, to act silly, it's okay to be exactly what I am. That's what I preach, and most of the time that's what I try to practice. I respect myself and my family, I go about my business without hurting anyone, and when I have the opportunity I bring a little laughter to people. That is who I am. It took me a long time to accept that—and even appreciate it, but I most certainly do. Well, at least most of the time. It was one of the very first talk shows I ever did, back in the early 1970s, that led eventually to *The Home Team Show.* To celebrate the opening of Burt Reynolds's restaurant in a new mall in Atlanta, Mike Douglas was doing his afternoon talk show from that mall for a week. That was the kind of TV specials they had at that time, *Mike Douglas Live at Some Mall*. But in that same mall they had an indoor skating rink—and they booked my wife, the top figure skater in America at that time, Jo Jo, to be on the show. I went to Atlanta with Jo Jo, and we had dinner with the producer of the show, a man named Erni DiMassa, and during dinner I told him about the time I accidentally put a new skylight in the roof.

It was a true story. Jo Jo did not like living on the ranch. Jo Jo liked being in the city; she liked the fancy restaurants, the crowds, the noise. I loved just being on the ranch. If cows had been cabs, we probably would've gotten along better. But Jo Jo was just never comfortable on the ranch. One night we were in bed, and there was a big windstorm. I was asleep when Jo Jo woke me up and whispered, "Terry, someone's trying to break into the house."

I've been robbed, I've also had people just come around the house to see where I lived, I even woke up one morning to find several Dallas Cowboy fans sitting on my front porch. But soon as I cleared the cobwebs, I heard a banging sound. "That's nothing," I told her, "it's just the wind blowing the screen door out back."

"No," she insisted, "someone is trying to break in."

Ever since I got shot at the summer I was working as a religious counselor, I've slept with a rifle under my bed and the bedroom door locked and chained. "Okay," I said, "I'll go see." So I got my thirty-ought-six rifle, unlocked the door, and went round back. Sure enough, it was the screen door banging open and shut. I latched it and went back into the bedroom. I locked the door and chained it, then I put the rifle on the floor next to the bed and laid down. I closed my eyes and . . .

"Terry, I can't sleep."

Hmmm. "What's the matter, sweetheart?" She was really scared. Every sound on the ranch seemed frightening to her. "Look, don't worry about it," I told her. "I promise you, there's nobody gonna bother you." Then I closed my eyes and . . .

"Well, what would you do if we did have a burglar?"

Hmmm. I sat up. "Now just look here. If a burglar breaks in here," I said, reaching over and picking up the rifle, "I'll just take this thirty-ought-six, and I will simply point it at him—"

That was when the gun went off accidentally. Fortunately I was pointing straight up. The noise of a rifle going off in a confined area can be deafening. My ears started ringing. But even that wasn't loud enough to drown out Jo Jo's screaming. Any little part of her that hadn't been scared before was now officially terrified. She was screaming, my ears were ringing, a cloud of gun smoke was drifting up. Finally I got up and turned on the lights. I wanted to see what damage I had done. It was real hazy in the room, so I couldn't make it out at first. When I looked at the ceiling, it looked like a little bullet hole. There was just a little piece of night coming in. "Oh, that's nothing," I said, "it's just a little bullet hole."

"AAAHHHHHHHHH!" Jo Jo screamed.

We did not sleep for the rest of the night. At dawn I went outside to see how much damage I'd done to my house. Truthfully, I was surprised. I had never known that one single hollow-point thirty-ought-six could do so much damage. I blew a hole clean through that roof maybe eighteen inches in diameter and splintered other places. Eventually I had to replace just about the entire roof.

While that didn't end the marriage, it didn't exactly endear me to my wife.

This was the story I told Erni DiMassa at dinner when Jo Jo went to Atlanta to ice skate at the opening of the mall. He was suitably impressed and decided to put me on the show. That was one of my very first real television interviews, and it went so well that thirty years later I found myself letting people paint my toenails and put a tarantula on my head.

NINE

You shoot one little hole in the bedroom ceiling, and thirty years later they still haven't forgotten it. Which is how I came to have my own daytime talk show. Erni DiMassa never did forget that story. While I completed my playing career, he went on to become one of the most successful producers in daytime television. Among the people he worked with were Mike Douglas, Regis, and Oprah. In the early 1990s he was running King World Productions, the biggest syndicator of television programming, and he wanted to create a show for me. I went to meet the King brothers, but my friends, I honestly believed there was about as much chance of my own show happening as me winning the Daytona 500 on my lawn tractor.

Not only didn't they give me my own show, they wouldn't even let me be on *Celebrity Jeopardy!* I'll have songs of love and despair for $500, Alex. But a few years later Erni DiMassa was asked by another group to suggest a personality who he thought could become a star in daytime television. He told them, "Terry Bradshaw." Then about three minutes later I believe he said, "Hello? You still there?"

One of the biggest cable companies in the world, Comcast, had formed a company named C3 to produce programming. C3 and the restaurant chain Planet Hollywood wanted to do a daytime talk show. Supposedly Planet Hollywood would get the top movie stars to make guest appearances, during which they would promote the restaurant. I met all the main people, and eventually they invited me to host the show: *The Home Team* with Terry Bradshaw. I couldn't believe it. My own show. Move over Oprah! Regis who?

If I couldn't believe it, imagine how people who weren't me felt. For a time after the program was announced I thought my name had been changed to Y. Terry Bradshaw? A lot of people were asking why they would hire a bald former football player with no experience in this field to host a show appealing mainly to women.

Well, I have always appealed to my mother, and she's a woman. If I'd had a sister, I feel real confident she would have liked me too. Admittedly though, after that my support among women got kind of thin. Truthfully, my qualifications for this job were not staggering, even including the fact that I once cohosted *The National Cheerleaders Competition*. But I believed completely I could do this. The part of me that is best known is the do-anything-for-a-laugh, crazy, outlandish, creative buffoon part of my personality, that's the part that makes my family wear phony name tags when they go out in public; but there is an equal part that is much less known. I have serious interests that most people would be very surprised to know about, knowledge about many things that I've successfully kept pretty well hidden from the public. I read books with big words in them, I know a lot of interesting stuff; if a person happened to come upon the books sitting on my shelves—most of which I've read—they would never suspect they were in Terry Bradshaw's house. There is a reasonably good mind hard at work inside my head.

So the concept of hosting an entertainment show in which I got to express the different parts of my personality appealed to me. The opportunity to meet every single one of the girls on *Baywatch* had absolutely nothing to do with it. Originally I was supposed to be the quarterback of *The Home Team,* my team consisting of a group of regularly appearing contributors on a variety of subjects, among them a "Mrs. Fix It," a woman who could fix things around the house, a stand-up comedian who was our roving reporter, a personal trainer, and a style reporter. We were going to have a whole lot of different segments, a cooking segment, a do-it-yourself without having to go to the emergency room and then get into a fight for payment with your medical insurance company segment, a fashion segment, a finance segment. We were going to borrow a popular segment from Art Linkletter's show and have me interview some young kids, then we were going to have inspirational pull-the-kid-out-of-the-hole, barking-dog-saves-family human interest stories, and finally I was going to do serious interviews with major celebrities supplied to us by Planet Hollywood.

Hello there Planet Hollywood? I'm still waiting for those major celebrities to show up.

Fox bought the show for its entire daytime network, although it didn't have much of a daytime network. Eventually we were on the air in about 150 markets, 98 percent of the country. We lasted thirteen weeks. The show failed for a lot of reasons. In a lot of cities we were on against Oprah and Rosie, so we definitely had no shot in those places. Planet Hollywood never was able to get us the celebrities we had been promised, so we had no big names to draw viewers. The show was constantly evolving as the producers tried to find the formula that would work. The show was never really promoted; a lot of people didn't even know we were on the air. We didn't have enough time to find our rhythm. I mean, it did take Regis twenty-four years to become an instant success. And finally, the show really just wasn't very good.

We did have fun doing it, though, and at times it was a very good show. Just not consistently enough. After a couple of weeks we added a cohost, a lovely woman named Cynthia Garrett. There were subjects we did that I just felt unprepared to do, I felt they needed a woman's viewpoint. That was Cynthia Garrett, who was absolutely wonderful.

I think a big part of the problem was that the producers of the show never really understood why they had hired me. Y. Terry Bradshaw. I'm best when you just let me be, when I open my mouth and whatever words are waiting there just come rushing out. When I have to read from a script or follow specific direction, I'm not as entertaining. Let me call my own plays. Just tell me, We're cooking shrimp today, go. I'm going to give you all of me. But too often on this show I was directed. What I offered was unpredictability; in football it was hard to call the right defense against me because sometimes even I didn't know what I was going to do till I got right up there at the line of scrimmage. Anything was possible. The same thing should have been true on this show, but it wasn't. The producers defended me pretty good.

Almost from the first day I kept getting these notes from the "suits" about improving my performance. Could Terry tone it down a little bit? Or Terry is speaking too southern, can he be more midwestern? One of my favorites was, "Terry is appearing too bright on the air and the audience doesn't expect it. Can you ask him to dumb it up?" First time anybody ever accused me of being too smart. Another time they complained I was being too deferential to my female guests. But the best complaint of all was, "Can you ask Terry not to sweat so much?"

I was willing to do just about everything possible to make the show work. I did things that if anybody had told me I was going to do them before I did the show, I would have said they had been sacked one time too many, they had played too long without a helmet, they were permanently one yard short of a first down. I let them put a tarantula on my head. I don't mean an itsy-bitsy spider, I mean a big, hairy tarantula. Maybe I didn't inherit my father's fear of spiders, but I didn't need it to be afraid of this thing. I was terrified all on my own. Don't worry, Terry, they told me, it can't hurt you. Then they explained why. Well, my friends, when you have a tarantula crawling on your head, you're not real interested in details. Maybe tarantulas on your head don't hurt you physically, but they can sure do some serious psychological damage. They are big, and they are ugly. I knew big and ugly—I played fourteen years of professional football, so I definitely knew big and ugly—but I had never experienced anything like this.

But even worse than a tarantula on my head, I allowed them to paint my toenails. All of my toenails. Erni DiMassa talked me into it. Shaquille O'Neal was coming out with a line of nail polish for men, Dennis Rodman was wearing lipstick and a wedding dress, so Erni came up with a plan. This was going to be a big secret. Cynthia and I would talk about big athletes doing silly things, and then I would shock her by taking off my shoes and showing her my painted toenails. Do I really need to do this? I asked him.

"It'll be great, Terry, it'll be fabulous."

What I did not know was that years earlier DiMassa had produced *Candid Camera*. And that he had hidden a camera in the makeup room and taped me having my toenails painted. As the very attractive makeup lady was doing my nails, I started fussing, "Well, dear, I think I like that color better . . . that looks so good . . . Can't you pretty please paint a little face on it?"

During the taping of the show I surprised Cynthia by revealing my painted toenails—and then she shocked me by introducing the tape. I have never been so embarrassed in my entire life. I didn't know where to hide, so I crawled under a table. Well, dear, I think . . . Oh, man, I was wishing for a sinkhole to appear so I could jump in. After the show I chased that man DiMassa around the studio. He was hiding all over from me. I believe that the only thing that prevented me from finding him and playing God Bless America on his head was my fear that I might chip my toenail polish.

Well, I mean, you know, as long as I had it done . . .

The cooking segments on the show almost always turned out to be funny. I can cook. Read this clearly now: I can cook. I've been divorced three times, I had to learn how to cook. It was either cook or die. I've got this big old lake on my property just filled with fish, and I live in that big old ranch house all by myself, ladies, I said *all by myself,* so I've got nobody there to fry fish for me. If I want fried fish, I fry my own. That's all by myself. Daytime talk shows usually take the cooking segment real serious. One of our first guests on the show was the executive chef from Planet Hollywood. Anybody who had ever eaten at the old Planet Hollywood will understand that we weren't that serious about our cooking segments. Usually we'd run into some sort of unusual problem—for example, I would eat the ingredients before we needed them. And I also know that some food is better for throwing than eating, and I would throw bits of it at Cynthia. We didn't exactly have food fights, we sort of had food skirmishes.

I also got to conduct some very good interviews. We had a hard time getting the major talent that we had been led to believe would come on the show. It probably says right on the menus, Planet Hollywood doesn't deliver. But we managed to get a splattering of great stars. We had 'N Sync—that was the first TV talk show they ever did—Kenny Rogers, Joan Collins, Trisha Yearwood, and Garth Brooks. We had Toby Keith, David Foster, Kenny Chesney, but the two interviews I most enjoyed were with Charlton Heston and Whoopi Goldberg. That covers just about the entire political spectrum.

The key to being a good interviewer, I learned, is being a better listener. I was reminded about that by a cabdriver who watched the show. As he was driving me to the airport, he said, "Can I give you a little constructive criticism? Let your guests finish the answers to your questions." That was the first time I had ever been given a tip by a cabdriver. But he was right. I was concentrating so much on getting all my questions asked that I wasn't paying any attention to the answers. The worst interviews I did were just me asking a list of prepared questions. It was like my subject said, ". . . So that's when I met the undercover agent who tried to slip me information about the nuclear balance of power," and I responded, "Oh, that's just great, so do you have another picture coming out soon?"

While it definitely is necessary to prepare all the questions you want to ask, then you need to pretty much forget about those questions. When you really listen to what people say, they will tell you what the next question should be. If you listen real carefully, the person you're interviewing may be hinting that if you follow up with the right question, they might be willing to talk about things that aren't even on the list.

I believe I got better at doing the show every day.

So by the time we got canceled, I was ready to start. And I probably wasn't even sweating so much. While I do not enjoy failing at anything I do, I really wasn't unhappy that the show was going off the air. I did feel bad for all the nice people who got involved with it, but it was too much, I had no life of my own. With the show, with my responsibility to Fox, with the commercials I was doing and the special appearances and the speeches, I was living on the road. I was never home. In the weeks when I wasn't really busy, I would leave my ranch every Friday and fly to Los Angeles. On Saturday and Sunday I did my football job. Monday morning I reported to the studio for my daytime talk show job. We taped two shows a day Monday through Wednesday, and when I wasn't at the studio, I was preparing for the next day's shows. Wednesday at 5:00 P.M. I got a flight back to Texas. I'd get there late Wednesday night, spend all day Thursday at home, and start the whole cycle again on Friday. It was a brutal schedule. In fact, it darn near got me killed.

It was usually real late by the time I got home Wednesday night. Everybody was asleep. One Wednesday night, I remember, I took off my boots because I didn't want to wake my wife or my girls and started walking across the living room and . . . whoosh, I went sailing. Landed splat on my back. I had slipped on the highly polished hardwood floors, which was very surprising to me—mostly because we didn't have highly polished hardwood floors. At least we hadn't had them when I'd left. We had nice thick carpet. Turned out that while I was gone, my wife had ripped out the carpets and had the floors done.

That was just the beginning. After that, just about every time I came home the house had been changed dramatically. Soon as I got on the plane, my wife and her best friend would begin making changes. I never knew what to expect. One night I made it safely through the living room into our bedroom——where in the pitch black I proceeded to break my toe kicking the newly placed $12,000 chair. I did that twice, actually. Just when I got used to that chair being in one place, she moved it—and I banged into it again and smashed the same broken toe. From week to week I never knew whether we had carpets or finished floors. One time when I left, we had a sunken den; I came home a week later, and that den had risen! I had a raised den. Another time I came home, and as I walked through the living room, I glanced outside into the backyard pool area and it had disappeared. All of it. She had torn out the whole back wall and added a smoking room. A smoking room! It was such a nice smoking room that I wasn't allowed to smoke in it because she thought I would mess it up. Nobody else in the whole world could get things done as fast as she could; her father was a builder, and every week just about the time I was sitting down on an airplane he must have been bringing in the heavy equipment. I went from a large game room one week to three small bedrooms a week later. I opened my closet when I came home one night and this huge cylinder with holes in it had grown out of the floor all the way to the ceiling; I was supposed to keep my socks and underwear stuffed in the holes. When I left one Friday I had a beautiful white bathroom; I came back and turned on the lights and . . . oh my, what in the world is that! The room was a bright, splotchy red.

I can't begin to mention all the changes that got made while I was gone. Carpet, paint, tile, furniture, a new roof. All I knew was that the more I traveled, the smaller my area got. Eventually I ended up keeping my clothes in an upstairs guest room. If that show had lasted much longer, that house might've killed me.

One of the first things I did when the show got canceled was shoot my cell phone. I can't stand cell phones. I hate them. I don't understand why people can't have a life without being attached to a telephone. I see people darting in and out of traffic with their head buried in a cell phone. When I play golf with my friends, they complain because I tend to cheat, but they have that cell phone tied to their belt. I just get sick of it. So I took my cell phone down to my lake and set it down on a rock. Then I stood about forty feet away and took my .300 magnum elephant gun and just disintegrated this thing. The only reason I used the elephant gun is that a cannon would have been too much. It definitely did the job—that cell phone wasn't going to ring no more; it was technological roadkill.

The people with deals still managed to find me, though. Three failed TV shows didn't even slow down the offers. In 1999 Jeff Quinn decided I would be a natural for talk radio and put together a deal for me to do my own show on a sports talk radio station in Los Angeles. What do I have to do? I asked. Talk, they told me. What do I have to talk about? I asked. Anything you want, they told me. I definitely could do that.

I had never hosted a radio show before—but I had

been divorced before. I was getting divorced again, so I knew that I definitely needed the money. It also sounded like it would be fun.

My show was called *Lunch with Terry*. The idea behind the show was that there was no idea behind the show. For one hour five days a week I was permitted to talk about anything I felt like talking about. Just about 90 percent of the time it was chaos, while 10 percent of the time it was organized chaos. At first I thought I might have a problem because this was a sports talk station and, besides football, I don't really like sports. The only thing I know about baseball is that I don't like it. I once went to a Lakers basketball game, but I was so bored I left early. Hockey I haven't come close to figuring out. Horse racing, I enjoy that. And golf, I love golf. But all I know about golf is hit and chase, hit and chase, sometimes hit and search and drop another one. But that didn't seem to matter very much, because we never talked sports on this sports talk station. This was the Dodgers' flagship station, but I personally thought it was a bad sign that no one objected when I told listeners that nobody cared about the Dodgers.

Basically, the show was a platform for me to talk about whatever was on my mind. It was a guided tour through my mind. I would just make it up as I went along. "Hello, everybody," I told my listeners, "how is everybody out there? This is my award-winning radio show. I just call it that because it makes radio people mad. Howie Long asked me, Yo man, you really got an award-winning radio show? I told him I did. He asked me, What are they paying you over there? I told him the truth, 'One point nine million, but that's for the full five months.'

"He looked at me and asked, 'You think they got room over there for me?'

" 'No,' I told him, 'you got to have personality. You got to have charm, you've got to be able to talk to the garbage collectors as well as the tax collectors. You've got to be able to spread it out, and Howie, that is not your forte. According to *People* magazine, you're one of the fifty most beautiful people in America, and that's not who this show is for. We're not talking to the beautiful people, with a few exceptions. All the women out there are gorgeous, but not the men, the men are not.

" 'The Welders Society in Los Angeles and surrounding counties voted us their favorite talk show. We received the famous gold-plating welding torch award. We had a pretty special night over at the union hall.

" 'I'll tell you what, Howie, when we first started, the only people who would advertise were strip joints. My momma pitched a fit, we got rid of the strip joints, and the beer people don't call in anymore. We picked up so many good listeners, milk people advertise on this show now. Pampers. It's a family show.' "

As always, I just opened my mouth, and this show poured out. I had several regular characters I liked to talk about. There was my ex-wife. Now, this was not my real ex-wife who is a lawyer and knows a lot of lawyers. I would never say anything poor about this fine lawyer ex-wife. The ex-wife I talked about who was not my real ex-wife was a very sweet lady. I used to tell people what a wonderful dancer she was. Nobody slid down that pole like she did. And if someone had a problem with their front lawn, I would suggest they invite my radio ex-wife to come over and graze.

Now my radio mother on the other hand, sadly, that was my true mother. I told people how terrible it was when she finally lost that tooth. She called me to complain, I reported, " 'cause now she can't whistle anymore. She just puckers up and goes, *pfffttt, pfffttt.* It's a real tragedy, squirrel hunting season opened, and she can't go because she can't call the dogs back in."

One thing I liked to do on the show was call up people and talk to them without telling them they were on the radio. I think there is a word to describe that: illegal. I called one friend who asked, Aren't you supposed to be doing your radio show right now?

No, they gave me the day off. You want to go play some golf?

I wish. I can't play golf today, I got to go to this $#%$#%& bowling deal tonight. I'm busy up to my ass. And my boss . . .

I did have the good sense to stop before anyone could wreck their entire life. I called up my brother once and accused him of bed wetting. "Are we on the show?" he asked. Oh man, what kind of brother do you think I am? Do you *really* think I'd call you up and make fun of you while tens of millions of people were listening?

He didn't even pause for respect. "Of course I do," he said. That boy had been my brother for a long time.

I did use the opportunity to talk about some of the things that I didn't like. As I explained one day, I had done an infomercial for a body-shaping device with

Dorothy Hamill—which brought me to the king of infomercials, Tony Robbins. "When I saw him," I said, "I wondered, how would you like to be his dentist? He has the biggest teeth I have ever seen. But I don't like him; I don't like anybody telling me they have all the answers to my problems, and I don't like people who flaunt their wealth."

I did on occasion talk about my real third ex-wife; well, at least I did until I got that letter from those lawyers, which enabled me to reveal my true feelings about lawyers: "We don't have too many attorney listeners out there, and if we do, they can't be very good attorneys, because they should be busy working, figuring out ways to screw people out of their money." I talked a lot about football; most of the telephone calls I took were football questions. And on occasion I did get real serious and talk about some of the things that were hurting me inside.

At times the show became Terry's on-the-air therapy session. I was going through a painful divorce at that time, and I allowed my feelings to be known. As I might have sung, I unleashed my heart to AM radio. That was good for me, but I also received many phone calls from other people going through the same thing, and they told me it helped them to know that someone understood their feelings and shared them. It helped for them to know that they weren't going through it alone. It helped me too.

One thing I did say that I knew was a big mistake. I played a song and offered my listeners one million dollars if they could tell who was singing it. That switchboard lit up brighter than the Christmas tree in

Rockefeller Center. The phone inside the studio also started ringing pretty loudly. It was the head of the station calling to inform me that there is no kidding on radio. No way. No million dollars either. So I immediately went back on the radio and told my listeners I'd made a slight mistake. I'd meant to say a quarter, I told them, twenty-five cents. I'd give them a quarter.

When I was hired, the station executives told me they wanted to see some movement in the ratings. As I later pointed out to them, they never did say which way! I don't think I really fit into the middle of their broadcast day; it was sports talk, sports talk, Terry talk, sports talk, sports talk, "My job," I told listeners, "is to take a little bit of the friction off between the morning shows and the shows coming up. I'm just a kind of buffer, I'm the shocks in your car, the disk in your neck, I'm just here to slow down the bumps so things aren't so bad. I'm the Teflon on your pans so nothing will stick. I'm here to make life better for everybody, I'm here for all the women in the world who ought to get a free lunch, I'm here for all the men who don't mind getting their toenails clipped . . ."

I was there for about six months. The problem with the show for me was that I couldn't get it to fit easily into my schedule. While I really enjoyed doing it, it was smack in the middle of the day, so it was difficult for me to find time to manage my other important affairs—like golf. And speaking engagements. And being home in Texas. There were too many times when I was almost late getting on the air or simply couldn't do the show because I was in an airplane flying somewhere.

The radio station people were very nice and deserved the kind of commitment I just couldn't give them.

I was glad I did the show, but I was also glad it ended. Most times, when my jobs have ended I have been ready for it and content with it. When my TV and radio shows were not renewed, I wasn't disappointed. When I left my job at the cosmetics company, I never looked back. I was thrilled when I drove away from that pipeline. My playing career ended when I no longer was healthy enough to play football. Every once in a while I think that if I had just taken that last season off completely, if I had just let my arm heal . . . I wouldn't have been me. I can hardly wait until the next sentence, so waiting a whole season just wasn't possible. But one thing I do regret is giving up on singing. I sang professionally. I made four albums. I had one minor hit song. But I wish I had pursued it seriously.

Probably the best thing I can say about my singing career is that I never got hurt physically. My professional singing career started as a bet. I met a record company executive on an airplane, and he bet me one hundred dollars he could get me a recording contract. Now this was before I had won four Super Bowls; this was when I'd won only one Super Bowl. He called a man he knew in Nashville. I auditioned on the telephone, singing "I'm So Lonesome I Could Cry." I got my contract with Mercury Records. It was a simple equation: You win a Super Bowl, you get a recording contract.

I'd been singing my whole life in church. My brothers did too. I had a pleasant voice. I sang country-and-western and gospel, the music I'd grown up loving. My problem was that singing came so naturally to me that I never took it very seriously. I never spent the time bouncing tunes off the ceiling and catching them. Most people spend a good hunk of their lives trying to get a recording contract; I happened to be on the right flight.

My first recording was "I'm So Lonesome I Could Cry." Nobody mistook me for Hank Williams—nobody even mistakes me for Ted Williams—but my record got into *Billboard's* Top Ten. It was definitely a hit. One record, one hit. Music sure is easy. I decided to go on tour and hired my teammate Moon Mullins to be my road manager. Moon had the right qualifications for this job. It was the off season, and he was available.

My first professional appearance was at the famed Palomino Club in North Hollywood. But to prepare for it I performed in front of a much tougher audience: I sang for my Steeler teammates at a party held at the Bruiser Pub during training camp. This was a bar filled with football players relaxing after a really tough day. Imagine it this way: the bouncers were the smallest people in the place. I sang the song "Release Me," and one of the reporters covering the team wrote, "If Too Tall Jones had had a hold of Bradshaw at that moment, I believe he would have let him go! The man delivered real feeling. There was earnest applause."

I never did put the effort into my singing career that it deserved. If I had been serious about it, I would have rehearsed for hours, I would have worked with a voice coach to learn how to breathe correctly, I would have found the right people to help me put together a professional show, and I definitely would have learned how to play the guitar. Instead I learned a few chords on the guitar, then put it aside.

But none of that mattered. As I discovered, people were coming to see me sing. They didn't care about the music, they just wanted to see the Super Bowl–winning quarterback. They weren't there to hear me. It could have just as easily been an autograph signing with a soundtrack.

Just about my only preparation for my big debut was writing out the lyrics of the songs I was going to sing. I gave them to a good friend who was sitting in the front row. Then I walked out onstage, looked at the audience—and completely forgot the words to the song. I mean, I didn't just forget the words to the song, basically I forgot my own name.

The band kept playing. Longest introduction in music history. It was pretty surprising to me that I could freeze up and start sweating at the same time, but that's what happened to me. But pretty quickly my friend got me the lyrics, and I caught up to the band. I don't know how good I sang, but at least I sang fast.

My hope was that eventually I would get as comfortable singing onstage as I was during my speaking engagements. I hoped that people would simply enjoy my show. Singing is not just putting words to music any more than throwing a pass is simply tossing the ball into the air. How you sing what you sing, how you relate it theatrically to the audience, how you present it, is the difference between "That boy can't sing a lick" and "Boy, that surprised me. I sure had fun." Getting to "I sure had fun" was my goal.

The success of my single led to my first album. All the loving care, preparation, and technical skills that could be packed into three whole hours went into that album. We recorded it pretty much in one take. But it sounded as good as if we had spent a whole entire day on it. It was to support this album that Moon Mullins and I went on tour.

We worked across the country for two months, me singing in clubs and bars and roadhouses, Moon out in the audience peddling pictures and souvenirs. We'd work until two in the morning and then have a very late dinner or very early breakfast, usually with the club owners. The next morning we'd be up early to catch a flight to the next show. After a while one city looked just like the next, one state was the same as every other state. One morning, I remember, we were supposed to fly to Albuquerque, New Mexico, but we just couldn't get up. We missed the flight. What we did not know was that the owner of the club I was playing had arranged a big welcome for us at the airport. He had the mayor there, he had high school bands there, he had the local newspapers there. The flight arrived, and we weren't on it. The owner convinced everyone to stay at the airport until the next flight arrived.

Unfortunately, we weren't on that one either.

It was early evening when we finally got there. A kid in an old car was there to greet us. "Whoo," he said, "wouldn't want to be you. The owner is one angry man, and people around here know he has a real bad temper." I know for sure I heard him use the word "embarrassed," but maybe I'm just imagining I heard him say "kill" and "maim." I like to think of myself as a stand-up guy, so in this case I stood right up and pointed at Moon—It's his fault. Moon, however, would have none of that. "It's your problem" were his exact words.

I spent the drive into town practicing apologies to see which one fit best. When we got to the club I apologized to everyone, the owner, the bartender, people were walking past outside and I apologized to them. It was good, those people forgave me. Finally it was time to perform. I didn't know how those people were going to respond, so I just got up there and told them as honestly as I could muster, "If I was ever going to die and be born again, I'd want to be born right here and live in New Mexico."

Wherever that came from, I was eternally grateful. Those people were in awe. In awe. I was just thrilled that I remembered what state we were in.

Eventually I recorded four albums, country-and-western and gospel, in addition to collaborating on a single with Glen Campbell, "You Never Know How Good You Got It 'til You Ain't Got It No More." I recorded an album of gospel music with legendary gospel singer Jake Hess called, appropriately, *Terry and Jake.* That had some wonderful music on it. But I also did a Christmas album for kids that just wasn't very good. The only real problem with it was that I was singing on it. Eventually though, it became obvious to me that people were never going to take me any more seriously than I took myself. I was never going to be more than a singing football player.

I did try to get some help. I was the opening act for several country stars. I asked one of them, a major star, to come to my rehearsal and offer some suggestions. The main suggestion he made was that I stick to football. The man told me, "You can't sing a lick," and practically laughed at me. Well, I certainly was a better singer than he was a football player. But the very worst moment of my entire singing career took place in 1979, when I performed in my hometown of Shreveport, Louisiana, with Larry Gatlin. A lot of those people are Cowboys fans, and we had just beaten Dallas in the Super Bowl. Larry Gatlin asked me to join him to sing "Your Cheatin' Heart," and as I walked out onstage most of the 8,000 people in the audience started booing me. Now, some people might have said it was "good-natured booing," just acknowledging the fact I'd beaten the Cowboys. But I can tell you as an experienced booee that when you're being booed there is absolutely no way to tell the difference between good-natured booing and just plain we-don't-like-you-at-all booing. Boo is boo.

I really was surprised. These people were booing me *before* I sang. Man, if I had wanted to be booed, I could have stayed in Pittsburgh. I am proud to be from Shreveport, I know it's a Cowboys town, but I was very disappointed in that response.

What I came to appreciate though, was how hard these people worked to hone the craft that they felt God had led them to love with such a passion. I grew to respect and admire all those people who had worked so hard to achieve even the smallest success. Too often I felt like a fraud. It made me uncomfortable. I didn't get into the NFL because I was a good singer; I started at a young age and worked incredibly hard to get there— but I got the chance to sing professionally because of my success in the NFL.

Just about everybody in my family can carry a tune. My brother Craig sings gospel music professionally. And my daughters, Rachel and Erin, both have the most beautiful voices. I have to admit though, that most people don't know about my singing career. Many times when I'm speaking to a large group, I'll ask everybody out there, how many of you have one of my albums?

Not one person has ever raised his hand.

Speaking is what I do best. I've been speaking just about my whole life, but I've been speaking professionally only since the late 1980s. Growing up in the church as I did and listening to the great Brother Buck Buchanan praising the Lord loudly and firmly every Sunday, I learned how the right words could move people toward emotion. As an active player I was never found lacking the words to answer a reporter's question. Most of the time I was as interested as the reporter in hearing my response.

The first corporation to hire me to speak was Frito-Lay. I had absolutely no clue what those fine people expected of me. Both of us were under the impression the other one knew what it was doing. All I knew was that they offered me $5,000 to talk. I'd done a lot of talking for a lot of money in my life. I had been making appearances at corporate events for a long time: How you doing, Terry Bradshaw . . . Bradshaw . . . Brad-Shaw . . . B . . . r . . . a . . . Usually they were just meet-and-greet events for which I was paid about $2,000 for the entire day. So when I learned I would be speaking to the fine people of Frito-Lay in Destin, Florida, the first thought that popped into my mind was: Florida! All right, let's play golf! So I packed my clubs and put on a real brightly colored golf shirt and my interestingly colored golf pants. The man who met my plane was wearing a tie and jacket. "We'll go over to the hotel," he said, "so you can change."

Change? Unless he was talking about my personality, I was in serious trouble. I hadn't brought any other clothes with me. "Oh," I said, "I don't need to change."

Apparently I did. I ended up borrowing clothes from the bellman at the hotel. I hadn't prepared a speech. I just got up there and talked to those fine people. I told them what was on my mind. I spoke completely from my heart. I can't remember anything I said, but knowing me, I suspect I told them to cherish the simple things in life, do whatever it is you do to the very best of your ability, and make sure you carve out time to love your family. And I'm pretty certain I said some things that made them laugh.

My speech was videotaped and eventually sent to the Washington Speakers Bureau in Washington, D.C., the very best speaker's agency in that business. A year later—literally, one year later—they finally got around to looking at it. They loved the tape and needed publicity photographs. This time I put on a tie and jacket with my jeans and went downtown. I had some nice pictures taken—from the waist up. I didn't really go into this business very seriously, but it didn't take me long to love it. Public speaking was another area in which my image hurt me for a while: Terry Bradshaw? What is he going to speak about, the years he spent placing his hands on the posterior portion of a hunched-over man? There were a lot of companies that didn't particularly feel the need to be addressed by the man whose image was that he was so dumb that blonds told Terry Bradshaw jokes! At one point when I was just getting started, a certain company was reluctant to hire me. I actually offered to speak on a contingency basis; if they didn't enjoy my speech and feel it was valuable, they didn't have to pay me. I spoke, they paid.

Ladies and gentlemen, believe me when I tell you there is nothing, I mean nothing, like the high I get speaking to a live audience. The response is an instant report card. I don't have a written speech that I deliver to each audience, but I have prepared in my mind what I want to say. So every speech I give is different.

It's a real challenge. When I walk out onstage, there are often more than a thousand people looking at me and thinking, So you're Terry Bradshaw, huh? Go ahead now, tell me something real useful to my life and entertain me while you're doing it, make me think and make me laugh. I do have a theme when I speak, but most of the time I lack a real strong structure. What often happens when I'm speaking is that I'll say something that reminds me of something else I want to say, and I'll take that path. I end up skipping around a lot. The problem then is getting back to my starting point, particularly when I can't remember where I started. When that happens my brain goes on red alert, sirens start going off in my head, and I'm thinking, stall, stall, stall. My brain is telling me, Brad, my man, go back to point one. And the other side of my brain is asking, Excuse me, could you remind me, what exactly is point one? That's when I start sweating. But eventually I do manage to retrace my steps, get back on the path, and neatly tie together all the points I wanted to make.

But much worse than that is to be in the middle of a really impassioned part of a speech, just exhorting these people to show their passion for a company, and then forget the name of the company. Oh my Butkus, that is a terrible thing to happen; I know, I can feel it in my heart, that you people know there is no other company in the whole world like . . . like . . . this company. It's not that I take these speeches for granted, but sometimes my brain just takes a little vacation: See you, Brad, you just keep talking, I'm just going to go over here and lay down for a few minutes. Oh, okay, brain, come back soon. When that happens I start looking everywhere for a corporate logo. I know there has got to be one somewhere in that room.

One time I gave a great speech to a life insurance company in San Francisco. There were at least 5,000 people in the room. The first half of my speech went well, I was just ripping it up, but sometime during the second half I lost them. I could just feel that they weren't with me. When that happens I try to come back to the company, "But here at this company I know how hard you people work . . . ," "At this company the emphasis is on integrity. . . ." Nothing worked, nothing, and I couldn't figure it out. When I finished, I received a polite smattering of applause. A few minutes later I went to meet the CEO to thank him for inviting me.

That's when I found that throughout the speech I had been referring to the company by the wrong name. I was real close, real real close, but unfortunately so was the name of their largest competitor. I was mistakenly using the name of their competitor. I have rarely been so embarrassed in my life. The CEO was absolutely furious. I think we decided that maybe we shouldn't charge for that speech.

Since that speech to Frito-Lay I've given hundreds of speeches to companies in just about every field.

I became an effective public speaker because I speak from my heart as well as my head. I'm not reading lines somebody else wrote, I'm just telling people in an entertaining fashion what I believe. The themes of my speeches are pretty basic: Keep it simple. Smile. Make other people feel good, and you end up making yourself feel good. The value of a good day's work. Self-pride. This is not complex stuff. I don't claim to have discovered the mother lode of wisdom. My speeches are filled with the kind of down-home good sense it has taken me my lifetime to learn. "Every morning when I get up," I might say, striding around the otherwise empty stage—I don't use a podium—"I sit on the edge of the bed. Now this is the gospel truth. I sit on the edge of the bed and get myself together a little bit, like everybody does. Then I draw in some air, and I think, Ahhh, this is pretty good. This is good. I'm alive! What a glorious thing to realize. I'm alive. Can I have an Amen just for being alive. Amen, Brother Terry, Amen."

This is not the most controversial material my audience will ever hear. No one, I assure you absolutely no one, is sitting out there thinking, Hmmm, he's alive. I wonder what he really meant by that?

I will confess something to you right now: there are no subtle messages hidden behind my words. There is no deeper meaning that the audience will understand when they have an opportunity later to reflect upon it. It's just good sense packaged with many laughs. I'm telling people what I know to be true; if you're nice to other people, they will usually be nice to you. If you make people laugh a little, they're probably going to like you. And if people enjoy being with you, life can be sweet.

I make it very clear I don't have the answers. If I had the answers, I would have passed that test and gone to LSU. "You want to be more successful?" I tell them, "Well, I can't help you there. You're flat out on your own . . . 'cause if I knew the secret, I wouldn't be sharing it. That's why it's called a secret. People who tell you they're going to tell you secrets shouldn't be trusted; if they are telling you, it isn't a secret. If I knew the secret I'd be using it to make a lot of money. But you can always go buy a book or a tape or tune in those people on the television at three-thirty in the morning. Especially that guy with all the teeth in San Diego who flies around in his helicopter talking about his house. That's not real. If you're here to get advice on how to run your business, I can't help you. I don't know. What can I possibly offer you? You've seen me on television, do you really think I can help?"

But I can make people laugh. And I do. To do that I've created some recognizable characters. "My momma taught me to be able to laugh. My momma only has one tooth. We love her, but we can't eat with her 'cause it's kind of awful-looking. I cooked a steak for her, and then we hid with a camera when she tried to eat it. We videotaped that and sent it to that video show and won $10,000. You ever kiss a woman with one tooth? My experience is that it is like a plunger. She latches onto me, and we can't get loose till some-one pulls us apart."

While I rarely, very rarely refer to my football ca-reer when I'm not working—I've never worn my Super Bowl rings—I do make references to it during my speech. Although admittedly those references might be a shade less than completely accurate. "Rocky Bleier was synonymous with work," I might tell my audience. "He was a working man. He represented every one of you. He was an overachiever. Like some of you. People ask me, 'Terry, how do you call your own plays?' Sim-ple, I tell them, if you remember them, you call them. One time I called Rocky's number on every single play: Toss 33, Toss 33, Dive 34, Wham 38 Special, 34 Spe-cial, 35 Lead Speed—we moved ninety-nine yards down the field. It was unheard of, the man carried the ball seventeen times in a row, seventeen carries, ninety-nine yards, Rocky Bleier. Folks were falling out of the stands, they were so excited. We are on the one-yard line. The one-inch line. Who is going to score? Am I going to sneak it in? No way. Is Franco going to score? No way. Swannie is telling me in the huddle. 'Throw it to me, Terry.' I ain't throwing no pass.

"The Rock . . . will run it in. But I hear this noise, and I look over to my left, oh my goodness, Rock has done passed out. His eyeballs were laying back in his head. Stuff is coming out of his mouth. He's turning ashen gray. Lot of people don't know this, but one of our linemen believed in voodoo. Rock had passed out in this man's arms, and he was hollering and danc-ing . . .

"I turned to Franco and told him, 'Go drag Rock over here.' Franco dragged him back into the huddle. I got down in the huddle and called the Rock's number. 'Wait a minute,' someone said, 'we got to get this man some help.' I said, 'Yes, we will, we'll get him some help, but he'll score before he gets some help. You think this man carried the ball seventeen times for ninety-nine yards and eleven inches, and he ain't going to score? He's going to score the touchdown, and when he does, we will get him some help. You understand me?'

" 'But Terry, the boy has passed out.'

" 'I don't care. I'll ride him across the line of scrimmage with the ball, turn the ball loose, touchdown, and then we'll get the doctor out here to save his life. But right now this boy is going to carry the ball one more time.' I called the play, Ride 32 Trap. Franco asked me what I wanted him to do. I told him, 'What you are going to do with him is hold him up. You get behind him, when we snap the ball, you shimmy him up. I'll ride him across the goal line, the referee'll signal touchdown, and then we'll get the ambulance out here and get the boy saved.'

"The ball was snapped. Franco stood him up. I rode him across the goal line. Soon as he broke the plane, I turned the ball loose. The referee signaled touchdown. Fans fell out of their seats in glee. Rocky rolled over and began turning purple. I jumped down on my knees and whomped him on the chest. 'Get up! Wake up!' I was going to give him mouth-to-mouth re-suck-I-tation, but I eyeballed the junk coming out of his mouth, and I ain't touching that boy. The ambulance came out, and the doctor slit Rocky's throat open, put tubes in him and pumped him, electroshocked his ass, and got him into the ambulance and to the hospital and saved his life.

"Until that moment I did not know that poor old Rocky smoked five packs of Camels a day. But Rocky was dedicated to success. That's what it took for him to reach the end zone."

I do tailor my message to the needs of each audience. The next time I gave that speech, for example, Franco might be the ball carrier.

When I first started speaking to corporate groups, particularly in cities like Dallas and Houston, I would always get a little heckling. In Dallas it was always, "You beat my Cowboys." I have never heard that particular phrase used in another NFL city. I never heard anybody say, "You beat my Giants." "You beat my Saints." Well, I mean, everybody beats the Saints, so it probably wouldn't pay to get too riled about it, but in Dallas it is always, "You beat my Cowboys." And then people tell me, "I really used to hate you," as if I'm supposed to be grateful to them that they don't hate me anymore. Oh well, thank you very much for not hating me for beating your team. What I generally say when someone tells me that is, "Then you need to grow up and get over it, 'cause I don't hate you." People, it is only a game.

Most of the heckling I got came at night, after people had been out in the sun all day and maybe had one or two or ten too many. I learned to deal with it mostly by ignoring it. But one time in Cleveland, this was in Cleveland now, I was giving a speech and this . . . person really wouldn't quiet down. I was surprised; at corporate outings people tend to be a little more subdued. Not this gentleman, he just wouldn't quiet hisself. Finally, I'd had enough. I stopped in the middle of a sentence and started tapping on the microphone. "Excuse me, ladies and gentlemen," I said, "but this is amazing. Until this very moment I truly had not realized that I was a ventriloquist. But I must be, 'cause every time I talk into this microphone, it comes out of that dummy up there."

The room just exploded into laughter. Everybody was turning around to see who I was talking about. I guarantee you, that man never shouted another word to me.

Usually I don't get heckled, though; usually when I finish speaking, people in my audience stand up in appreciation: That ol' boy sure knows a lot of good words. I know by their recognition that they have enjoyed themselves and perhaps even gained a little insight into their very own lives. It'd be a good thing if they did so. But standing there just hearing those cheers—without having to get carried off the stage on a stretcher and having a teammate warn me, "Don't move your head, Terry, they love you. They think you're dead"—is truly one of the greatest things I have ever experienced. I do love it. When I hear that applause, when I hear that laughter during my speech, I know that I am bringing happiness into the lives of some people primarily by letting them know what a mess my own life is. It feels very good. I enjoy making people happy at my own expense, and fortunately I've lived the kind of life that makes it easy to do.

In my life I have enjoyed success and suffered through considerable failure. I don't brag about my victories, and I am not ashamed or embarrassed by my defeats. I've been living my life with a wide-open throttle. I haven't backed off too many challenges. I've ridden all the roller coasters with my kids. I even went parasailing with my soon-to-be-ex wife.

That was a truly bad time for me. I was gathering a lot of material for that portion of my speech when I speak about dealing with tough times. My wife and I had pretty much decided to end our marriage, but we took one last trip as a family. I don't know why we went, but I found myself being with a person who did not want to be with me one little bit. I felt about as desirable as a toothache.

But I did everything to make this vacation fun for our little girls. And maybe even remind my wife that we had once had such good times together. We went on all the rides. We went on the submarine. The roller coaster. And then I saw the parasailing operation. Parasailing, I thought, yeah, that's what we need to do. That will swing her around. We'll go a few hundred feet up in the air harnessed to a kite, pulled along on a cable attached to a speedboat. We'll be terrified together. Then we'll come down, and maybe that experience will bring us closer together. All we had to do was survive.

Before going up, I asked the guide if it was completely safe. He assured me it was absolutely, perfectly safe. The very last question I asked him was, "You ever have one of these cables break?"

"Never," he said flatly.

Good enough for me. We parasailed into the sky.

We were just gliding along at about 350 feet over the ocean. It was so peaceful, so quiet, so beautiful. I was thinking, This is very cool, when the cable snapped. Poof, broken. It took maybe half a second for me to fully comprehend the situation: I was flying 350 feet high through the air with the woman who was going to divorce me as soon as we got down. Assuming we did get down.

I've heard people say that at times like that, your entire life passes in front of you. That didn't happen to me at all. But if it had, it would have been great. I have lived a wonderful life, and I wouldn't mind reliving a lot of those moments—although assuming I stay away from bulls, I expect to live a lot more years. No doubt I also would have found a few things that I would have done differently, but at that moment the only one I knew for certain that I definitely would have done differently was going parasailing.

"Don't move," I said to her, pretty much ignoring the fact that we were flying along at a pretty good pace. It probably wasn't the most valuable advice I could have given her, but there wasn't too much else available right at that moment. Don't sing? Don't lose the cable remote? Don't divorce me? The whole point was to make it seem like one of us was in control, keep her from panicking. There was no sense in both of us doing that.

I didn't have the slightest idea what was going to happen. My fear was that we were going to splat straight into the ocean. For the first time that divorce began to look pretty good. Instead, we just kept sailing, coming down slowly.

About two years earlier I had had my wrist fused. We hit the water pretty hard, and that wrist got bent backward like it was never supposed to. While my wife had no problem getting free of the sail, I got caught up in it and dragged underwater. I felt like I was about to drown. I managed to get loose and looked around to make sure my wife was safe, but she was already on the boat. I finally managed to get into the boat, and I just laid there. The guide was in a total panic. "Mr. Bradshaw," he said over and over, "Mr. Bradshaw. I'm so sorry, you can have a free ride anytime you want. No charge, anytime."

Now there was an offer I really intended to collect on. "No charge?" I said, "no charge?"

"No charge," he agreed.

Not only didn't this experience save my marriage, it almost got me killed. So I guess it helped me put things back in perspective. We did get divorced, I redecorated the entire house, and since then I haven't broken even a small bone.

Just like I tell people when I speak to them, I try to keep my life simple. I try to make people feel good. I smile a lot; I even smile sometimes when inside I don't feel like it. I try to lift up everybody else, and just like I learned from Brother Buchanan, it comes back to me many times over. I call my mom and dad, and when I do, I tell them that I love them. My father doesn't show too much emotion, my mother worries that the last cookie in a box is going to get lonely. In that regard I am my mother's son.

My daughters are as lovely as their mother and as strong-willed as I am. When Erin was maybe ten years old, she came home from school one day and asked me, "Dad, would you teach me how to throw a football?"

We went right up to the Wal-Mart and bought a small football and spent the next several hours tossing it. I showed her how to roll her wrist, and gradually she got it. She got pretty good at it. She could throw nice tight spirals pretty much every time. And when we were out there tossing it back and forth nothing else mattered to me, not the TV show, the commercials, the speeches, my whole celebrity being. I was right where I wanted to be, throwing a football with my kid. Sometimes the world just treats you perfect. Amen to that, Brother.

And did I happen to mention that I called my own plays?

**POCKET BOOKS
PROUDLY PRESENTS**

KEEP IT SIMPLE

Terry Bradshaw

**Now available from
Pocket Books**

**Turn the page for a preview of
Keep It Simple. . . .**

The happiest times of my life were the summers I spent with my family in Hall Summit, Louisiana. The entire family would stay together on my Paw-paw's place. I remember most of all the comfort that came from just being with family. But I also remember that it was hot. I mean, it was hot. How hot was it?

Thank you for wondering; I'll tell you, it was so hot that the flies preferred to walk. In that heat it seemed like everything slowed down, even time. Saturday nights were my favorite time of the week. That's when the men would go on down to Slim's Barber Shop to get our hair cut. We went every Saturday whether we needed it cut or not. We'd sit around that barber shop listening to the men telling their hunting and fishing lies and family stories while the Grand Ole Opry was playing on the radio. "HowwwDe!" Minnie Pearl would sing, and talk about her own family, "We took Brother to Nashville to try and get him a job. A man offered him $30 a week and told him in five years he'd get $200. Brother told him that was fine, he'd be back in five years."

It was such a simple time. It was a time before money had begun to play a role in my life. I didn't know anything about money. My idea of wealthy would be my grandmother's brother's son. He was a wonderful man who owned a big farm. We would ride over to his house on an old dirt road and he would serve steaks for dinner. Steaks! He served steaks and it wasn't even a holiday. That's how rich he was. I remember one day he took all the kids to the store—he let us ride in the back of his truck, which was pretty exciting—and bought us a whole case of soda pop. I couldn't believe it, he could afford to buy the entire case of soda pop at one time. To me, that was pretty much the definition of rich.

I own a horse ranch in Texas and another one in

Oklahoma. I got a lake on each spread. I got cars, I got big-screen TVs, if I really wanted to I could buy a whole bottling plant worth of soda. I have earned a lot of money. And if there is one thing I truly regret it's the fact that I cannot enjoy my life. I appear to enjoy it. And I do have a good time. I work with nice people, I get to travel to wonderful places, and I have a job—several jobs—that I enjoy which don't involve being run down by a 330-pound lineman who doesn't know the meaning of the word "mercy," and a lot of other words too! But the truth is that to afford those material things that bring me pleasure I have to spend most of my life away from them. At best I get to spend two or three days in a row at my ranch, then I'm off to a hotel room somewhere.

I could live very happily without the ranches, without the horses, the cars, without all of it. It probably wouldn't even make me too sad to see all of it go. I am not someone who has ever been possessed by my own possessions. I don't need a big house and I don't need a fancy car. For too many people the size of their house is inversely proportional to the amount of time they get to spend in it. They have put themselves in a position where they spend their life working hard to buy things that they never get time to enjoy because they're working so hard.

Most of us, including me, too often take the really important things in life for granted. We don't really recognize the things that make a difference in our lives. Many people come to my ranch and see the house and the horses and the lake and are overwhelmed by it. When I go to Hawaii I cannot stop staring at the ocean and the meadows of pineapples and the gorgeous mountains and the island doves and the beautiful people and I'm overwhelmed by it. I find myself telling Hawaiians, "You don't really appreciate what you have, do you?"

And they tell me, "It's nice, but it's not as nice as a horse ranch in Texas." Okay, maybe they don't actually say that. What they do say is, "It's home." Just like I say it. So maybe the best place to start is to look at your own life and appreciate those things that really matter; someone to love, your family, good health, your friends.

It's nice to have nice things. Anyone who tries to tell you that money doesn't matter in life really means it doesn't matter in *your* life. Money definitely does not guarantee happiness—I know many people who have a lot of money who aren't very happy—what money can do is make life a little easier. But in the top-ten list of the happiest days of my life, "cashing a check" does not appear.

Let me ask you this question: How many of you people reading this book right now would like to know how to double—I said double, my friends—the amount of money you have in the bank? How to guarantee that you would never have to worry about having enough money again? How to have more money than you ever dreamed possible?

I can practically hear you singing, amen to more money than we ever imagined, brother Terry, amen.

Of course you want to know. Well, me too! Who wouldn't? Believe me, if I knew that you'd be saying, "'Member that guy Terry Bradshaw we used to see all over the TV? Whatever happened to him? After he got all that money we never heard from him again." But as I've already explained, I don't have the answers. I do know that in just about everybody's life money causes considerable problems. Everybody. There are probably more women in this world who want to date me for my good looks as there are people who feel they have just enough money to make them happy. How much money is enough? That's an easy question to answer: Just a little more than you have.

No matter how much money you have, or don't have, the problems we all face are pretty much the same. I work to meet a payroll, support my kids, pay the mortgage on my house, pay the mortgage on my third former wife's divorce attorney's house. And the fears are the same too: what am I gonna do if I can't make the bills this month?

Admittedly in my case the bills are probably a little bigger than many other people's. When you don't have money the problems are obvious and extreme: food and shelter. But in my case, in addition to paying the rent, child support, all the bills and my personal expenses, I have substantial business expenses. There are a lot of people who depend on me keeping the Circle 12, my horse ranch, in operation. And it is expensive. Believe me, people who tell you money "ain't hay" have never had to pay for hay. I'm responsible for the livelihood of all the people who work on the ranch. It's a responsibility I take seriously. It's a commitment. I have to be away from the ranch just to pay for the ranch.

My parents used to say our family was rich in love, which was another way of saying we weren't rich in money. I began learning the value of money when I was three years old and staged my first and only robbery. I went with my mother to visit a good friend of hers. I remember it was raining that day. As my mother and this woman socialized I played in the back of the house—and in the back bathroom I found a whole jar of money. Oh my goodness gracious, I had never seen so much money untended in the entire three years of my life. There were pennies and nickels, I don't know how much money it was, it could have been as much as one dollar. That jar was just singing my name, "Terrrrr—ry . . . Terrrrr—ry." Yes, Jar? "Take me home with you."

Well how could I resist. I took all that money and put it in my pocket. The Bradshaw family fortune was beginning to build. I got away with it clean too, at least until I got home and my mother the detective found it in my pocket. "Terry, where did you get that money?" She definitely did not sing my name.

I was three years old, I wasn't allowed out of the house without permission, so there were a limited amount of alibis open to me. "I don't know, Mommy," I said earnestly. This probably would have been a very good time for me to raise the subject of miracles.

"Don't you lie to me, Terry. Where did you get that money?"

I was sticking to my alibi, "I don't know, Mommy." I smiled broadly. I was playing the "cute" defense.

Nobody ever makes bank robbers bring the money back to the bank. But my mother put me back in the car, took me back to that woman's house and made me hand it to her. "I found this," I said.

"Terry . . ." my mother warned.

". . . in my pocket," I admitted. I got a Momma-whipping that day, which, while not as bad as a Daddy-whupping, was definitely bad enough.

Everyone in my family worked hard, following the example of my father. Growing up, he always had chores for us. The one we probably hated most was clearing out his vegetable garden. The thing about that garden was as we grew bigger so did his garden. I had an assortment of jobs growing up, not one of them requiring more brains than muscle. I did everything from hauling skids on a pipeline to selling used cars.

I never had an allowance. To earn money I mowed yards for a dollar a yard. One year I worked on my hands and knees digging weeds out of a football field for $42 a week. With my first week's pay I went down to the clothes store because they were having a sale on rayon short-sleeved shirts. There was a big stack of them right in the middle of the table. They were selling for fifty cents, and I bought every one of them that fit me. That was my very first purchase. I was so proud of those shirts because I had never in my life had anything so nice. They were nice too, right up until you wore them. Then they fell apart. The first time you washed them the strings came loose. When I put one on for the second time I looked like I was wearing a ball of string.

I worked in a clothing store on Saturdays. I was a machine welder on drill stem pipes. One summer I hauled hay. In college when I came home for Thanksgiving and Christmas vacations I worked all week building doors at a window-and-door-manufacturing plant for $1.75 an hour. I worked ten hours a day six days a week. There was no paying job beneath my dignity.

My rookie year in the National Football League I was paid $25,000. For me, that was a fortune. The most money I'd ever had in the bank at one time before that was $350, which I saved for college and had lasted me an entire year. I didn't know anything about handling money; I especially didn't know about taxes. I had never even filed a tax return. But at the end of the year a CPA told me I had to pay the government $7200. I had $7000 in the bank. So to earn money during the off-season I took a job at Bill Hannah Ford selling used cars. All my friends would come to see me and I'd give them the same deal I wished someone would give me. I gave them the deal of a lifetime. I may still hold the all-time record for most used cars sold without making any profit. As a salesman my selling technique is probably best described as "seriously pathetic."

Even after I became more successful with the Steelers I wasn't about to give up my summer job. I never knew when I might chance upon another pile of rayon shirts and I wanted to be ready to pounce. When I did begin to gain some recognition I began appearing in commercials for the used car lot. If anybody ever asks you just how badly you would embarrass yourself to earn a paycheck, I suggest you thoughtfully look up into the sky, rub your jaw between your thumb and forefinger, and say, "a whole lot, but probably not as much as Terry Bradshaw."

For one commercial I actually dressed up like a mountain hillbilly. I had the beard, the hat, the cornpone pipe. My dad had an old dilapidated shack on his farm and we filmed it there. I was supposedly sitting inside reading the newspaper, when suddenly something I read shocked me. My jaw dropped open, I stood up, flung open the door—which immediately fell off its hinges—

and yelled, "Clyde, lookee here. Bill Hannah Ford has an 'If you can push, pull or tow your old car in they'll give you somethum' for it.' Two people were crouching inside under the window frames and when I opened the door they started throwing chickens out the windows. Oh man, those chickens were petrified; they came flying out the window right into the camera as I was trying to remember my lines.

Winning four Super Bowls has made a significant difference in my life. Now instead of doing commercials with chickens I work with a puppet named Alf.

There hasn't been a time in my life when I haven't had at least one job. When I started earning a reasonable salary I decided that I needed to invest for the future. There were a lot of young divorce lawyers graduating from law school who were going to be depending on me. But truthfully I didn't know anything at all about investing. In fact, I knew so little about investing that as my first major investment I bought myself a brand-new boat.

I'll just wait right here, right at this comma, until all you boat owners stop laughing. When I got drafted I bought a life insurance policy. That was not meant to be a comment on the quality of the Steelers offensive line, the people who would be protecting me, it was just that I thought buying life insurance was what all adults did. The way I understood this policy was that if I died I would be a very rich man.

Then somebody told me to invest in the commodities market, invest in futures, they said. Well, that definitely made more sense to me than investing in the past. Linebacker Andy Russell was a graduate of the Harvard Business School, and he told me what to do. I bought some oil and gas stocks. I bought some Dr Pepper because that was my favorite brand. I probably owned less than five hundred shares of that stock, but every time I drank a bottle of Dr Pepper I felt like I was being loyal to my own company.

But primarily I invested in land. Once, when asked for investment advice, Mark Twain advised investing in land "because they're not making it anymore." More importantly, as every real estate broker knows, it isn't going to cost any less either. When I started buying land I very quickly learned the language of real estate. I found out what all those real estate expressions really mean. A lot, for example. I always thought a lot was . . . a lot. But one thing "a lot" isn't, for example, is a lot. It's usually a lot less than a lot, it probably should be called a little. One time a real estate broker was showing me some expensive farmland and I said, that's not a lot of land, is it?

He agreed with me, "You're right," he said, "It's almost twenty lots."

You know that expression "dirt cheap"? Well, dirt isn't cheap. Dirt can be expensive, and the more fertile the dirt the more it is going to cost.

And you know why the person who sells you lots is known as a real estate broker? That's because by the time you're finished doing business with him you're going to be a lot broker than you ever thought possible. A lot, in this sentence, meaning . . . a lot.

The only good investment I ever made on my own was buying a ranch in Louisiana. There is considerable competition for the worst investment I ever made. But I would have to admit that my ostrich egg venture certainly would be among the finalists. I was going to be to ostriches what Frank Perdue is to chickens: a mass murderer. Several years ago it seemed like everyone was talking about ostrich meat. Well, okay, maybe not in your neighborhood. But the rumor was that ostrich meat was going to become very popular. It was tasty, low in fat, high in protein. It was the perfect product for diet- and health-conscious America.

Man, that still sounds promising. So I decided I was going to become an ostrich farmer, Terry the ostrich king. I could almost hear people saying with awe, "Wow, Terry, you got the biggest ostrich I have ever seen. Boy, Terry, love your ostrich." I had four hundred acres of God's beautiful earth just needing to feel life. I had visions of a great herd of ostriches . . . doing whatever it is ostriches do, all over my land. ever seen in my life. I had been a cattleman, now I was going to be an ostrichman.

Lemme have an amen for ostriches, people.

So I bought a pair of ostriches. Truthfully, it wasn't exactly a pair of ostriches. It was a pair of future ostriches. Actually I bought two ostrich eggs. I thought I got a great buy on them too, I paid only $7000 for them. This is the truth, I paid $7000 for two bird eggs. So, my friends, if anyone ever asks you who the greatest salesman in history is, you just sit quietly waiting until everybody else has had their say and then you tell them, how about the guy who sold two bird eggs to Terry Bradshaw for $7000. Or when things are really going bad around the office; when your biggest customer is unhappy and the important shipment is late and those pictures they took of you in the stockroom at last year's Christmas party show up on the corporate Web site, you just lean right back and think, could be worse, could be a lot worse. I could have paid $7000 for two ostrich eggs like Terry Bradshaw.

When I finally got my two eggs I didn't even know what to do with them. I certainly wanted to protect my investment, but I wasn't going to sit on them. I wasn't going to put them in a safe deposit box. Let's be honest here, if God had intended ostriches to be raised in Texas he wouldn't have invented shotguns.

I definitely should have known better. When was the last time you opened a restaurant menu and saw they were serving poached ostrich? How many ostrich cookbooks are there on the market? What's your favorite ostrich recipe? When was the last time anybody served ostrich steaks and Dr Pepper? There is a reason for this: Normal people don't eat filet of ostrich.

Finally I went to the man who sold me these eggs and

told him they were killing my investment portfolio. I had some shares of IBM, of Xerox, I had my Dr Pepper stock, Red Man Tobacco, and I had these two bird eggs. He agreed with me that not every man is well suited for ostrich ranching and agreed to return my money. I didn't even get to name my eggs.

I've learned that money does not bring me satisfaction. Mostly it brings with it the need to make more money. I gave a speech to a group of young people and their parents in Oklahoma. I said to them that the real joy in life is life, living life day to day, you just have to be smart enough and aware enough to appreciate it. The good and the bad. It's no secret. It's no more complicated than that. Too many people spend too many years of their lives trying to reach a goal only to discover when they finally get there that the real joy is in taking the journey.

We are all on this journey, this incredible journey. There is nothing that stimulates the mind of a human being than a journey. We all want to take that trip, we all want to know what's going to happen around the next corner. It's the most exciting adventure of your life—because it is your life.

During most of my football career I was too busy playing football to appreciate the privilege of playing football. I'm sure most people believe that the most enjoyable moments of my career were winning four Super Bowls. But that's not true. The part of my career that brought me the greatest pleasure were the years when we were building a great team. Position by position I could see the Steelers getting better and better, preparing to win. When I started I struggled in football. I failed, I failed often, but I learned a little more each week, and gradually I became a pretty good quarterback. And gradually the team started winning. Finally we made it to our first playoff game. We didn't know if we could win at that level until we won. Then we went to a championship game and finally to a Super Bowl. It took a long time to get there and it required a lot of hard work; we had to confront a lot of self-doubts, a lot of insecurities, a lot of bad breaks. We had to believe in Chuck Noll's plan. And all that time I was so focused on getting to the future that I forgot to enjoy the present. I was so focused on reaching the summit that I neglected to appreciate the beauty of the climb.

The great joy in winning the Super Bowl was magnified because it had all those building years wrapped into it, that's what made it so special. The journey. The trip. Same thing in the horse business. If my dream was owning a world champion stallion I could go to the bank, borrow the money, and buy a world champion stallion. But what would be the joy in that? It would bring me no satisfaction. About the only thing I could do would be to take people over to my barn and say, "Look at my world champion. Ain't he a beauty!"

But then somebody might say, "Wow, Terry, you raised him?"

Heck no, I bought him. But I raised the money to buy him! That would bring me no satisfaction at all.

But if I could answer, Oh yeah, I raised his momma and I bred her to this other horse I raised and I remember the day she dropped and then there was the time he had that little bout with colic but he came through . . .

If I could answer it that way it would bring me incredible satisfaction. Just let me point out to you that the Declaration of Independence identifies the basic human rights as life, liberty, and the pursuit of happiness—not the pursuit of money. I have been diligently pursuing happiness my whole life. On many occasions I've caught it, but it just keeps getting away. What I have learned during that pursuit is that I don't find my personal happiness in those things money can buy.

Actually there are a lot of things that bring me happiness. Most importantly, being with my girls, Rachel and Erin. I'd like to say that as a father I'm a tough disciplinarian; I would like to say that definitively but it wouldn't be true. I'm about as tough as Jell-O with my girls. One time we went to the Quarter Horse competition in Columbus, Ohio. Erin was showing in the youth class. But while I was looking at horses they followed a sign that pointed them in the direction of puppies.

I warned them before I let them go that I was not going to get them a puppy. Each of them had animals at both my house and their mother's house. I had dogs and horses and cats, I just didn't have room for any more animals. About an hour later they came running up to me all excited, "Oh, Dad," Erin said, "we found the most beautiful puppy . . ."

We are not getting another puppy.

". . . and you ought to see it, Dad, and it's so beautiful, Dad, and you'd love it so much, Dad, and we told the lady that we were your daughters and she told us that she hadn't intended to sell this puppy, Dad, she wanted to keep it to breed and raise it herself because it is so special, but because it's you, Dad, she'll let us buy it. Dad, you have to come see this puppy."

We are not getting . . .

I held out for maybe another hour. All you parents know how tough this situation can be. It's a good opportunity to teach children the most important lessons in life: You say "Daddy" in the right tone and you can have anything you want. I explained logically why we couldn't buy this dog. I laid it out for them clearly and rationally. But I had no chance, I was being attacked by the worst of all combinations: a salesman, my daughters and a puppy.

I agreed to look at this puppy. They grabbed my hands, c'mon, Daddy, and we walked six hundred yards up a hill. As we got closer they let go and took off running. I reached in my wallet and pulled out four hundred-dollar bills, hoping it wouldn't cost me any more than that.

Three hundred, the puppy salesman said. This was a pure breed Corgi, she added, suggesting that I think of it as an investment.

No, ostrich eggs were an investment. This was simply me caving in to my daughters. I couldn't resist, they'd called me "Daddy." We took it back to the hotel. The girls promised me they would take care of this dog forever, or twenty minutes, whichever came first. This dog was so happy to be coming home with us that she peed all over the carpet. Her name is Sammy. She does all these little things to endear herself to me, like ripping up my very expensive carpet.

So my daughters bring me happiness. Animals bring me happiness. I've learned good lessons from animals. Animals don't demand anything from you. They never ask to borrow your car, complain about the weather, or charge movies on your pay-TV. The sweeter and gentler and kinder and more respectful you are to an animal, the more it will respond to you. Many times I've stepped into the stall of a nervous horse and just squatted there; I have literally stayed still in a stall for more than an hour and eventually that horse understood that I was not there to hurt him, and came over to me and nuzzled me. Horses have what's known as "horse sense." It means horses understand one of the basic rules of happiness: Be nice to me, I'll be nice to you. Most living things respond real well to a kind hand. What could be simpler than that, my friend?

But I warn you, don't try that behavior at home with someone you love. Trust me, you try walking into a room and squatting down in a corner without saying a word and I guarantee you it will inevitably lead to three questions: Why are you squatting in the corner? What's wrong with you? Are you completely out of your mind? That's what is known as "nonsense."

I don't ride horses. This is not due to any strongly held belief about the exploitation by man of the noble beast, it's just that I have a bad back and it hurts too much when I ride. Riding is therapeutic for some people, not me. I get my enjoyment from walking amongst my horses, loving on them, hugging on them, watching them interact with other horses. Every horse is different, physically and temperamentally. Some don't want you to touch their ears. Some don't want you to touch their nose. You learn these traits when you pick yourself up off the ground. When we buy a horse I always ask the owner, does he have any bad habits.

Yessir, he does, Mr. Bradshaw, he smokes too much and hangs out with the mares all night.

I love my dogs. When I sit down in my big chair, my dogs fight over my attention. Including Sammy. My dogs think I'm special and they can't even bark the words *Super Bowl*. All they want me to do is pet them and let them know that I love them. And I can express that with the palm of my hand. Dogs are not impressed by status. Find your dogs a filthy fireplug and they're happy. They communicate with other dogs by pee-mail. Remember this: Dogs get to see you naked—and they still like you!

Of course, I don't know if any of this is true concerning ostriches. But I can tell you from experience that ostrich eggs don't make good pets.

Close friends bring me happiness. The great game of golf on occasion brings me happiness. Lake fishing makes me really happy; I'm a catch-and-release man, which definitely makes the fish happy. Reading my Bible makes me very happy. The quiet of the early morning brings me happiness, that time when there's nothing going on, when I can make some coffee, sit down, and just be. Winning a football game always made me happy, even if personally I hadn't played well; but playing well when we lost did not make me happy. There are a lot of things that make me truly happy; a pretty lady with a smile, kind words from people who know my work—whatever that is exactly, old people holding hands just crushes me, and most important of all just being with my family. And not one of these things requires a substantial amount of money. Not one.

I don't know what it is that makes other people happy. In my life the evidence is particularly strong that I definitely don't know what makes a wife happy. That is something each person has to determine for himself. For some people happiness is a big car, a big house, big toys, the material things. There's nothing wrong with that. Some people catch fish and hang them up on a wall, showing people how proud they are that they outsmarted a fish.

My friends, and by this page you are my friends, happiness is where you find it. Just don't spend so much time looking for it that you miss what's right in front of you. In all the years I played pro football, only once—in the last minutes of my final Super Bowl, when we had the game won—did I actually stop and take time to look around and savor the moment.

I have earned a lot of money, and much of it has gone to make other people happy. Sometimes people stop in front of my ranch and they see the beautiful house, the barns and the horses, the lake and the pasture; my oh my, they must say, that boy Bradshaw has done good for himself.

But most times what they don't see is me—because I'm usually on the road earning money to pay for it all. And what they don't see are my girls, because they're living with their mother down the road.

It really is very simple: Stop, take time to look around, and savor this moment.